THE MAN
WHO SHOT
McKINLEY

THE MAN
WHO SHOT
McKINLEY

by A. Wesley Johns

South Brunswick and New York: A. S. Barnes and Company
London: Thomas Yoseloff Ltd

A. S. Barnes and Co., Inc.
Cranbury, New Jersey 08512

Thomas Yoseloff Ltd
108 New Bond Street
London W1Y OQX, England

*Unless otherwise credited, the illustrations in this
book are reproduced through the courtesy of the
Buffalo and Erie County Historical Society*

SBN 498 07521 4
Printed in the United States of America

Contents

Acknowledgments

I WOULD LIKE to express gratitude to those who have so graciously and consistently helped me in this work.

These include my wife, June Blair Johns, who has been of invaluable assistance in every phase of the book. Others who have aided me in one phase or another are: Roy W. Nagle, Niagara Frontier historian; Edwin Valentine Mitchell; Dr. Julian Park, former president of the Buffalo and Erie County Historical Society and son of Dr. Roswell Park; Dr. Oscar Lang, Dr. Sanford Greenberg, Mrs. Margaret M. Mott, former acting director of the Grosvenor library; William Farley, of Spartansburg, Pa.; Richard Farley of Linesville, Pa.; and these members of the Buffalo and Erie County Historical Society: Walter Dunn, director; Lester Smith, associate director, and staff members, Miss Alice Pickup and Ivan Whitney.

I should like to express appreciation to the Buffalo and Erie County Public Library staff for help in locating research material. Thanks also go to Peter Andrews, Washington correspondent for the *Buffalo Courier Express,* and Joseph Ritz, staff member of the same paper, for reading the manuscript and offering valuable suggestions; also Leslie Bialler, of A. S. Barnes and Company, for editorial guidance.

Appreciation is due Justice John F. Dwyer, former district attorney of Erie County; Justice Carman Ball, also former district attorney of the same county, and Michael Dillon, present Erie County district attorney, for giving me an opportunity to examine statements in the district attorney's office pertaining to the trial of Leon F. Czolgosz.

The author is grateful for the permission to reprint the following quoted material:

The Buffalo Evening News for "Perhaps McKinley's Life Could

Be Saved Today," by Arthur Goldberg (in Chapters 11 and 28) ; "What Wasn't Told About the McKinley Operation," unsigned (in Chapters 8, 11, 17, and 28) ; "Dr. Mynter's Daughter Disputes Story of McKinley," unsigned (in Chapter 28) ; "T.R.'s Famous Surrey Ride Through the Adirondacks to Presidency," by C. R. Roseberry (in Chapter 19).

HARCOURT, BRACE & WORLD for *The Presidency*, by Clinton Rossiter (in Chapter 28) ; *The Robber Barons*, by Matthew Josephson (in Chapter 4).

HARPER & ROW, Publishers for *The Big Change*, by Frederick Lewis Allen (in Chapter 4) ; *The Assassins*, by Robert Donovan (in Chapter 11).

HOUGHTON MIFFLIN COMPANY for *Life of William McKinley*, by Charles S. Olcott (in Chapter 3).

THE MACMILLAN COMPANY for *The Autobiography of William Allen White*, by William Allen White (in Chapter 26).

RANDOM HOUSE, INC. (Alfred A. Knopf) for *Living My Life*, by Emma Goldman (in Chapters 4, 14, 15, 26, 28).

SCIENTIFIC AMERICAN for "Operation on President McKinley," by Selig Adler (in Chapter 28).

CHARLES SCRIBNERS AND SONS for *From McKinley to Harding*, by H. H. Kohlsaat (in Chapter 20).

FREDERICK UNGAR PUBLISHING CO., INC. for *The President Makers*, by Matthew Josephson (in Chapter 28).

THE MAN
WHO SHOT
McKINLEY

Part I

THE DAYS BEFORE

1

"A Fair Sort of Man"

ON THE NIGHT of August 31, 1901, a young man in his late twenties walked into the barroom of J. Nowak's saloon-hotel on the east side of Buffalo and asked for a room. The young man was Leon F. Czolgosz.[1] Like scores of other arrivals in the city that night he had come to attend the world-famed Pan-American Exposition.

John Nowak was an old hand at sizing up people. The newcomer seemed "a fair sort of man." He was neatly dressed in a gray suit and wore a black shoestring tie. Probably, thought Nowak, a clerk or a bartender on holiday. Something about the stranger's dreamy eyes even suggested a writer. His face was handsome except for a slight, almost imperceptible scar that ran along his lower left cheek. In one hand he carried a telescope-shaped valise; in the other, a brown hat with a yellow band.

The rates were $2 a week, Nowak told him, payable in advance. As the guest laid that amount on the bar, Nowak called to his clerk, Frank Walkowiak, and handed him a key.

"What name shall I write on the receipt?" Nowak asked, then raised his eyes for another quick appraisal when the guest replied, "John Doe."

Nowak prided himself on his practical knowledge of human nature. The man had looked all right; he still did. Handing him the receipt, the proprietor nodded to Walkowiak to take him upstairs to his room.

As the clerk led the way, he turned and asked bluntly, "What made you say John Doe?"

"Well, I'll tell you," the stranger answered, "I'm a Polish Jew and I didn't like to tell him or he wouldn't keep me in the house."

---

1. Pronounced chôlgôsh.

13

Walkowiak, who besides being Nowak's clerk was reading law in the office of Nowak's attorney, pushed his questioning: "What is your real name?"

"Nieman, Fred Nieman," was the reply.

"What are you going to do here?"

"I'm going to sell souvenirs."

The man's explanations didn't entirely satisfy the clerk. Still, why worry? Many of Nowak's guests were queer fish. This one was better dressed than most.

Six doors opened on the second floor hallway. Walkowiak unlocked one of them. Then after exchanging a few more words with the visitor, he left.

What thoughts surged through the head of this strange young man after the door closed and he found himself alone in his small room at J. Nowak's?

These can only be surmised from what came to light about him much later. But by then he had performed his mission—and the whole world was agog, trying to solve the mystery of his shocking behavior.

Perhaps on this night, as he had on many nights before, he drew from his coat pocket a worn and crumpled newspaper clipping. No need to take it to the lamp. He knew its contents by heart. He had recited the details of the story over and over again. Its hero, Gaetano Bresci, was a simple, unknown man like himself. A silk-weaver and member of the Right to Existence, an anarchist group from Paterson, New Jersey, Bresci had set sail for LeHavre, France, on May 17, 1900. During the next few weeks there had been a deadly directness about his movements, which culminated in his murder of the King of Italy, Humbert I, near the Italian summer palace in Monza. Bresci had fired five revolver shots at the monarch, who was distributing prizes to young athletes. All but the last bullet had found their mark. The monarch died on the spot.

This act illustrated perfectly the ideal of the branch of the Anarchist movement that subscribed to "propaganda of the deed." No vague theorizing for its adherents! They demanded the annihilation of all rulers, all governing heads, capitalist magnates—even members of the clergy.

Bresci had performed a great act of liberation. But soon this strange man, too, would perform a "noble" act—for sometime within the next few days he, Leon F. Czolgosz, was going to kill the President of the United States.

2

"Who Would Want to Shoot Me?"

"WHO WOULD WANT to shoot me?" asked President William McKinley; and as if to allay all possible fears for his life, he smilingly added, "The American people are too intelligent for that."

His sanguine observation on the mentality of the American public, however, did not convince Attorney General John W. Griggs. Indeed, the list of those fearful for McKinley's life was impressive. It included not only Griggs, but the burly Republican boss, Mark A. Hanna; Cleveland banker Myron T. Herrick; Chief John E. Wilkie of the Secret Service; the President's personal secretary, 39-year-old George B. Cortelyou; as well as the Secret Service operative, George E. Foster, who had been sent to Canton, Ohio—the McKinleys' home town—to guard the President during the summer of 1901.

Foster, a professional sleuth, was clearly recognizable as such at a block's distance. A derby tilted rakishly on one side of his thatch of gray hair, a pair of drooping mustaches, a cigar clenched belligerently in his teeth, and an air of imminent discovery stamped him clearly for what he was. Strangers, and even the President's friends, were subject to Foster's scrutiny as they drove down North Market Street or ambled along the brick walk in front of the President's rambling frame house.

McKinley, as he had at the White House, took a complacent view of the doughty guard and eluded him whenever possible, slipping away for a solitary walk or for a drive with Cortelyou or the First Lady. The Secret Service man appeared to be only an unwelcome supernumerary until mid-August, when suddenly, as if to justify his presence, he spotted a suspicious looking figure flitting through the area between the McKinley home and the adjoining property. Suddenly unleashed, Foster sprang into action, pursuing his prey through the downtown area. Canton, aroused from its midsummer lethargy, sizzled with excitement. The incident, which mushroomed as it passed from lip to lip, furnished the town with dinnertime conversation for the rest of the summer.

The shadowy suspect was never brought to heel, and the President, who took his customary light view of such alarms, went on pacing his garden and smoking his twenty cigars daily, as he enjoyed what had been his first real vacation in years. To mollify alarmists, however, he did consent to have the livingroom shades drawn at night.

Fears for McKinley's life had started at the time of the Spanish-American conflict, when the usual trickle of threats and crank letters had swollen to a torrent under the excitement and strain that swept the nation. There were reports of infernal machines being delivered to the White House. Even though McKinley was the most popular President since Lincoln, unrest seethed under the veneer of increased prosperity and the sweeping naval victories over Spain.

The President had been severely censured on the one hand for his dilatory entrance into the conflict, and on the other for grasping the fruits of victory.

Security arrangements for the President, as Chief Wilkie of the Secret Service soon discovered when he took office in 1897, were lamentably weak. Wilkie, a former Chicago newsman, found the department shot through with inefficiency and hobbled by men who had been appointed only because of their political connections. But Wilkie had cleaned house. He insisted on picking men for their ability and ordered a stop to third-degree and stool-pigeon methods. Measures to protect the President were stepped up.

About this time two of Wilkie's Philadelphia operatives, Ahern and Griffin, reported that they had supposedly eavesdropped on a plot to murder McKinley. Concealed in a coal chute, the sleuths were on the verge of learning the name of the murderer when they were deluged by a load of coal and all further information was blacked out—an incident which, if true, makes one wonder exactly how much the department's efficiency had been improved.

At this time neither the Secret Service Department, nor for

that matter any other bureau, was officially empowered to protect the President. Wilkie, in fact, exceeded his official authority by providing Foster as a personal bodyguard. Since he had no legal authority to pay men out of funds allocated to his department, Wilkie risked official censure by charging the costs to counterfeiting.

Other factors besides the war contributed to fears for McKinley's life. One was the alarming growth of Anarchism since 1875. Anarchists were at first mere theorizers. They beheld somewhere in the vague future a Utopian society where mankind would feast upon a common manna, unfettered by economic woes, untroubled by the shackles of state, where every man—as Bakunin and Proudhon and their followers had preached—would live in a world of unworried splendor where free love would reign. But terror had followed theory, and by 1901 at least two monarchs lay moldering in their royal graves while others had been nicked by bombs and exploding infernal machines hurled by the more rabid of the malcontents.

With increased industrialization and a widening rift between the classes, Anarchistic ideals found fertile ground on which to propagate. Bitter labor disputes led to bloodshed. In 1886 the famous Haymarket Riot erupted in Chicago. Later, in Homestead, Pennsylvania, steel magnate Henry Clay Frick's hired Pinkerton men battled in open warfare with striking Bessemer furnace workers. In 1894 President Cleveland sent government troops to quell the Chicago Pullman strikers.

As the arrogant rich piled fortune upon fortune, resentment smoldered among the masses. The underpaid sweatshop-workers and tenement-dwellers were hardly cheered in their misery by the fact that the *nouveau riche* often lavished enough money on a single night's revelry to support a thousand families for more than a year.

Meanwhile the yellow press, led by the young multimillionaire William Randolph Hearst, was fulminating. After the conclusion of the war, which he had so vigorously helped to instigate, Hearst continued to flay relentlessly both McKinley and Republican Boss Mark Hanna. The President was little more than a puppet (as depicted by Hearst), manipulated by the crafty Cleveland industrialist.

One of Hearst's writers, the querulous but talented Ambrose Bierce, had on the occasion of the assassination of William Goebel, a contender for the governorship of Kentucky, penned a verse which read:

> The bullet that pierced Goebel's breast
> Can not be found in all the West;
> Good reason, it is speeding here
> To stretch McKinley on his bier.

Hearst's attacks on the President reached their lowest point on April 10, 1901, when his *Journal* printed an editorial which asserted, "If bad institutions and bad men can be got rid of only by killing, then the killing must be done." Though responsible for many venomous attacks on the President, Hearst claimed later that this editorial, generally attributed to Arthur Brisbane, had been published without his personal knowledge. When he became aware of it, he said that he had ordered the presses to be stopped and the editorial to be softened. But a number of *Journals* had already reached the streets.

More disturbing to Hanna, however, than the puerile spewings of Hearst's *Journal* was a report that came into his possession in the summer of 1900. Unearthed by Secret Service man Ralph D. Redfern, it had actually been compiled by a temporary Secret Service operative named E. Moretti two years before and had evidently remained buried in the files ever since. By some devious means Moretti had managed to infiltrate an Anarchist grotto in Paterson, New Jersey, then acknowledged as the fountainhead of American Anarchism. His report was a hair-raiser: it ticked off in order a number of high-placed personages who were to be liquidated. The whole plot was so bloodthirsty in its systematic fingering as to seem fantastic; yet among those proscribed two had already fallen victim to Anarchist assassins. These were the world-renowned beauty Empress Elizabeth of Austria, wife of Franz Joseph, and King Humbert of Italy. Others doomed by the timetable but still alive were the Czar of Russia, the aged Queen Victoria of England or her son Edward, the President of the United States, and the Kaiser of Germany.

Empress Elizabeth had been killed in September 1898, but Humbert's death had occurred in July 1900, only shortly before

Redfern submitted the report to Hanna. Hanna may also have recalled that the Prince of Wales (later Edward VII), an alternate for the third place upon the list, had been fired upon in a Brussels railway station the preceding April.

Big, bluff Hanna, who had survived and even thrived upon the jungle savagery of industrial warfare, quailed when he scrutinized the report, which proposed to destroy the man he had helped to put in the White House. He hastened to effect ways to improve the Presidential guarding, as he warned the President of needlessly exposing himself to danger. (Incidentally, upon Hanna's recommendation Redfern received an appointment as Assistant Sergeant at Arms at Republican headquarters in Chicago as a reward for his sleuthing.)

Of the President's menage perhaps no one was more fearful of an attempt on his chief's life than his secretary, the alert and efficient Cortelyou. A Georgetown graduate and holdover from the Cleveland administration, the secretary had become a general factotum in the McKinley summer household, as well as in the President's official life. Now Cortelyou's fears were not vague but centered specifically upon the President's planned September 6 appearance at the Buffalo Pan-American Exposition, where McKinley was to greet thousands of exposition goers at a reception in the ornate Temple of Music.

Following his intuition, Cortelyou cancelled the Temple appearance. However, the President restored it—not once but twice. Fearing Presidential censure, the secretary let the reception stand though later, his fears still undiminished, he took precautionary measures that he thought would safeguard the President.

3
"A Model for Every Boy to Emulate"

THE PRESIDENT'S APPARENT LIGHT VIEW of his own safety was no doubt partly temperamental, but was also the result of a self discipline that the circumstances of his life had forced him to cultivate. Journalist William Allen White, calling upon him in Canton one swelteringly hot summer day in 1900, was impressed by McKinley's cool, calm, unruffled manner. No wrinkle or sign of care appeared to mar his unblemished face. He looked, White thought, as if he had been "buttoned up" in early youth and never unbuttoned.

Now 58, portly, balding, of less than medium height, McKinley was still a handsome man. He looked every inch the President. Yet his dignity was softened by geniality. Behind his seriousness were hidden fires of humor, which often broke into boyish practical joking.

The most impressive features of his pale face, all agreed, were his eyes—gray and penetrating, almost fixed in their intensity of expression. Behind them lay only a hint of personal tragedies—a chronically invalid wife and the deaths of their two daughters in infancy.

All his old Canton friends still referred to him as "The Major," the brevet rank with which he had been mustered out of the Union Army and which he had worn in all its newness when he had come to practice law in this thriving little community 34 years before.

By this time the President was an institution—a model for every boy to emulate. Most everyone in Canton could recite the highlights of his career. He had been born of hard working middle-class parents in Niles, Ohio, and had been educated at

21

Poland (Ohio) Seminary and for one term at Allegheny College in Meadville, Pennsylvania.

At 18 he had enlisted in the 23d Ohio Volunteers in June, 1861, and had seen service in some of the bloodiest encounters with the "Rebs" at Antietam, Kernstown, Opequan, Fisher's Hill, and Cedar Creek. Colonel Rutherford B. Hayes, under whom McKinley was serving in 1862, referred to him, then a second lieutenant, as "an exceedingly bright, intelligent and gentlemanly young officer."

After serving throughout the entire war and emerging without even a minor wound he entered the law office of Judge Charles E. Glidden. There ensued a term at the Albany Law School, following which he had come to Canton, largely at the instigation of his older sister, Anna, who was teaching there. After this Mc-Kinley's political ascent had been steady. In Congress, where he served seven terms, he espoused the high protective tariff, mastering its intricacies and driving home his defense of it with telling oratory on the house floor. Two terms as Governor of Ohio—successful but not particularly distinguished—had followed. Then —the Presidency.

What was probably recognized only by fellow politicians was that behind the dignified, bland façade was a political shrewdness without peer in his time. Smooth as a velvet glove, he gained his ends by tact and indirection and a capacity for making friends of enemies.

McKinley was now six months into his second term. Behind him—solid achievements all—were the return of the country to prosperity after the Cleveland doldrums, the staving off of the Bryan silver peril, the victorious war with Spain, the emergence of the United States as a world power, and overseas expansion with the annexation of Hawaii and the acquisition of the faraway Philippines. The President had sweated out the 90-day conflict from the White House war room, now heartened by the news of Dewey's and Schley's spectacular victories at sea, now depressed by Shafter's bumbling campaign in Cuba. He had survived the calumnies heaped upon his head when he hesitated to plunge the nation into war and the cries of imperialism when he sought to grasp the fruits of victory.

Of course, there were those who charged that the protective

tariff, far from protecting the masses, only subsidized the rich. Still, McKinley had found no difficulty in gaining a second term, *again* defeating the platform mesmerist, William Jennings Bryan. Stumping the country on his way to defeat, Bryan was brilliant. McKinley conducted his campaign from his North Market Street front porch. Hanna loaded up trainloads of Republicans who made the pilgrimage to Canton, where the "safe" GOP candidate warned of the dangers of a weakened currency and regaled the faithful in his bell-like voice with campaign oratory.

McKinley had rightfully interpreted his reelection in 1900 as a mandate of all the people, and now he looked to possible reciprocity treaties and, it was rumored, some curbing of the big trusts whose tentacles had been strangling competition.

But the past few years had been hectic, and before leaving Washington for the beloved haven of his North Market Street home, he had definitely throttled the growing demand that he seek a third term.

As the warm summer days slipped by, the President delighted in the simple, relaxing activities of which he had been so long deprived—family outings and picnics, drives about town in the McKinley runabout, evening hymn-sings and an occasional game of euchre. Once traveling in Colonel Herrick's private railroad car, he paid a visit to Minerva, Ohio, where he inspected the farm inherited from Mrs. McKinley's father. A second excursion took the President to Zoar, seat of a group of German refugees, who until recently had lived a communal life. Then there was a day at the Stark County Fair.

Charles G. Dawes, at this time the 36-year-old United States Comptroller of the Currency, visiting Canton in mid-August, found the President "in his best mood." The First Lady also was in excellent spirits and fully recovered from the bone felon and blood infection which had almost claimed her life during the Presidential tour of the Western states the previous spring. The lank, red-mustached, young comptroller, who enjoyed an almost filial relationship with the President, records in his 1901 diary that the couple was "passing a quiet pleasant summer" in their Canton home. "The callers are many," Dawes wrote, "but not so pestiferous as when they come bent on getting office."

It was not delicacy alone that withheld from common knowl-

edge the true nature of Mrs. McKinley's emotional and physical
condition. While Republican newspapers no doubt suppressed
information along this line out of consideration for the President's
feelings, the Democratic press did not wish to show McKinley in
a role where he was assuredly near perfection. Certainly as a husband he was without peer, if not a true martyr.

When the 27-year-old Major McKinley, then on the first rung
of his political career as prosecuting attorney of Stark County,
married the attractive Ida Saxton on January 1, 1871, everyone
gathered for the wedding in the newly erected Presbyterian
Church must have thought that the new year could not ring in a
more promising match. Here was a handsome, ambitious, serious-
minded groom—obviously a comer. To spark his solid worthiness,
the bride offered a cultivation acquired from Brooke Hall finish-
ing school in Media, Pennsylvania, and an eight-month sojourn
in Europe. Ida's father, one of Canton's leading bankers, was
apparently well-pleased with his elder daughter's choice, for his
wedding gift to the pair was their North Market Street home.
This they occupied until McKinley went to Washington for his
first term in Congress, then later repurchased in 1899 for $14,500.

The couple's first child, Katie, arrived on the Christmas Day
of their first year of marriage. Soon a series of tragedies overtook
them which culminated in Ida's complete collapse. Shortly before the arrival of their second child, Mrs. McKinley's mother
died. Then five months later the baby Ida also died. These events
appeared to have plunged Mrs. McKinley into a severe depression
from which she had not rallied when little Katie was taken from
them in 1876. Ida emerged a seriously handicapped invalid, unable to walk without assistance, an epileptic, definitely a neurotic.
McKinley emerged stronger, more solid than ever. Patiently, un-
ceasingly, he watched over his wife. Later, as President, he chose
to break with protocol in order to sit beside her at state dinners
and on other formal occasions. There was never a moment when
he was without anxiety for her. If his wife's face was contorted by a
seizure he covered it quickly with a napkin or handkerchief, as
unperturbed as though this were a common gesture of Presidents.
To his wife's condition he never specifically alluded.

Over the years the two continued to dote upon each other as
fondly as young sweethearts. "My Precious" was one of Mrs. Mc-

Kinley's favorite terms of endearment for her husband. He in turn addressed her with all the ardor and courtliness of a lover.

Though Ida received far more than she could give, she was capable of deep loyalty for, as well as pride in, her husband. Once she tartly corrected a friend who inadvertently had referred to McKinley as "a politician," reminding him that "statesman" was the appropriate word to describe her husband.

In 1893 when the bankruptcy of a friend whom McKinley had backed with notes amounting to $100,000 threatened to ruin him financially and politically too (he feared), Mrs. McKinley insisted upon making available for his use her inheritance, valued at some $70,000. To her objecting attorneys she retorted, "My husband has done everything for me all my life. Do you mean to deny me the privilege of doing as I please with my property to help him now?" Fortunately through the efforts of some of McKinley's friends, notably Hanna, it was not necessary to dip into Mrs. McKinley's small fortune.

During McKinley's term as Governor of Ohio the couple lived in a suite in the Neil House across the street from the capitol. Every morning as he entered the executive building McKinley turned to raise his hat to his wife in the window opposite. At 3:00 every afternoon he suspended all gubernatorial duties to wave his handkerchief from his office window and receive an answering wave from his wife.

Though Ida was incapable of taking on any of the usual house-wifely duties, she kept her fingers busy with the needle and crochet hook. The number of bedroom slippers which she crocheted and her maid sewed to cork soles was rated in the thousands. She also hand-sewed black satin neckties, which her loyal husband wore tied in large soft bows.

When McKinley was elected to the Presidency those in his intimate circle, as well as the townspeople of Canton, shook their heads at the idea of Mrs. McKinley's taking on the responsibilities of First Lady. But it soon became evident that Ida McKinley intended to bask in the full sunshine of her husband's exalted position. There were to be no proxy First Ladies.

The ineptitude of her performance at the time of the first inauguration set the pattern for the years ahead. The Presidential party had arrived in the capital in seven Pullman cars from

Canton on the day before the ceremony. Though Mrs. McKinley had slept badly, she valiantly refused the wheelchair that awaited her, and carrying a large bouquet in one arm and clinging heavily to her husband with the other, she trudged through the Washington railway station.

At the Ebbitt House reporters and well-wishers were greeted by members of the McKinley and Saxton families. Notable among them was the President's frisky, self-reliant 87-year-old mother, Nancy Allison McKinley. But Ida rested in her room, later sending her regrets to the Clevelands, who had invited her for an evening at the White House to discuss the domestic takeover.

At the inauguration ceremony, though stylishly attired in royal blue velvet, sealskin cape, black bonnet edged in white, by her pallid face and unsteady gait she gave onlookers the impression of a very ill woman.

In the evening the inaugural ball furnished a brief glimpse of the First Lady, befeathered and resplendent in a silver and blue dress, diamonds, a corsage of violets, a lace fan, and silken evening cape richly edged in white fox fur. Half a turn around the ballroom as she clung pathetically to her husband's arm—and the promenade came to an abrupt stop. Quickly she was whisked into the supper room and was seen no more on that momentous day.

Fortunately, Mrs. Garret A. Hobart, the wife of the Vice-President[1] during McKinley's first term and a woman of unusual perception and kindliness, took over some of the more exhausting duties of the First Lady. At formal receptions Ida would sit complacently in her blue chair holding a bouquet of flowers to ward off possible hand-shakers while her husband eased the person he was greeting gently past her to shake the hand of Mrs. Hobart, standing on her other side.

In an age when extreme courtliness is obsolescent the picture of the President, ever watchful, apprehensive, ready to spring to his wife's side at the slightest provocation, suggests sentimentality even with a touch of hypocrisy. But there is every indication that the same tender solicitude they displayed at public functions was present in their private life. Charles S. Olcott in his *Life of William McKinley* quotes a neighbor in Canton, " 'A thousand

---

1. Garret A. Hobart died in office on November 21, 1899.

times . . . I have seen him spring from his chair with an almost startling speed of movement to those not accustomed to his watchful care.' " Even when he was called from an important meeting or conference upon one of her vagaries "as to express a preference between two shades of ribbon, or to help select a present for a friend," he would respond to her request, then inquire, "Is that all, Ida?" excuse himself and go back to the matter under consideration.

Ida did not like cigar smoking, so his twenty Garcias a day could not be smoked in her presence. Ida was fearful of taking cold, so the President rode in closed carriages and lived in close, stuffy rooms.

Though McKinley's solicitude for his wife was well known to Cantonians and in Washington circles, it came to the attention of the general public in the late spring of 1901. Shortly after his second inauguration an extensive tour of the country was planned, which would culminate in Buffalo for the Pan-American Exposition. President's Day was at that time slated for June 13. A group of 43 in all—cabinet members and their wives, officials, staff members, newspapermen, servants—left the capital in a special train late in April bound for the West Coast. Mrs. McKinley was pleased to have as a companion her favorite niece, Mary Barber. She was attended by her personal physician, Dr. Presley M. Rixey, and of course her faithful maid, Clara Tharin. It became evident from the ovations given the President in Memphis, New Orleans, Houston, San Antonio, that the Republican former Yankee war hero had won the hearts of his Southern constituents.

Then at El Paso Mrs. McKinley became ill. Dr. Rixey lanced the bone felon that seemed to be the seat of the trouble, but she became increasingly worse. Against his strict Methodist scruples the President traveled on the Sabbath to get her to San Francisco. There she sank into a stupor. After two weeks of critical illness she rallied. Meanwhile, the President had cancelled all engagements to remain at her side. He watched and prayed, while thanks to the reports of the press the whole country was able to share his anxiety.

Two days after the crisis had passed the President attended the launching of the battleship *Ohio*. In his address the chief executive expressed gratitude "to the Ruler of us all for His goodness and His mercy," Who had made it possible for him to perform his duty on that day.

When the First Lady felt able to travel, the Presidential party returned directly to Washington. The return route into the Northwest and the proposed visit to Buffalo were both cancelled. President's Day at the Pan-American Exposition was rescheduled for September 5.

Amid the homey pleasures, which with slight variation had occupied the McKinleys during the intervening summer of 1901, slowly the President's forthcoming Pan-American speech began to take shape. During the day spent at Minerva with Colonel Herrick, Dr. Rixey, Cortelyou, and others he had been mulling over ideas for what would prove to be his most important and his last address.

In the evening after dinner he led Mrs. McKinley to her chair in the sitting room as was his custom and excusing himself retired with Cortelyou to the library. As he sat by the open window smoking a cigar, he suddenly turned to Cortelyou and said, "Expositions are the timekeepers of progress." Cortelyou jotted down the statement. The President continued, "We'll build the speech around that." Later, back in the sitting room with his guests, he explained to Colonel Herrick that his advocacy of a high tariff in 1890 had been necessary "to get my bill passed," adding that he had planned to "make necessary reductions later." He was conscious, he remarked, that larger markets were needed as an outlet for American producers. "The period of exclusiveness is past," he stated, and these words were to become the keynote of his Pan-American speech.

As the speech neared completion, Cortelyou ventured his final plea that McKinley forgo his Temple of Music appearance on September 6. At best, the secretary reasoned, the President could hope to greet only a few of the thousands who would wish to shake his hand.

"Well," replied the President, "they'll know I tried, anyhow."

Still disturbed by fears for the President's life, and also concerned about the First Lady, Cortelyou shot an admonitory telegram to Buffalo warning officials that no precaution should be spared during the couple's visit. The First Lady, Cortelyou stressed, was to be spared undue disturbance of any kind. She would attend a luncheon in her honor on September 5 and would appear with her husband on the platform when he delivered his principal address, as well as accompany him to the evening display of fireworks. Otherwise, engagements were politely but firmly declined. Fearful of a repetition of the contretemps that had frightened Mrs. McKinley in Pittsburgh, when shots had caused carriage horses to rear up, Cortelyou especially warned that all gun salutes should be fired from an ample distance.

In Buffalo, meanwhile, General William Bull, the 58-year-old superintendent of police, who had fought in some of the same Civil War encounters as McKinley, was laying plans to ensure the President's utmost safety at every turn during the three-day visit. Four crack detectives were to be assigned to the President along with Foster and two other Secret Servicemen, Al Gallaher and Sam Ireland. In anticipation of the Presidential visit and to cope as well with a heavy influx of petty thieves, 75 policemen had been added to the Buffalo force. These would be augmented by the Pan-American guards, Coast Artillerymen, Pinkerton men, and railroad detectives.

The protection—on paper at least—looked perfect and, considering McKinley's disdain of guards, top-heavy.

4

"He Pays His Bills Doesn't He?"

DURING THE NEXT FEW DAYS after Czolgosz had made his first appearance at Nowak's saloon his routine varied little. He rose early, read the papers, and left his barren room to saunter along Broadway or visit the Exposition. He bought cigars at the tavern but no meals.

Walkowiak was often on duty at the bar evenings when Czolgosz returned. The clerk's suspicions had never been entirely allayed. Once he spoke to Nowak about his feelings, but the saloonkeeper had more important matters on his mind. Nowak only shrugged his shoulders. Why should he bother about flimsy suspicions? "He pays his bills, doesn't he?" asked Nowak.

As far as Nowak was concerned, Czolgosz was an exemplary roomer. He came and went with little fuss or bother. He had little to say. Nowak noticed with approval that he always ordered good whiskey, never that five-cents-a-shot stuff. At night when he returned to the tavern he usually carried a sheaf of newspapers under his arm and retired to his room.

Occasionally he lingered a few minutes at the bar or watched a card game. One night he volunteered the information that he had attended St. Casimir's Church.

Soon Czolgosz had become a minor, unobtrusive figure in the area of the East Side tavern.

Now and then he struck up a conversation with someone in the vicinity like John Romantowski, who lived nearby in Sycamore Street. Romantowski was impressed but apparently not suspicious when Czolgosz flashed before his eyes a $50 bill from a roll he had.

With Joseph Rutkowski, a barber, Czolgosz talked about Socialism while he was being shaved, though he disavowed any adherence to the theory himself.

Possibly the only negative impression he made in the circle around the saloon-hotel at 1078 Broadway was upon Alphonse Stutz, another roomer at Nowak's and a retired German army officer, who resented being aroused from sleep one morning by Czolgosz, who was in search of a pitcher of water.

In the city papers Czolgosz took to his room each evening there was plenty of information to help him formulate his strategy for the grand gesture he was planning during the President's visit to the Exposition. *The Express, The Courier, The Times, The Commercial*—in any he could have learned precisely the schedule the President would follow.

The Presidential party would reach the city after an all-day journey by train from Canton, Ohio. The President and First Lady would be guests in the Delaware Avenue home of John G. Milburn, Exposition president.

Had Czolgosz ever set foot on the broad, tree-shaded Delaware Avenue its very name would have sent shivers of resentment coursing through his entire body. Its opulent mansions, luxuriously landscaped and set upon wide expanses of close-clipped lawns, bespoke the highest in wealth and privilege that the city could offer at the time.

The Presidential Special, outfitted like a miniature White House, was to roll into the Amherst Station on the Pan-American grounds at 6:00 on the evening of September 4.

From his many visits to the Exposition grounds it is probable that Czolgosz could recall this low frame building well enough, for it had been painted violet as part of the Exposition's rainbow color scheme. It stood at the northern end of the grounds, surrounded by a block-long platform, and separated from the grounds proper by a fence.

The President would be closely guarded as it was conservatively estimated that he would be greeted by a crowd of 40,000. In spite of what he had read about the guards and the crowds Czolgosz decided that he would be on the platform of the violet-colored station on the evening of Thursday, September 4, to meet the President as he alighted from his special train.

Who was this solitary, erratic man, Leon F. Czolgosz; and what were the currents driving him toward the horrendous act he was so coolly planning in his little room above Nowak's saloon?

Like millions of others in the ranks of the poor and the oppressed he had brooded over the injustices and the inequalities that surrounded him. In the country as a whole, a chasm wider than the distance between the mansion of John G. Milburn and the saloon-hotel of John Nowak divided the rich from the poor. Unhampered by federal restrictions and guided only by their elastic and often slippery consciences the rich indulged in pleasures which recalled decadent civilizations of the past.

As if to flaunt the downtrodden and the hungry, some Sybarites of the period capered until dawn at Sherry's or Delmonico's or reveled in Lucullan feasts served up on gold plates. The Bradley Martin fancy dress ball at the Waldorf—reported to have cost $369,200, its ten-course feast washed down with cognac and champagne—made for spectacular reading in the press but hardly cheered the thousands who went to bed hungry.

J. P. Morgan, the gruff master of Wall Street, was spending the summer of 1901 on his yacht, *Corsair III*, riding off the New Jersey coast, from which he commuted daily to New York—but not because of a lack of housing. Besides his town house at 291 Madison Avenue, New York City, he had his country estate at Highland Falls, his London double house, his 1000-acre Adirondacks place, his Jekyll Island apartment, his "fishing box" at Newport, his palatial suites in Rome and Paris, not to mention a private steamer especially designed for navigation of the Nile River.

Few of the privileged bothered to ponder the injustices of the order of things. Had not Providence in its wisdom ordained it this way? "God gave me my money," piously stated John D. Rockefeller.

The magnates who dominated industry usually thought of themselves as munificent masters of slaves they expected to be obedient. Mine operator George F. Baer best expressed their reasoning in describing business as "not a religious, sentimental or academic proposition."

At the same time coal miners laboring in the Pennsylvania

fields, amassing fortunes for their masters, struggled along on wages of $358 to $450 a year.

Conditions for the workers were, for the most part, dismal. At times they rebelled. Anarchism found fertile ground in which to thrive. In 1887, four men went to the gallows in Chicago as the result of an Anarchist-fomented strike, but long after the case had been officially closed the silhouettes of their gibbeted bodies dangled as symbols of their cause. The Haymarket Riot in May 1886, arising from a demand for an eight-hour working day, ballooned into a *cause célèbre*, its leaders enshrined as martyrs in the eyes of their followers. "Let the world know," cried August Spies, one of those sentenced to die, "that in 1886 in the State of Illinois eight men were sentenced to death because they believed in a better world."

In 1892, labor and capital clashed in another bloody struggle at the Carnegie Steel plant at Homestead, Pennsylvania. When a strike erupted there, Henry Clay Frick ordered in scab labor and 300 Pinkerton men to guard them. In the ensuing battle three Pinkerton men and ten workers were killed.

The blood of workers flowed freely again in 1894 during the Pullman strike in Chicago. After four days of terror and fires, 14,000 state and federal troops managed to restore an uneasy peace after scores had been killed and wounded.

The situation was exacerbated at times by inflammatory statements made by the spokesmen for capital—and by the champions of the underdogs. Although removed from its original context, William H. Vanderbilt's remark, "the public be damned," made no friends for the rich—nor did steel magnate Andrew Carnegie's wire to Frick at the conclusion of the Homestead strike, "Congratulations—life is worth living again."

The brooding discontent of the poor flamed into diatribe. "The great common people . . . are slaves, and monopoly is master." cried Populist leader Mary Ellen Lease; and the outraged Anarchist editor Enrico Malatesta cried out, ". . . every bit of bread they [the rich] eat is taken from your children."

From behind her pince nez glasses a Jewish Anarchist leader, herself disillusioned with the American system, watched the struggle between the classes, convinced like her companions that the time had come for action. This short, snub-nosed radical, who burned with the injustices of the system and who had been embittered by her own sweatshop experiences, was Emma Goldman, known as the High Priestess of Anarchism.

Still seared in her memory were the days of her youth when she had witnessed the gendarmes beating Russian peasants with knouts until the blood dripped from their naked backs. She remembered the pogroms, and she could not forget the ghettoes into which she and her fellow Jews had been herded. An immigrant from frozen Russia, she had arrived in New York City in 1885, full of plans and ideals that were shortly shattered. She found want and misery, sweatshops, low pay, and disease side by jowl with staggering wealth and ostentatious luxury.

After several disillusioning experiences in Rochester, she decided to return to New York City. Here she sought out the radicals and met Alexander Berkman, who became her lover. Berkman took her to hear Johann Most, the German Anarchist.

Emma had already come under Most's influence through his paper, *Freiheit,* but at her first meeting with him she was repulsed by his twisted, bearded face. His facial disfigurement—the result of a bone infection—had caused him to abandon an acting career. Instead, he became a radical spellbinder whose ability to sway workmen led after his arrival in the United States to his leadership of left-wing forces.

Most, who soon became Emma's idol, recognized her latent ability as a speaker, adopted her as his protegee, and sent her on a speaking tour to Buffalo, Rochester, and Cleveland.

Both Emma and Berkman had in their several ways reacted to the Haymarket affair. The America of their idealistic hopes, they concluded, was far too similar to the Russia of their childhood memories. Learning of the Homestead incident, they decided the hour had struck for action. Berkman appropriated for himself the role of assassinating Frick. With this as his goal he boarded a train for Pittsburgh, where he managed by a ruse to gain access to Frick. His attempt on Frick's life failed. The industrialist, not seriously wounded, emerged as a hero. Berkman, at 22, was sentenced to spend his next 22 years in prison. As an aftermath Emma broke with Most.

Despite the rupture with Most, Emma nevertheless continued to appear frequently at radical meetings, which were often held under police surveillance. After one explosive tirade in New York City she was whisked off to Blackwell's Island for inciting to riot.

Then on May 6, 1901, she spoke before the Franklin Liberal Club in Cleveland, where she laid down the principles by which she expected universal Anarchy to prevail. In her speech she did not condone violent measures and pointed out that education was the real answer to social betterment. Nevertheless, she gave a rundown of the recent violent measures enacted by Anarchists, obliquely praising them because they could not stand aside while workers suffered. Their motives were high and noble; their means in which they acted upon these motives was a matter of temperament. "Men, under the present society are products of circumstances," she said. "Under the galling yoke of government and ecclesiasticism, it is impossible for the individual to work out his career as he could wish. Anarchism aims at a new and complete freedom."

One of the audience that night was Leon F. Czolgosz. The magnetism of the woman probably more than her words (for on this occasion they were not especially inflammatory) reached out to him. After Emma Goldman had finished, he moved down the aisle to greet her. Would she recommend some reading matter for him, he asked. Yes, she would be glad to, she replied.

Scanning him, she saw a handsome young man of moderate height, fairly muscular and well built with a shock of wavy blond hair. His eyes were the most unusual feature of his physiognomy —the eyes of a visionary. She was favorably impressed. Months, even years later she could recall his face. A highly sensitive being who could not accept complacently the injustice and inhumanity he found in the world without doing something about them—in this way she later was to explain away his act of violence. She elevated him into the company of martyrs—the forerunners to a better and a nobler life.

Indeed, the sensitive soul that Emma Goldman recognized in Czolgosz had been exposed from birth to the harsh injustices and inequalities that so often surrounded the typical worker of the day. From babyhood Leon had to cope with a hostile world, for even in his own family he was looked upon as odd. As he grew up, he became silent and withdrawn. Leon's father, Paul, now 58, but as bent and gnarled as a man of 80, had emigrated from Russian-dominated Poland a few months in advance of his wife and three children. Leon was born in Detroit in 1873, about a month after his mother's arrival. When she was 40, she died following the birth of her eighth child. Paul Czolgosz's remarriage furnished much of the unhappiness Leon experienced in his home. He looked upon his stepmother as a virago. As the years passed their hatred of each other deepened.

In 1902, Emma Goldman searched out Leon's father and stepmother, whom she described as "dark people—the father hardened by toil, the stepmother with a dull, vacant look." A skeleton in the family closet involved Paul Czolgosz in complicity in the murder of his boss, a man named Molitor—an accusation the Czolgoszes hotly denied.

Leon had five brothers—Waldeck and Frank were both older than he, and Jacob, Joseph, and Michael were younger. A sister, Ceceli, was married; but Victoria, only 17, was as yet unmarried and worked as a waitress.

Seeking to improve their lot, a bleak one at best, Leon's family moved frequently during his early life, spending seven years in Detroit, then moving to Rogers City in northern Michigan, and later to Posen and Alpena, both regions dominated by Polish culture.

Although regarded as the family intellectual because of his propensity for reading, Leon attended school for only five and one-half years. Apparently he derived some benefit from his limited schooling since he could both read and write English.

In 1889, when he was 16, the Czolgoszes moved to Natrona, Pennsylvania, where Leon found his first regular job as a bottle forker. When the family moved again two years later to Cleveland he worked in a wire mill, first as a winder, then as an assistant in charge of some machinery. In 1893, he joined in a strike for higher pay. When he returned to work, fearing that a new boss might think of him as a trouble maker, he used the alias Fred C. Nieman for the first time.

Up to this time Leon had always been a strict adherent of the Catholic church; but during the strike he and his oldest brother, Waldeck, who worked at the same mill, began to rebel against the tenets of the church. Unemployment had stirred serious doubts in their minds. Their prayers to God, they felt, had gone unanswered. The parish priests counselled the brothers to continue to pray. When they received no help—at least not the kind they wanted—the brothers decided to explore the mysteries of religion for themselves. They sent to New York City for a Polish Bible.

Both Leon and Waldeck appeared to become more skeptical after their reading of the Bible. Waldeck later revealed that they felt that the priests had "told it their way and kept the rest back." Leon, Waldeck said, compared the priest's trade "to a shoemaker's or any other." By 1896 Leon's break with the church was complete.

Leon voted only once—in 1894 when he was 21. That year he met Anton Zwolinski, president of a Polish educational group that discussed Anarchism and Socialism. Their discussions, Leon later confessed, raised doubts in his mind about the American form of government. The country's system of voting, he decided, was wrong and therefore he would not vote again.

Though in the group no mention was made of killing anyone, Presidents were generally regarded as "no good." His doubts grew when he attended meetings in the upper room over a saloon and grocery store which his father had bought in 1895 at Tod and Third Avenue in Cleveland. He sat in a back seat, silent, contributing nothing but listening, rapt, to speakers castigating the wealthy and privileged, the government, Wall Street, the capitalistic system, even religion.

Until 1898 regarded by his family, his employer, and the community as a steady worker Leon suddenly announced that he was quitting his job. Illness was the reason he gave. His foreman was dubious. "Sick!" he exclaimed, "You look well enough."

"Yes," was Leon's reply, "but I don't feel well; I'm quitting."

The days of his unemployment passed slowly. Most of his time was spent on the 55-acre farm that the family had pooled their money to buy near Warrensville, about twelve miles from Cleveland. Some days he got out his breech-loading shotgun. At other times he used a revolver—a weapon he used well—to hunt rabbits and other small game on the farm.

He slept a lot, and on hot summer days with flies and bees droning around him he curled up under an apple tree, read, then dozed off.

His stepmother thought he was crazy and told him so. He began eating in his room to get away from her, but his appetite was gone. A bowl of bread and milk was all he wanted. Occasionally he fished in a pond on the farm. When he was alone he might fry and eat his catch. If his stepmother or others intruded upon his cooking, he would burn the fish and throw it away.

Life on the Czolgosz farm was bleak, but there were occasional happy moments. He liked to read newspapers when he could get them. The yellow papers sparked his interest for they often lambasted the President and revealed him for what he was, Leon agreed, a hypocritical friend of the powerful. One day he happened upon an account of the Humbert assassination. He read it over and over, captivated by the bold way in which Gaetano Bresci had stalked and finally shot his royal quarry. Leon was so fascinated by the story that he clipped it and put it in his wallet, and even took it to bed with him.

During this period Leon showed clear evidences of hypochondria. He sent for and dosed himself with nostrums; he pored over the back pages of cheap magazines seeking for panaceas. Once he ordered an inhaling machine. To Waldeck at least there was some justification to Leon's claim of poor health. Once robust enough, Leon grew pale; he coughed; he had chronic catarrh. Waldeck thought his brother looked "gone to pieces" and suggested that he enter a hospital. Leon, however, waved aside the suggestion. "If you have lots of money you get well taken care of," he grumbled bitterly.

Their father also believed that Leon was sick and did not insist that he work. Besides if his mood was right Leon could do odd jobs on the farm like mending machinery and wagons or taking milk to the cheese factory. At times he did a little horse trading.

Although the physicians who examined Czolgosz before his trial recorded no illnesses at this time, in 1898 Leon had actually furnished a doctor's certificate to the benevolent order to which he belonged—The Knights of the Golden Eagle—and drew 16 weeks' sick benefits.

At this time Leon's personality suffered a change. He became restless and moody. He had always been withdrawn, having no real confidants except perhaps Waldeck. No one had ever seen him with a girl. In fact, he was so bashful that he would cross the street to avoid speaking to one. Yet his foreman described him during the seven years up to 1898 as "as good a boy" as he ever had. He never got into trouble, never quarreled, and was quiet and cheerful.

To Dr. Walter Channing, an alienist and Professor of Mental Diseases at Tufts Medical School, who made a detailed study of Czolgosz's case in 1902, Leon's 1898 illness was of tremendous importance. It transformed him from a steady, quite normal person "into a sickly, unhealthy and abnormal one."

"While in this physical and mental condition of sickliness," wrote Dr. Channing, "it is probable that he conceived the idea of performing some great act for the benefit of the common and working people." This resulted in the delusion that it was his mission to kill the President of the United States, who was to Leon at least the enemy of the people.

In March 1901, Leon's behavior—strange for three years—grew even stranger; his family was baffled. As he became more restless and mysterious, he demanded the return of the $400 he had contributed toward the purchase of the farm. At the same time he began to take two- and three-day trips, but where he went no one knew—his family least of all. When his brothers or sisters, naturally curious, asked him, he would snap "To the city" or "To meetings." Since he was so secretive and close-mouthed, they pressed the matter no further.

One day when Leon and Waldeck were standing under a tree, Leon brought up the subject of the farm money. "If I can't get my money now I want it in the summer," he told Waldeck.

"What do you want it for?" demanded Waldeck.

"Look," replied Leon, "it is just the same as a tree that commences dying—you can see it isn't going to live long."

Leon then revealed that he planned a trip to the West, where he hoped to land a job as a conductor or fixing machines or binding wheat.

Sometime later in a paper he was reading he came upon a

notice stating that Emma Goldman was to appear before the Franklin Liberal Club in Cleveland. He had often heard of the famous woman radical, and he decided to go.

The High Priestess was speaking as he entered the hall. Her spitfire delivery set him aflame. This was what he had been seeking—a gospel of action. In the spring days that followed her strident voice dinned in his ears. She was much more dynamic than the Cleveland radicals he had met. He once had belonged to the Social Labor party and to the Sila, an organization whose name meant *force*. Their ideas, for the most part, were piddling, he felt.

On May 19, Leon called upon Emil Schilling, the treasurer of a Cleveland Anarchist group known as the Liberty Club, saying he had been sent by a friend named Hauser. He passed himself off as Fred C. Nieman; but, Schilling noted, he spoke English, not German. He talked about capitalists in a way that Schilling considered revolutionary. Schilling gave him a book called *Chicago Martyrs* and some numbers of the Anarchist organ, *Free Society,* and also invited him to stay for dinner. At the time of this visit Schilling thought that Leon was all right.

In about three weeks Leon returned to Schilling. The Anarchist leader became rather angry when he learned that Leon had not read the literature lent him; also Schilling was suspicious of Leon's questions, asked in a very quick way, like, "Say, have you any secret societies?" Leon referred to Bresci's assassination of Humbert and wondered if the Anarchists were contemplating such an act. Schilling denied that the Anarchists did any plotting. His caller, Schilling felt, was always laughing at his answers, either because he felt superior or because he had a plan in mind and was putting out a "feeler."

After this visit Schilling decided to check with their mutual acquaintance, Hauser. Hauser vouched for Leon as a good and active member of the Polish Socialist Society of the Labor Party but said that his name was not really Nieman. However, Hauser could not at the time recall his right name and advised Schilling to "watch out" if he had any suspicions.

Leon's third visit to Schilling took place about a week later. This time he was dressed in his Sunday best. He told of his harassment by his stepmother and claimed he was sick of life. He wanted a letter of introduction to Emma Goldman. Schilling refused the letter but told Leon she was in Chicago. Leon then expressed a resolution "I go Chicago." Schilling decided that he would not accuse Leon as yet but lead him on a little longer, then tell him not to come again.

After Leon's return to the farm, Emma's voice kept dinning at him. He must, he decided, see her again. But he needed money to go to Chicago. When he demanded the money he had contributed to the purchase of the farm, there were scenes—shouting and wrangling. Finally, his father gave in and handed him the first installment of his share, $70.

By the time Czolgosz caught up with Emma Goldman in Chicago, she was on the point of leaving the city for Rochester. He called upon her at the home of her host, Abraham Isaak, the editor of *Free Society*, and accompanied her to the depot. Here she presented him to the Czech emigré, Hippolyte Havel (one of her several lovers), Abraham Isaak, and others. After Emma's departure he continued to converse with Isaak for about 40 minutes. He addressed Isaak as "comrade" and inquired about secret meetings.

Isaak asked him whether he was an Anarchist and had read Anarchist literature. Czolgosz replied that he knew nothing about Anarchy except what he had learned from Emma Goldman's speech in Cleveland. He was, he said, a Socialist and had been a member of the Socialist party in Cleveland for seven years. Since the organization had split he had become disgusted with it. The American government's action in the Philippine Islands appeared to trouble him. "It does not harmonize with the teachings in our public schools about our flag," he complained to Isaak. Though Isaak was supicious of Czolgosz he felt there was a certain sincerity expressed in the eyes and words of the young man.

Czolgosz visited Schilling a fourth time in August. Again he was dressed in his Sunday clothes. Schilling was, coincidentally, in the act of reading a letter from Isaak about him when Czolgosz appeared. Schilling thrust it in his pocket and asked his caller where he had been. Czolgosz answered that he had been working at a cheese factory in Akron, but laughed, so that Schilling did not take him seriously. They went for a walk with a third man, a friend of Schilling. Czolgosz appeared to be tired and spoke very little. When the men parted Schilling asked him where he intended to go. Czolgosz answered, "Maybe Detroit, maybe Buffalo."

At the time Schilling did not think that Czolgosz had a plan. He had not expressed himself as being against the President but against the party. Things, he said, were getting worse and worse: there were more strikes; strikers were being more brutally treated. After the shooting, however, Schilling changed his mind and as he later told the alienists, "I assume he plan to do it some months before he done it and only waited a good chance and hoped to get some help from friends [sic]."

After an exchange of letters between Schilling and Isaak, at Schilling's suggestion, Isaak printed a warning in the September number of *Free Society*. Though ostensibly a warning, it may have been a means of exculpating himself and his associates from any possible involvement with the attempted assassination, which would occur only five days later. The warning was headed *Attention!*

> The attention of the comrades is called to another spy. He is well dressed, of medium height, rather narrow shouldered, blond, and about 25 years of age. Up to the present he has made his appearance in Chicago and Cleveland. In the former place he remained but a short time, while in Cleveland he disappeared when the comrades had confirmed themselves of his identity and were on the point of exposing him. His demeanor is of the usual sort, pretending to be greatly interested in the cause, asking for names, or soliciting aid for acts of contemplated violence. If this individual makes his appearance elsewhere, the comrades are warned in advance and can act accordingly.

Before his last call on Schilling, on July 16, he had appeared in West Seneca, a Buffalo suburb, and taken a room at the home of Antoni Kazmarek, a Lake Shore Railroad track worker. At the Kazmareks' he followed much the routine that he had on the farm. He arose at seven and was in bed by 10 at night. Here also he was unusually withdrawn, sending a boy out for food, which he ate in his room.

Perhaps this was the same boy he hired for 10 cents to carry his bag to the trolley car bound for Buffalo on August 29. At Buffalo he boarded a lake steamer for Cleveland but remained in that city only one day—to buy some papers and look around, he later explained. However, if, as Schilling said, Czolgosz visited him in August, it is possible that this was the day of his last call upon the Cleveland Anarchist. He may have wished to make one last appeal to Schilling.

On the other hand, if he actually was without funds (as his inability to pay the $1.75 balance due to the Kazmareks for room rent would seem to indicate) perhaps he returned for funds to some source in Cleveland. At least, during his stay at Nowak's he seemed to have enough money—and if we can take at face value the testimony of Romantowski, who saw him draw out a roll of bills—even to be bountifully supplied.

Was Czolgosz's selection of the Buffalo area to while away the summer weeks a part of the "plan" Schilling believed he had in mind? Robert J. Donovan states that the President's visit to the Pan-American Exposition was not publicized until early August and suggests rather that Czolgosz may have sought out Buffalo on account of its large Polish population or because he was enticed there by the low excursion rates offered at the time of the Exposition.

Czolgosz himself said he went there to find work. If so, he made very little effort to do so and once during this time loftily remarked that he never worked when it was hot. There is no evidence to imply that Czolgosz was still on the trail of Emma Goldman except that she also visited the Pan-American city on August 13. Neither one ever confessed to a meeting at that time, but by the code of the Anarchists they might not have done so in any case. Of course, it might have also been pure coincidence that originally planted Czolgosz in the vicinity of his crime some six weeks before it was committed.

5

"Anarchists! They've Wrecked the Train"

TO MRS. McKINLEY the summer now waning had been one of the most enjoyable of her life. Was it a presage of danger to come that made her confide in her diary a reluctance to leave their Canton home?

A consolation perhaps was the inclusion in the party of the First Lady's favorite niece, Mary Barber, and the President's niece, Sarah Duncan, of Cleveland. Both the McKinleys delighted in having young people about them, a compensation no doubt for the loss of their own children.

The hours slipped away. Trunks and office files were stacked aboard the Presidential Special. September 4 dawned auspiciously, a warm, cloudless day, which might have graced the midsummer calendar. At ten o'clock a delegation of Canton friends waved farewell as the Special glided past the Cherry Street crossing bound for Alliance, Ohio.

Aboard, a gay spirit prevailed. Foster had preceded the party to Buffalo; in his place was Secret Service man Al Gallaher, hardly expecting trouble but on the alert. In the party, besides the indispensable Cortelyou, were two stenographers, M. C. Latta and N. P. Webster; T. J. Charlesworth, the Lake Shore Railroad representative; the President's valet, Charles Tharin and his wife Clara, the First Lady's personal maid. Since the First Lady's health demanded almost constant attention, two nurses were included in the group besides the President's personal physician, Dr. Presley M. Rixey.

Since 1899, the tall, bushy-moustached Naval surgeon had been the McKinleys' physician, succeeding Army Surgeon Leonard Wood, who had left Washington in 1898 as a colonel in the Rough Riders. Rixey quickly became an invaluable member of the

44

President's entourage on all of their trips. A native of Culpeper, Virginia, Rixey, after graduation from the University of Virginia, had studied medicine in Philadelphia. Of his 26 years of Naval service, 11 had been spent at sea in Mediterranean, African and South American waters. On shore he had served in the Philadelphia and Norfolk Naval Hospitals and also at the Naval Dispensary at Washington. While in official attendance upon Secretary of the Navy John D. Long and his daughter, he had first been called to administer to Mrs. McKinley on the Presidential trip to Atlanta in December of 1898. The President, impressed by the doctor's gentleness as well as his skill, had later in Washington asked him, "Why do you not come to the White House?"

Rixey had replied simply that he did not know he was wanted. The President then requested him to come, adding that he especially wished the physician to accompany him and Mrs. McKinley on their railroad trips around the country.

The President's departure competed with other frontpage news: Chicago's packing house workers were striking; a settlement in the steel negotiations had been reached; a $30,000 holdup had been staged on the North Cotton Belt passenger train as it roared through Texas.

At 2:25 P.M. the Special rolled into a private Cleveland siding to take aboard Sarah Duncan and Senator Hanna.

While the President's niece joined the party bound for the Buffalo fair, her uncle was closeted with the Cleveland industrialist for only a brief conference, directed no doubt to McKinley's coming visit to the Cleveland G.A.R. Encampment upon his return trip from Buffalo.

During their political and social liaison of many years Hanna had proved a tremendous asset, and at times, because of the unfavorable press he attracted, a liability. To many the Republican boss was a symbol of the trusts and money interests, a Svengali who called the moves that a vapid President executed. When McKinley entered the White House a Hearst writer had predicted that Hanna would "shuffle McKinley like a pack of cards." Even though the canard had been controverted by those who knew both men intimately, it clung to McKinley like an unwelcome burr. But their association had paid off too in handsome dividends. As a campaign organizer and collector of "boodle," Hanna was without peer. Though poles apart in temperament, the two men had remained friends through many vicissitudes as they guided the destiny of the country.

No doubt, Hanna admonished the President once more about his personal safety. Added to his fears for McKinley's life based upon his personal affection was the spectre of the young Vice President, Theodore Roosevelt, as McKinley's premature successor. Tom Platt, unctuous New York State Republican boss, had jockeyed Roosevelt into the Vice-Presidential post to rid his state of an unmanageable governor.

Hanna's aversion to Roosevelt was deep-seated. He mistrusted the former Rough Rider and threatened to bolt his party chairmanship if Roosevelt were chosen as McKinley's running mate. Angered at T.R.'s nomination, Hanna had kept his post but stormed—"there's only one life between that madman and the Presidency."

As the Presidential Special was rolling toward Buffalo, Vice President Roosevelt, who was headed east for a Vermont speaking engagement, stopped briefly in the Ohio city. Needless to say, there was no conference with Mark Hanna.

At 43, the man of "pure action" seemed to be safely tucked away in political limbo after a sensational career as a dude New York state legislator, a Western rancher, a reforming New York City police commissioner, an Assistant Secretary of the Navy, a colonel in the Rough Riders, and a one-term governor of New York State. His heroic sweep up San Juan Hill had endeared him to the public; his unpredictability and rash impulsiveness had not endeared him to certain leaders, like Platt and Hanna.

About the time the Vice President's train was pulling out of Cleveland the McKinley Special was stopping briefly at the small fishing village of Dunkirk, New York, to take aboard Buffalo's Mayor Conrad Diehl and Exposition President John G. Milburn, who headed a small welcoming committee.

By late afternoon the Special was roaring past the vast complex of steel mills and grain elevators that skirted the Buffalo waterfront. As the train sped under the Louisiana Street steel bridge, the flag-decked city, like a symphony suddenly released by its director's baton, poured forth a welcoming crescendo of bells and whistles.

Engineer Peck slackened the big, dust-covered locomotive and stopped abreast the red-brick Exchange Street depot, where Exposition Director William Buchanan—onetime U.S. Ambassador to the Argentine—joined the party.

Seconds later, headed along the serpentine tracks toward the Niagara River, the Special raced along to the Terrace Station, where a Coast Artillery captain, Leonard Wisser, commanding a green gun crew, waited to touch off the 21-gun Presidential salute.

As the train, in deference to the welcoming throng, slackened speed, there arose a chorus of cheers, punctuated by several resounding booms, followed quickly by blinding billows of smoke and a great crackling of glass.

The three-car Special shook as if torpedoed, then hissed to a clanking stop as the delegation recoiled. The cannon boomed on despite Cortelyou's desperate signals from the observation platform to stop. This was the very kind of salute he had so pointedly warned against; already it had thrown the Special's passengers into a state of consternation. A *Buffalo Courier* reporter and Trainmaster Charlesworth, as bewildered as his distinguished passengers, had both been hurled to the baggage car floor.

At this critical moment, McKinley, smiling, apparently unruffled, but as mystified as the rest, appeared on the observation platform, gingerly doffing his high silk hat as if to restore calm to a nightmarish scene.

Outside and within the cars confusion reigned. Not only had eight front car windows been blasted to smithereens, but dozens of windows in nearby office buildings had spewed their remnants into the street.

Dr. Rixey, summoned as the excitement was at its height, was pressing an improvised restorative to the First Lady's lips, hoping the shock would not induce one of her seizures, when Charlesworth gave the signal to pull away. There was a sudden heave of the engine—then the train began to roll along the tracks toward the Exposition grounds.

Meanwhile, around the station, mingled with the hue and cry, arose shouts of "Anarchists! Anarchists! they've wrecked the train!"

The crowd, seeking a butt for its suspicion, advanced upon a dark swarthy man who stood near the tracks. More serious trouble might have ensued except for the intervention of an unidentified but well-dressed man, who at this moment stepped from his parked carriage nearby. Raising his hand, he cried, "There's nothing wrong, gentlemen. This man had nothing to do with the blast. The explosion was caused by the cannon. Dynamite would have blown off the wheels of the cars."

Apparently this observer was the only one to realize that Captain Wisser, in his zeal to fire the salute, had placed his cannon too close to the tracks.

The explanation had clearly headed off an ugly situation. The crowd, however, continued to mill about long after the Special had left, still bewildered and still conjecturing on this weird contretemps, which had set the pattern for McKinley's Buffalo visit.

6
"I'll See the Buildings Tomorrow"

WHERE CZOLGOSZ OBTAINED THE REVOLVER he left
at the Kazmareks' and why he had it with him are still subjects
for conjecture. It may have been the one he used for hunting
rabbits on the farm; emulating his idol Bresci, he may have used
it for target practice.

After his arrest police while ransacking his room at Nowak's
discovered in his bag another weapon, which he had apparently
discarded—a single shot revolver. This would have been ineffectual in his plan. He was reconciled to capture and to exchange
his pitiable life for that of the President, but he was not reconciled to these sacrifices without the certain death of his victim.
To ensure the success of his plan, he needed an automatic revolver, one that would blaze away several times.

Sometime before the evening of September 4, the would-be
Anarchist entered Walbridge Company's hardware store at 316
Main Street and without arousing the slightest suspicion pur-
chased a nickel-plated .32 caliber Iver Johnson six-shot automatic. With this, should the first shot fail, he could be sure that
his mission would be successful.

Czolgosz's movements during the day of September 4 are unknown. It is likely that he spent some part of it in wandering
around the Exposition grounds. By late afternoon, shortly before
the President's arrival, he had edged his way through the dense
throngs around the Amherst Street depot and was about to gain
entrance to the inner area of the station.

It was here at the violet-colored station that most of the out-
of-town visitors arrived by steam or electric railroad. After alight-
ing, they passed through the station to the spacious Railway Exhibits building. Emerging from here, they saw for the first time

the Propylaea, an imposing structure consisting of two entrances connected by a colonnade.

Now several smart victorias were drawn up before the railroad gate awaiting the President's party. A column of mounted, plumed guardsmen stood nearby. The area swarmed with detectives, Pinkerton men, and uniformed guards. Just as Czolgosz was pushing himself through the gate a guard suddenly loomed in front of him. The guard yelled, brandishing his club. Terror-stricken, Czolgosz turned and began to run. He had taken only a few steps when he felt the guard's big hand on his collar. Then he went sprawling into the dust. He cowered there a moment, expecting to be seized and taken away. Suddenly he heard an ear-splitting train whistle. It seemed as if every whistle in the city had joined in. Fearfully Czolgosz looked up. The guard, along with other guards and policemen, had turned and was moving away from him toward the tracks.

Miraculously he had escaped. He picked himself up and ran. As he mingled with the crowds on the Plaza, he realized with tremendous relief that no one was taking the slightest notice of him.

At twelve minutes past six the Special ground to a stop beside the wooden ramp at the Exposition's Amherst Station.

The President made his appearance at once, emerging directly after Buchanan and Milburn had stepped onto the platform. Doffing his silk hat in response to the thunderous ovation being accorded him, he descended the steps. One of McKinley's assets was that he looked like a President. Now standing for a moment beside the Special, his hands raised, palms outward, as if to invoke a blessing on the thousands who cheered him, he seemed the quintessence of aplomb and benignity.

Then turning, he helped the First Lady to alight. She was dressed in black save for a narrow trim of gray on her hat. Despite the reported recovery from her illness of the previous spring, she impressed onlookers as "pale and feeble."

One by one, the rest of the Presidential party began to step down to the station platform—first the two nurses, then Dr. Rixey, to be followed by the other occupants of the special.

In response to Buchanan's gesticulations, a boy who had been posted in readiness darted forward pushing a wheelchair. But Mrs. McKinley, sensing that this was to be for her use, waved it aside, saying, "Thank you, Mr. Buchanan, it won't be necessary. I'll walk." Clinging to her husband's arm, she then moved slowly, as he measured his pace to suit hers, through the small station toward a cluster of carriages drawn up nearby. Harry Hamlin's elegant low-slung open victoria with its double span of superb horses had been assigned to the President during his Buffalo visit. As he and his retinue reached it, Dr. Rixey helped Mrs. McKinley aboard.

The day had been hot, with the temperature tipping 80 degrees, but now a coolness was settling over the city. Noting the change, the President, with his characteristic concern for the First Lady's comfort, called for a light wrap. Evidently in anticipation of such a request, one had been placed in the carriage. It was immediately discovered and draped about Mrs. McKinley's shoulders.

The coachman crackled his whip, and the carriages moved south through wildly cheering masses of spectators. The Exposition grounds, through which the Presidential party was passing, was a mile in length and three-fifths that distance in width. For months preceding its opening on snowy May 1 hundreds of wagons had rumbled across a sea of mud as thousands of workmen erected the scaffolding for the buildings and planted the lush gardens now in full bloom. Gradually out of chaos there had arisen a glittering myriad of lacy towers and ornate turrets. By day the sun spun its magic over the vivid hues of the buildings, predominantly Spanish Renaissance in style, over the winding canals and the dazzling Esplanade. By night the Exposition glittered under the refulgence of half a million electric lights, then novelties of the first order.

The cavalcade moved on. Before him McKinley could see, jutting skyward, the 389 foot Electric Tower, the dominating structure of the Exposition. The tower was a square shaft surmounted by a crown of three stages of diminishing proportions. On the last stage, or cupola, was poised a gilded statue of the Goddess of Light. From the ground she looked ethereal, balanced lightly on the toes of her right foot, but she actually weighed 1.5 tons. At the base of the tower curved colonnades, which terminated in pavilions, enclosed a semicircular basin some 200 feet across.

Beyond lay a maze of color, a conglomeration of architectural styles, a labyrinth of winding canals, a profusion of fountains, lakes and bays, glimmering in the ambience of twilight. Along either side of the broad vista that bisected the length of the grounds arose red-tiled roof tops, minarets, gilded turrets.

In deference to the theme of Pan-Americanism, Spanish Renaissance style of architecture prevailed, but, here and there, almost incongruously, appeared buildings modeled after those of ancient Rome and Greece. At the corner of the Esplanade and Court of Fountains, plainly within view of the President as his carriage whirled by, stood a domed building, overly ornate, the Temple of Music.

At a rise on the causeway the Hamlin horses were reined to a stop. Within the sweep of the President's view rose myriads of fountains, which spumed an iridescent mist skyward, gardens ablaze with color, and exhibits buildings, including that of the President's own native state.

The stop had been brief. Once more the carriage rolled southward, moving along with its clattering escort down a gentle slope, across a small bridge that spanned the entrance to North Bay, past the flower-filled conservatory, and at length into the cool shade of Delaware Avenue.

At the time of the President's visit the avenue was world-famous for its elegance. Of its almost solid two-mile display of wealth and luxury, the Milburn home was not the most pretentious, but it bore, like its neighbors, the indelible stamp of gracious living, and suggested, like the rest, in its substantial brick frame, the success of its owner.

In anticipation of the McKinley visit, the house had been refurbished from basement to attic; porches had been converted to wings and an entrance porch had been removed. Amply staffed with servants, within easy driving distance of the Exposition, it offered a relaxed atmosphere of luxury and comfort to its famous guest.

The President's host, John G. Milburn, a tall, genial and urbane man, was in his fiftieth year. Although he had started life in England as an engineer, he had forsaken that profession in favor of law with such success that by 1901 he was considered a leading member of the Buffalo bar.

As the President stepped from his carriage and led Mrs. Mc-Kinley up the Milburn walk, he gave his first impression of the Exposition. "The grounds are beautiful," he told Milburn; and as the latter smiled, the President added, "I'll see the buildings tomorrow."

Part II
T H E E V E N T

7

"The Earth Had Never Known a Fairer Day"

SINCE EARLY MORNING sunlight had streamed from a cloudless sky.

"The earth," noted a *Buffalo Express* reporter, "had never known a fairer day."

September 5 was President's Day—a holiday of promised magnificent spectacles, a day to be lifted from the mundane by scarlet and blue uniforms and the flashing of swords, a day when the silk-hatted Western envoys would mingle in a spirit of amity with the silken-robed emissaries of the Far East. Above all, it would be a day when thousands might glimpse the President, the First Lady, and their distinguished entourage.

As the city stirred to life a breeze, gentle, almost imperceptible, wafted in from the Niagara River, unfurling thousands of American and Exposition flags from office buildings, street corners, and front verandas of any consequence. Main Street blazed, a canyon of red, white, and blue.

On the East Side, a sportive mood prevailed. Fat German brewers forsook their beer kegs, joining Polish sausage-makers as they headed for a common destination. Nowak's saloon looked jaded and gray in the morning sunlight. It lay quiet and still and deserted, as if depleted by its nocturnal exertions. Nowak's guest, Leon F. Czolgosz, had risen early, bought a cigar, and left for the Pan-American grounds.

Although a crowd of 50,000 was expected and for months every minute detail had been carefully planned, police facilities at the big, purple-draped rectangular stand on the Esplanade were practically nonexistent as people poured into the area at the rate of 500 a minute. In they piled, helter skelter, unrestricted in any way except for a single rope barrier that two policemen had strung before the stand. The police had then vanished, leaving in their wake a confusion which aroused one Committee member's anger. Major Thomas W. Symons, viewing the scene, called the situation "deplorable."

Elegant carriages, runabouts, and other horsedrawn vehicles were rolling in, discharging passengers, who sought to reach their reserved seats in the stand—usually with little success.

In the midst of this chaos three Committee members, George L. Williams, James L. Quackenbush, and L. D. Rumsey, jumped into the breach, booming out orders and herding the milling throngs into some semblance of order as the minutes ticked by before the President's arrival.

At 9:30 across the broad causeway detachments of Marines and the Sea Coast artillery and National Guardsmen of the 65th and 74th regiments, in a blaze of red, blue, and gold, their rifles glinting, now swung into view, and advanced briskly in unison as bands blared martial music.

Now appeared the vanguard of the foreign diplomatic corps. In monocle and frock coat, the quintessence of courtly splendor, the Duke of Arcos moved across the stand to join a small cluster of his elegantly dressed fellow diplomats.

The Duke's appearance signaled the arrival of a fresh batch of carriages bearing other members of the corps, whose equipages descended with much thudding of hoofs and scrambling of liveried footmen.

Each diplomat was a distinct revelation of resplendency. The short, white-haired gentleman, venerable and kindly, was the Mexican ambassador, Senor Don Manuel Aspiroz. Around him and his son, Don Roderigo Aspiroz, clustered those of lesser importance in the Mexican service, though no less impressive in their gold-braided splendor. Other frock-coated emissaries from Latin America included Carlos Silva, the Colombian envoy, and Manuel Alvarez Calderon, the Peruvian representative. The Turkish minister wore a red fez.

But these diplomats paled when matched with a cluster of Orientals, whose dress shone like the plumage of exotic birds. In blue and gray and yellow silken robes they glided across the stand and mingled with their confreres of the West.

Shortly before 9:00 Czolgosz, gripping his revolver in his coat pocket, was trying to edge his way through the dense crowd toward the grandstand. From here the President would shortly deliver the speech that would mark the high point of his three-day visit. Czolgosz was seeking a position from which he could whip out his weapon and blaze away at his victim at close range. But that, he soon discovered, was not going to be an easy spot to find. For one thing the crowd was immense. Men, women, and children were pouring into the open area before the stand.

Suddenly Czolgosz heard the deep boom of a cannon. It came from the south end of the grounds, followed quickly by a second, third, and fourth rumble; the sounds continued, echoing lugubriously across the smooth surface of the lake, up the slope, and across the broad causeway. After the 21st salute, the roaring ceased and died away to an echo.

A minute later appeared the bobbing red plumes of the mounted soldiers, their metal helmets shimmering in the sunlight as they cantered into view. Czolgosz noted with misgivings that they encircled the President's entourage. Then the horsemen wheeled sharply, entering a cordon formed by red-coated Marines and National Guardsmen. When the carriages halted before the stand, the crowd surged forward. Amid storms of applause the President and First Lady alighted from the Hamlin victoria. With his left arm encircling his wife gently, McKinley led her through the cordon of gold-braided officers to the stand. Here the two paused dramatically to acknowledge the surge of cheers that welcomed them.

Czolgosz found himself squeezed in on all sides. Momentarily he lost sight of his quarry, who suddenly reappeared, bland-faced and smiling, as he moved among the diplomats, shaking hands. Presently, amid a blur of fluttering handkerchiefs Czolgosz saw the President stride to the platform and take a sheaf of papers from his pocket.

But now a sea of ladies' parasols blocked the speaker from sight. These quickly disappeared, however, in response to cries of "Down! Down!"

Cheers drowned out the President's first words. He held up his left hand for silence. The persuasive voice rang out in clipped, precise accents. "Expositions are the timekeepers of progress. They record the world's advancement. . . ." Each syllable was bitten off in neat emphasis.

Czolgosz must have writhed when he caught the words "unexampled prosperity." The country's prosperity, the speaker was saying, exceeded by far the demands of home consumption.

This would have been the perfect moment for Czolgosz's contemplated act, but no doubt with deep chagrin he realized it was impossible from where he stood. People pressed so tightly against him he could not move. He would have to wait—after the speech when the crowd began to disperse. He stood, an involuntary captive, as the President amid renewed applause went on: "We must not repose in the fancied security that we can forever sell everything, and buy little or nothing. Isolation is no longer possible or advisable. God and man have linked the nations together. The period of exclusiveness is past."

And then with greater emphasis: "Gentlemen, let us ever remember that our best interest is in concord, not conflict; and that our real eminence rests in the victories of peace, not those of war. We hope that all that are representatives here may be moved to higher and nobler efforts for their own and the world's good and that out of this city may come not only greater commerce and trade . . ." The persuasive voice was lost again amid a fresh surge of cheers.

The plaudits rang in Czolgosz's ears as the President concluded: "Our earnest prayer is that God will graciously vouchsafe prosperity, happiness, and peace to all our neighbors and like blessings to all the people and powers of earth."

There he stood, his arm around the First Lady, acknowledging the cheers and the congratulations of the diplomats who surrounded him. Once the felicitations were over, McKinley led the First Lady to her carriage. As the people began to break ranks, the pressure of arms and bodies around Czolgosz was being relaxed. He could move his arms freely. His eyes shifted to the stage. A group of important-looking men, perhaps some of them detectives or Secret Service men, were conducting the President to his victoria. Here was his chance.

He pushed forward a step, then two steps, then he broke into a trot toward the stand; but as he reached it, he stopped abruptly.

Two men were entering the carriage. From where he stood, several yards away, they looked uncommonly alike; both were clean shaven; both wore high silk hats and black frock coats. He realized to his horror and dismay that he could not be sure which was the President. As he stood there, grim and wavering, the two men entered the carriage, which moved away. He followed it a few steps, then stopped. The carriage was soon engulfed by the shouting, flag-waving crowd that packed the road beyond.

The President's resemblance to his host had spared his life, at least for the present.

There were few minutes or even seconds, not to be utilized in the day-long program ahead. McKinley must see the sights—and perhaps equally important—he must be seen by the flag-waving thousands who rimmed the Exposition's roadways, held back only by the presence of an almost solid line of helmeted police and guardsmen. Handkerchiefs fluttered; people yelled themselves hoarse as the President's entourage of 35 carriages wound its way toward the concrete stadium niched in the northeast corner of the grounds, which was described as America's most magnificent amphitheater (it had a capacity of 12,000).

Despite police vigilance, time after time, enthusiastic admirers broke ranks, stampeding into the road and blocking the carriage horses. One man wiggled under the horses and popped up beside the President's carriage. "I'm Hawaiian Joe," shouted the intruder in the President's ear. Far from annoyed, the President thrust out his hand and greeted the interloper. A small boy, held in his father's arms, was similarly rewarded. An old woman, thought at first to be Carrie Nation, the Temperance Hatchet Woman, worked her way to the carriage and thrust out a bony hand. Secret Service men rushed her away, crying and cursing "like a hard-boiled cattle hand."

Across the breadth of the vast Esplanade came the procession, past the ornate Temple of Music, where McKinley was to receive the people the next day, across the Plaza, with plumes waving and uniforms glittering in the late morning sun. The President, with Milburn at his side, bowed, smiled, and doffed his hat. Popcorn boys, souvenir vendors, sideshow spielers stopped their sales chatter to wave and shout their greetings. One spectator fought his way to the forefront and yelled, "Howdy, Chief!" The President waved and returned the greeting. "Hello, Frank," he replied. A moment later, another man broke from the ranks, eluded the guards, and snapped his suspenders which bore a likeness of the President. At this unscheduled buffoonery McKinley laughed heartily, accepting this incursion, like numerous others, good-naturedly.

At 11:40 A.M. the vanguard of the procession drew up before the stadium's southeast entrance, halting momentarily while Captain Damer with his Exposition police swept back the swarm of curious spectators who blocked the passage.

Presently, the road was cleared and McKinley's carriage rolled into the amphitheater, drawing up before the flag-emblazoned reviewing stand. Amidst the brilliant unfurled colors of Marines and National Guardsmen, General Samuel Welch with his staff drawn up behind him saluted the President. Now came the clear calls of the bugler, sounding the Commander-in-Chief's call—then 2000 rifle butts thudded to the turf to the booming commands of "Present Arms" and "Order Arms."

The President with his retinue moved from the stands. With Welch's staff he strode briskly to the west side of the field, passing from west to east in front of the troops, then from east to west along their rear.

As McKinley started back for the stands, a note of comedy—unscheduled but affording a welcome respite—relieved what might have been a sober ceremony. The Marine mascot, Billy (Goat) Marine, his whiskers neatly pleated, pranced onto the field, trotted directly over to the President, and acted as an unofficial orderly to the smiling Commander-in-Chief on his return to the stand.

The ceremony—including Billy Marine's impromptu performance, which the President seemed to enjoy as heartily as the rest—had lasted only five minutes. At 11:46 Welch boomed out the command: "Battalions, change direction—by the left flank." The guardsmen swung smartly about, facing west in columns of companies.

"Forward!" came the crisp command. The Marine band wheeled left, then started east along the south side of the field, headed by the irrepressible mascot and General Welch and his staff, while the Marine musicians formed a cordon through which the battalion could move. The Stars and Stripes were dipped; the troops marched out through the stadium's east gate; and the President, after acknowledging the greetings of a handful of people, introduced by Mrs. John Miller Horton, left the review exactly 23 minutes after his arrival.

The procession moved on, pausing momentarily to view 7000 carrier pigeons as they were released, then stopped at the Canadian exhibit, where the President's attention was occupied for the most part by a plump white porcupine. "Fine fellow, isn't he?" the President commented.

Now, there came extremely brief visits to the Honduran and Dominican exhibits, where the President was conducted through thick clusters of excited Latin functionaries and welcoming delegations.

At the Cuban exhibit a spokesman bowed low, greeting McKinley as the "great honored man who promised Cuba her liberty and has given it to her."

Here, as he moved swiftly past the various attractions, McKinley's attention was drawn to the famous Antomarchi death mask of Napoleon. Examining it, the President became grave, perhaps reminded that earlier in his career his facial resemblance to the French Emperor had caused comment.

While Mrs. McKinley was the honor guest at a luncheon given by the Women's Board of Managers, her husband was whisked off to the western end of the grounds, where stood one of the Exposition's most magnificent structures. This was the New York State building, a Grecian replica in Vermont marble, which commanded the crest of a gentle knoll, its columns shimmering in the green waters of a pool below.

At 12:45 McKinley stepped from his victoria, shook hands with President Daniel Lockwood of the New York State Commission, and moved through a line of Exposition police to the impressive entrance.

Feverish preparation had preceded the luncheon, to which United States Supreme Court justices, foreign functionaries, as well as Army and Navy brass, had been invited. Despite the beauty of the building it lacked kitchen facilities; this necessitated the hauling of 100 waiters and the entire menu of food and wine several miles across the city from the downtown Hotel Iroquois.

At 2:00, beaming and acknowledging a fresh surge of applause while an orchestra secreted in the balcony played "Hail to the Chief," the President strode down the marble staircase leading to the Hall of State, where he was seated under a bower of American Beauty roses.

Harry Winer, who had served McKinley at The Planter's Hotel in St. Louis during the 1896 Republican convention, had been chosen to wait upon the President.

Was it vague fear or an uneasy premonition of his coming fate which caused McKinley midway through the festive luncheon to ask Winer, "What's on the other side of that door, my boy?"

Behind the flag-draped door, Winer explained, were a pool and garden. He offered to open the door if the President wished. Smiling, the President said no, he was only curious. Over sixty years later, Winer, the proud possessor of McKinley's autograph and one of his cigars, still retained the uneradicable impression that the President felt a vague sense of apprehension.

An hour later, after coffee and cigars—and a brief view of the Exposition from the building's rear portico—the President entered his carriage for a short visit to the United States Government building.

Outside this building the crush was so great that police, brandishing clubs, were hard-pressed to open a passage for the President to the south entrance. After McKinley had managed to squeeze through, however, fifty others, including Milburn, were stranded outside, their progress halted several minutes by the wildly cheering spectators.

Perhaps tired and surfeited with the succession of his visits, McKinley moved rapidly past the government displays, glancing at them rather perfunctorily. At length, he took up his position in the rotunda to shake hands with a swarm of guests, among whom were the Spanish-American War hero, Captain Richmond E. Hobson—who had sunk a collier in order to plug up the enemy fleet at Santiago—and a lesser known man, Dr. Herman Mynter, erstwhile surgeon in the Royal Danish Army and Navy. As he passed, Mynter, then practicing in Buffalo, gripped the President's hand, saying, "I hope I can return the favor."

By 4:35, the reception over, the President entered his carriage which headed for Milburn's, where he and the First Lady were to enjoy a much-needed rest before attending Henry J. Pain's brilliant pyrotechnic display on the grounds that evening.

Seldom had an evening promised so much. Had P. T. Barnum devised the program it could not have been improved upon or offered such a variety of happily contrived, sure-fire attractions. Besides precision marching by columns of brilliantly uniformed soldiers and that perennial favorite, the Marine band, thumping out martial airs, there would be a water nymph ballet performed upon a mid-lake float. Henry Rustin's illumination display, which had been astounding visitors nightly, was to be rivaled by a show of fireworks by the world-famous pyrotechnist, Henry Pain. But top billing would have to be given to the illustrious visitor himself, who with the First Lady and their entourage would be the chief attraction for the 115,000 spectators.

A salute of 21-inch aerial maroons fired from steel mortars was to open the program at 8:05. McKinley and his party were to witness the illumination from the grandstand where he had spoken only a few hours before. Half an hour before the President's arrival the area was packed with diplomats and other distinguished spectators, including Mayor Diehl and his wife. They waited expectantly—but in vain, for as darkness enveloped the grounds, the President's victoria with its escort drew to a halt on the bridge of the Triumphal Causeway.

At this moment the Marines were swinging along the Esplanade in their "twilight" drill. A bomb from the military camp had signaled the President's arrival. Simultaneously, the Marine band began to march into the Esplanade, where, after coming to parade rest, they struck up a medley of patriotic tunes.

Presently, the music ceased; the band reversed its position to face the President. Milburn raised his hand. As he did, ripples of incandescent light, like streaks of lightning, ran through the buildings. Only one, the Ethnology Building, remained in darkness. "A fuse must have blown out," said John N. Scatcherd, Executive Committee chairman of the Exposition, who was standing near the President's carriage.

"That will break Rustin's heart," replied Milburn. "He was so anxious there be no flaws tonight."

The President, attempting to assuage their disappointment,

remarked, "It's always on such occasions that accidents happen."

He had barely spoken when the Ethnology lights appeared.

Meanwhile, myriads of fountains, which until now had been shut off, began to send up a crimson spray, reflected from lights beneath. The band struck up the national anthem. The President, uncovering, rose to his feet. The lights increased in intensity and the fountains in volume. The music swelled. The big search-light, perched under the Goddess of Light, shot its powerful rays over the Causeway. The lights continued to grow stronger, until the national anthem reached its final bar. Then the lights and music seemed to blend in a grand crescendo.

The President's carriage was about to pull away at this exciting juncture when McKinley suddenly countered an order previously given. He wanted, he said, to enjoy the spectacle "as long as possible." He had remained standing in his carriage. Now raising his hat and waving, he pivoted his body slowly while his eyes appeared to drink in the magnificent scene stretching around him.

"Never," wrote the *Courier* reporter, "had the grounds been so gorgeous—never had a President been welcomed so warmly."

At length, the President's carriage was turned toward the Art Building. Here the occupants stepped down from the carriage, walked a short distance to a floating dock nearby, then boarded the largest boat from the Exposition Life-Saving Station. McKinley and his wife took rear seats, upon which cushions had been placed. Cortelyou, Dr. Rixey, and Milburn sat facing the couple. Captain Henry Cleary took the tiller of the craft, manned by ten picked rowers; and it moved slowly over the surface of the Park Lake to the opposite shore.

The rest of the Presidential entourage, including Secretary of Agriculture James Wilson, had been driven to the Life Saving Station. They were waiting, ready to rejoin the President when his boat glided into a slip at that point. The First Lady seemingly had enjoyed the short trip by water; she was smiling as her husband conducted her to a seat at the top of a stand erected in front of the boathouse. From this vantage point they were soon engrossed in watching the graceful movements of a water nymph ballet performed at mid-lake upon a floating stage.

Then a hush fell over the vast concourse. A pause. A signal. Pain's renowned fireworks display was about to begin.

At the turn of the century fireworks were often used to welcome heroes or to commemorate important events. As a drawing card they were unbeatable; and Pain was the acknowledged master in this field.

Known as "Pyrotechnist Pain" and "The Fireworks King," he had brought the ancient Chinese art of pyrotechnics to a point of perfection. He employed crews of men skilled in operating his batteries of heavy mortars and manipulating his intricate equipment, which produced bombs that burst, releasing stars, flowers, sprays of exotic hues, and other celestial wonders. On several occasions he had been hired by William Randolph Hearst to celebrate American war victories or to boost some of the publisher's promotions. Hearst had once hired Pain to take his two creations, "The Blowing up of the Maine" and "The Battle of Manila" on tour. The latter "showed twenty glowing battleships maneuvering on wheels as guns boomed" and was pronounced (by the *Journal*) "Pain's masterpiece."

Engaged by the Exposition, Pain had outdone himself in creating a super-spectacle for the evening of September 5. In breathtaking succession there blazed across the blue-black sky bursting bombs, shooting stars, flaring rockets, which rose and dipped with miraculous speed. Next came the ascent of five mammoth meteoric balloons of dazzling brilliance, changing as they rose to spiral formations and leaving in their wake beautiful coruscations, which fell to the earth.

Each glittering outburst was accompanied by the collective gasp of wonderment by the viewers, as Pain's aerial wonders continued—"The Southern Cross," "Shower of Pearls," "Spirit of Niagara," "The American Navy" (the largest ever exhibited in the World), a timely novelty produced by a giant combination shell, which at 1000 feet released a large bomb representing the United States, followed by a gold shell representing Cuba, a silver shell for Puerto Rico, and finally a number of smaller shells for the Philippines. To conclude, a likeness of the President bore the caption "Welcome—McKinley—Chief of Our Nation and our Empire."

As the last rocket zoomed across the sky, dipping beyond the horizon, the President's carriage was heading for the Lincoln Parkway entrance. The Exposition's giant searchlight probed the darkness ahead, beaming its rays along the roadway, "as if to say good night."

The day now nearing its end had seen the President at the zenith of his popularity—acclaimed, cheered, beloved. The program honoring him had run smoothly for the most part. Protection afforded him seemed almost topheavy; yet there had been at least a dozen incursions on his privacy. The mounted escort, the Secret Service men and detectives who walked or jogged by his side, the scores of helmeted Exposition policemen who rimmed the roadways, the 65th and 74th National Guards—all these, at times, despite their show of vigilance, had been ineffectual—a shortcoming which the President's great personal popularity and his willingness to shake hands with anyone who could reach his side only abetted. These incursions were serious faults, which at the moment—amidst the great carnival spirit and joyousness prevailing—were passed by lightly. The President was not one to complain or to reprimand a subordinate. The incident at the city's Terrace Station on the evening of September 4 had passed without a word of censure. Indeed, during his entire visit McKinley made only one comment on his guards, and that was complimentary. While visiting the South American exhibits, he had, at one point, praised his guards for their vigilance.

Perhaps motivated by this remark, detectives shortly after had spotted a boy following the President's carriage. Pouncing upon him, they opened a suspicious-looking bundle, which, they discovered to their chagrin, contained only the boy's lunch.

One of the most serious incursions came after the noonday military review when 250 spectators, eager for a closer view of McKinley, spilled over the field to engulf him.

Again, at least in the opinion of two members of his party, the President had exposed himself needlessly during the fireworks display. The tall, bearded Secretary of Agriculture, Scottish-born "Tama Jim" Wilson, who with his daughter Flora was accompanying the Presidential party during the Pan-American visit, admitted that his pleasure that night was dimmed by the dread prospect of what could happen. Wilson and Cortelyou, whose fears for McKinley's life had never subsided, both anticipated the coming Temple of Music reception with a sense of foreboding. They agreed it was an occasion where some half-crazed malcontent could easily assault the President.

At 10:00 P.M. Leon F. Czolgosz walked into Nowak's saloon. He carried a bundle of papers under his arm. As usual he didn't linger in the barroom but went directly to his room.

8

Early Morning

AT 7:10 A.M. ON SEPTEMBER 6 the Milburn front door swung back, and the President of the United States appeared. Even at this hour he was immaculately dressed, ready for the day ahead. He came down the steps briskly, his silk hat perched sedately, his arms swinging, the flaps of his frock coat drawn back exposing a black bow tie and a Piccadilly collar above a broad expanse of boiled white shirt. He nodded graciously to the sentries and Secret Service men, then set out alone for a morning constitutional. He strode south along the avenue, crossing West Ferry Street and, as the Secret Service agents watched anxiously, continued on to Utica Street.

Foster chucked away his half-smoked cigar, his eyes riveted upon the President, who after crossing the avenue was moving along its east side. To Foster this was an old story. In Canton and Washington the President frequently took solitary walks like this, slipping away for drives, often without his guards. Fortunately, the President at no time was out of sight. Within five minutes, apparently refreshed, he returned.

By this hour the gray mists drifting in from the river had lifted. The skies, as on the previous two days, were blue and unflecked; already it was growing warm. By 7:30 a small vanguard of the curious, eager for a glimpse of the President, was gathering along the avenue near the Milburn house. Smart victorias and barouches swung by, each with liveried footmen and coachmen, each drawn by superbly groomed horses, which were better cared for than thousands who would later view them. The procession glided along—elegantly, confidently; all bound for the same destination; all assured that many days like this one lay in the future.

70

In other parts of the city men destined to play roles in the drama ahead were preparing for the day.

As he arose, Director Buchanan sensed a vague apprehension, which he attributed to nerves. It would wear off in the course of the activities of the day.

Young reporter John D. Wells of the *Buffalo Morning Review* looked forward zestfully to his first really big assignment—covering the President's afternoon reception at the Temple of Music. He intended to vivify with words every detail of this occasion.

Giant six-foot-six James Parker, a Negro waiter from Atlanta, was pulling on his shoes, glad that he had "laid off" from his job with the Bailey restaurant concessions, for today was his chance to realize a life-time ambition and shake the hand of the President of the United States.

Captain Louis L. Babcock, a 32-year-old attorney from Milburn's office and a veteran of the Spanish War, felt the weight of his responsibility for the day. As marshal of the Exposition, he must provide at the afternoon reception an easy access to the President for as many hundreds of people as possible, yet at the same time establish perfect security measures to protect the President's life.

Dr. Herman Mynter was making ready for his morning routine in his home at 566 Delaware Avenue a few blocks south of Milburn's. Certainly this sturdily built, black-mustached surgeon could not have forseen the part he would play in the events of the day ahead. Having been presented to the President at a small reception the previous afternoon, he had no intention of braving the crowds to attend the Exposition grounds on this last hectic day of the President's visit.

Mynter, now 56, had studied medicine at the University of Copenhagen in his native Denmark, then after two years' service in the Royal Danish Navy and one year in the Royal Danish Army had set out for America, coming directly to Buffalo in 1875. Here he had established a considerable reputation, particularly as an authority on appendicitis, and as Professor of Post-Operative Surgery at the University of Buffalo Medical School. Recently he had returned to Denmark to lecture on his specialty and to be honored by his native land for his work in his field.

Though plain-spoken, often brusque, he was great-hearted, as many men of the 65th Regiment and other Volunteers from Northwestern New York could attest to. On their return to Buffalo from disease- and fever-infested Camp Alger, Mynter had managed to bring back the trainload of sick, crazed men without a single casualty enroute. One dying man he had picked up in his arms like a child, winning him back to life long enough to see his loved ones at home.

In his Delaware Avenue home not far from Dr. Mynter's Dr. Roswell Park was preparing to leave for Niagara Falls, not to accompany the President's party, but to perform a delicate neck operation in the Memorial Hospital of that city. Educated at Rush Medical College in Chicago and in Europe, Park was at 48 at the height of his very considerable powers. Tall, powerfully-built, urbane and witty, this ambidextrous dean of the area surgeons, had gained international renown. His world-famous, 1200-page text, *Modern Practice of Surgery,* would not be published until 1907, but he had written several other books. Although an expert on cancer, he was interested in other phases of medicine. After a study of the Garfield case he had written and lectured on the treatment of gunshot wounds. As a surgeon he was rapid, clean, what is professionally termed a "pretty operator."

From the moment of his appointment as Exposition medical director, Dr. Park had insisted upon having on the grounds "a sufficiently-equipped hospital in which care could be given to any emergency cases that might occur within the exposition limits." Not without difficulty Park had convinced the officials of the need for such a building, and eventually "a small but convenient structure" had been erected near the Elmwood Avenue entrance. Of Spanish Renaissance style in keeping with the architectural theme of the Exposition, it had a frontage of 90 feet. The first floor was given over to the "usual hospital purposes," with two male wards in the western wing and a women's ward in the eastern. The main entrance from the Mall opened directly into a small rotunda decorated with tropical plants, pictures, and drapery. Back of the rotunda a rear wing contained an operating room on one side of a corridor with a patients' waiting room on the other. Farther back were a kitchen and dining room. The upper floor contained rooms for the superintendent, Miss Adelia

Walters, and for half a dozen nurses. Each of the latter served for only a month, so that as many trained nurses as possible from various parts of the country could combine a tour of duty with sightseeing. The facilities offered by this small building would ultimately prove its worth, for by the close of the Exposition a total of 5567 cases of aid or comfort would be recorded in its books.

On this morning the young medical students on the staff of the small hospital were looking ahead to the usual calendar of minor casualties for the day. Perhaps the list would be a bit longer with the press of crowds everywhere to catch a glimpse of the President or to shake his hand. Burton T. Simpson and Burt J. Bixby had just completed their sophomore year at the University of Buffalo Medical School, T. Frederick Ellis his third year. They had spent their summer dressing minor injuries and treating minor emergencies, but their most thrilling job was driving the hospital's electric ambulance. Serving as resident physician was senior medical student Edward D. Mann, the son of the city's foremost gynecologist, Dr. Matthew D. Mann. Also on duty was young Dr. George McK. Hall, an intern. In case more seasoned medical help was required, the hospital staff included Dr. Vertner Kenerson, who was Dr. Park's deputy; Dr. Nelson W. Wilson, medical inspector of the Exposition; Dr. A. F. Zittel, and Dr. Alexander Allan.

Across the city at 1078 Broadway Leon F. Czolgosz was also astir early. Dressed neatly as usual, he went downstairs, bought a cigar at Nowak's bar, and left. In the right-hand pocket of his gray flannel suitcoat he carried a white handkerchief and as he had the day before, his newly bought nickel-plated .32 caliber Iver Johnson six-shot automatic.

9

"I Don't Know If I Will Ever Get Away"

A CHEER FROM THE SMALL GROUP of people in front of the Milburn house greeted the President as—with Mrs. McKinley on his arm—he appeared in the doorway. The coachmen and footmen aboard the Hamlin victoria, and those who were to man the carriages behind, stiffened perceptibly. The sentries snapped to attention. Foster and the detectives ran to take their positions around the Chief Executive as he and the First Lady moved down the walk.

One could sense a carefree gaiety this morning. The President was smiling as he waved his silk hat. Mrs. McKinley, though she looked pale and worn, seemed happy. She chatted happily as the entourage, including the couple's attractive nieces and Flora Wilson, entered the carriages.

Once Mrs. McKinley was seated, the President took his place beside her; Milburn, as he had done on the previous days of the McKinley visit, faced the couple.

Cortelyou, Dr. and Mrs. Rixey, and Secretary Wilson entered the carriage directly behind. Once the Secret Service men and detectives had scrambled into a third carriage, the beplumed escort under Colonel Chapin's command formed around the entourage; the whips were flicked lightly, and the party started for the Exposition railroad station, less than two miles to the north.

There was nothing even faintly ominous or suggestive of the tragic events to come. From rooftops, from windows, even from trees, from the curbs and the sidewalks, people cheered as the horses cantered along the shady avenue. The President's popularity was amply attested to on this morning as it had been on the day before.

"This is President McKinley's day at Niagara Falls," *The*

74

Buffalo Commercial noted. "Yesterday, the nation's chief executive viewed the masterpiece of the creative genius of the nineteenth century; today he is viewing the triumph of nature's handicraft, powerful beyond conception, yet harnessed by men, lending an infinitesimal portion of its energy to create the fairy City of Light. The one would be incapable without the other—to appreciate man's achievements as exemplified in the Pan-American Exposition, one must see Niagara which made the exposition possible; to grasp the majesty of the mighty cataract one needs to see what can be done by diverting a small portion of the water from the channel provided by nature and forcing its flow over turbine wheels."

At a point just beyond the Lincoln Parkway entrance the prancing horses were reined to a halt. While for a moment McKinley lolled at his ease to view the Lion's Bridge, a program boy named Kloenhammer eluded police and darted to the President's carriage. "Here's a program for you, Mr. President," cried the boy.

Smiling, the President extracted a fresh dollar bill from his billfold; but the boy, after handing the Chief Executive the program, backed away, saying, "No, sir, that's a gift."

The President was pleased—he smiled more broadly. That was payment enough for Kloenhammer.

It was now 8:35. The morning seemed expressly created for the occasion. "Dew still glistened on the grass, and the flowers, as if refreshed by a night of rest, were holding up their gayly colored heads," wrote one lyrical reporter.

As the carriage rolled along the Esplanade, carpenters who were ripping down the stage from which the President had spoken so forcefully the day before, stopped their work and bared their heads.

The area around the station swarmed with carriages, each disgorging a bevy of fashionably dressed men and women. Presently, McKinley's carriage drew up. Slowly, deliberately, the driver jockeyed it into position alongside Engine 390 and an excursion train of five cars.

After helping the First Lady aboard the car *Columbia*, the President reappeared on the station platform to smoke a cigar and thread his way through the clusters of frock-coated diplomats, exotically attired foreign visitors, high-ranking Army and Navy officials, and Buffalo socialites.

McKinley seemed happy and relaxed. As he stood chatting with Dr. Rixey, Milburn, and Cortelyou, he remarked, "The Exposition seems more beautiful than ever this morning."

The bidding had been furious among local socialites to join the Presidential excursion, but necessity had limited the party to 104. These chosen few, as 9:00 approached, jammed their way aboard the train—convinced beyond a doubt that they were the luckiest people in the world. Many had been fortunate enough to exchange a few words or a handshake with the President as he strolled about the station; others had received at least a nod or a smile. All were to treasure memories of the President in this intimate mood and later to congratulate themselves upon their good fortune.

At two minutes to nine amid laughter and gaiety and a buzz of conversation, Engineer Murphy signaled for departure. The President, who had taken his place beside the First Lady, pressed his face against the car window, smiling, and bowing to those along the platform. Engine 390, trailing a thin plume of smoke, chugged away toward the Niagara River. Within the cars the excursionists laughed and chatted, seeking where possible points of vantage close to their famous guests.

Past little farmhouses the train moved on. A gentle haze, the first harbinger of autumn, lay upon the orchards and the patches of still-green woodlands.

"Nature," said one of the excursionists who viewed the placid scene, "was in her most happy and accommodating mood."

The rasp of saws, mingled with the pounding of hammers, arose from the Temple of Music. At 9:00 Captain Louis Babcock began driving his crew of workmen hard. McKinley was to enter the Temple at 4:00 and proceed along the main aisle to a small cleared area where, surrounded by members of his immediate entourage, soldiers, and guards, he would greet the public.

Babcock's men formed the aisle to the reception area by pushing the backs of chairs together and draping them with blue bunting. Thus arranged the chairs formed a large V. After shaking the President's hand, the people were to move quickly along and exit on the other side. Flags were draped at the point of the

V. As a decorative touch two potted bay trees and other shrubs were brought from the grounds and placed in front of the draped flags. McKinley was to stand amidst this bower of greenery.

Some lingering instinctive sense of danger may have lurked in Babcock's mind this morning, for he summoned Harry Hamlin to discuss the possibility of an attack from the President's rear. This possibility seemed to both men so remote as to be fantastic; yet after a brief conference Babcock ordered the workmen to build a wooden blind to preclude any approach from the President's back.

By noon arrangements were completed. Over a glass of Pilsener beer Babcock, Hamlin, and Quackenbush reviewed the morning's work with satisfaction. Their mood was light. As they drank their beer and munched sandwiches, Quackenbush remarked facetiously, "It would be Roosevelt's luck to have McKinley shot today."

The possibility at this moment appeared so ludicrous that the three joined in a hearty laugh.

Czolgosz's movements during the morning and early afternoon are uncertain. Contradictory accounts exist, both supposedly based upon his confession made that evening. One has him following the President to Niagara Falls; another claims he remained on the grounds and secured early a position in the line that was forming outside the Temple of Music. If Czolgosz did indeed go to Niagara Falls, he must have found it easier to make an expeditious return, making his way through the throngs at the Falls and on the grounds and by the use of public conveyances, than Dr. Park was later able to accomplish by special arrangements with top priority in response to the nation's number one emergency. Of course, Czolgosz may have made a very short stop at Niagara Falls, realizing almost at once that this was not the place to afford him the opportunity he was seeking. In any case early afternoon found him in the vanguard of those waiting to meet the President and shake his hand.

According to one version of the "confession"[1] the idea of the handkerchief ruse occurred to Czolgosz almost on the spot. Since

1. The confession extracted from the prisoner during a grilling in Chief of Police Bull's office on the night of September 6 was read to newspapermen in a condensed form. The actual confession is missing from the files of the Erie County District Attorney's office. No other copy appears to be in existence.

the day was hot, handkerchiefs were much in evidence to wipe perspiring hands and faces. Perhaps as he used his own for that purpose, Czolgosz suddenly conceived the idea of wrapping it as a bandage around his right hand. Thus he could hold his weapon in his hand without arousing suspicion. Otherwise, it would be unlikely that he could carry it under the watchful eyes of those surrounding the President and have it ready to fire and continue firing until his mission was completed. Somehow he felt this would work.

Now all was in readiness!

The excursion train cut through the ripening fruitlands, stopped momentarily at the Falls Street station in Niagara Falls, then chugged on toward Lewiston, a small hamlet to the north. This circuitous route would enable the party to return to Niagara Falls by the picturesque Gorge Route, which skirted the river along the eastern escarpment excitingly close to the Lower Rapids.

Here the Niagara River, reunited after having made its stupendous leap in two gigantic cataracts, roars through caverns at forty miles an hour and plunges among boulders as high as a house.

Although the river forms a short segment of boundary between two friendly nations, it winds its turbulent course through country bristling with memories of their former enmity. From Lewiston the President could view on the opposite bank craggy Queenston Heights and spot atop a Doric shaft the stony likeness of British General Sir Isaac Brock, who had repulsed the Americans on this very site in 1812 and paid with his life for his victory.

Lewiston, niched into the craggy precipice on the eastern flank of the Niagara, itself abounded in literary and historical associations, for here James Fenimore Cooper had found material for his Revolutionary War novel, *The Spy,* and in this area John Jacob Astor had once plied his lucrative fur trade.

In this village there was a brief delay, which one of the reporters present explained: "The reason for it was a slight misunderstanding as to which track the President's Special train was to run on. The result was that the four elegant observation cars which the Gorge Route had provided for the party had to be backed to meet the train."

The President and his party alighted while this took place. The First Lady leaned heavily upon her husband's arm as he led her slowly to a chair near a weather-beaten railroad shed. The President, much to the amusement of his party and a crowd of villagers who had gathered around them, opened the First Lady's black silk parasol and held it over her head as a protection against the sun.

This was an intimate scene that even the hinterlanders realized was a rare treat. They had, no doubt, heard of McKinley's unfailing gallantry toward his invalid wife; now as they edged closer, they saw him, uncomfortably hot in formal black, shading his wife with a parasol. No reception had been planned and certainly none would have ensued but for an aged man with a long white beard who mustered up sufficient courage to step forward and shake McKinley's hand. The others, including a delegation of Toronto excursionists who had crossed Lake Ontario that morning, now sensing the President's friendly spirit, inched forward to be rewarded with handshakes.

"In the meantime," the reporter wrote, "the special trolley cars were brought up. They were run on the tracks of the New York Central to the end of the trolley wires. They were fully one hundred feet from where the President's party was gathered, and as it was decided that Mrs. McKinley should not be compelled to walk even that short distance, orders were given that the cars should be shoved back by hand as far as the train.

"Detective Geary placed his shoulder against the rear platform of the leading car and although there was a slight upgrade at that point, he succeeded in getting it in motion and forcing it to the position desired. George Urban, Jr., and Mr. Scatcherd tackled the second car, and, by starting the perspiration, and getting very red in the face, succeeded in duplicating Mr. Geary's feat. In the meantime, employees of the company had gotten the remaining two cars in motion; all were in position a minute afterward. . . .

"When all was ready the engine was attached to the Special train and it shoved the four cars until the trolley wires were reached."

The President had accepted this awkward interruption in the best of spirits. In fact, as he watched, he laughed and joshed with

Milburn and Urban, as well as the others who had joined in the pushing.

Once this sweaty task had been performed, the President and his wife boarded the first car, from which a moment later photographers snapped him as, in an anticipatory mood, he looked through the open window of the car.

On the return trip to Niagara Falls along the river's edge the Gorge Route cars were spaced at intervals of 300 yards. As the cars raced along, only a few yards above the rushing stream, the President caught a glimpse of the site of the famous Devil's Hole Massacre of 1763, where a portaging detachment of British soldiers had been swept by the Seneca Indians over the chasm to their death.

For many in the party this was their initial view of the river, and on this September day it was a most spectacular one. It out-stripped any man-made attraction the McKinleys had seen. The river especially delighted Mrs. McKinley, affording her more pleasure than any other single phase of her Buffalo visit. Her favorite view, she confided, was below the Cantilever Bridge, where the broad river's surface was peaceful, with only the slow, widening circles to suggest the mighty forces at work beneath. Here, as one of the excursionists noted that day, "the river stretches away with a smooth green surface between green-clad, rock-bound banks until it ends in a burst of foam and hanging clouds of spray and a mighty rush of water at the point where Niagara's torrents tumble into the great Gorge."

Clearly the excursion had relaxed the President. Surrounded by friends and obviously enjoying the mild late summer morning, as well as the relative lack of constraint and formality, he lolled back in his cushioned chair, joking with detectives and others in the car. His joshing became more pointed as the cars neared Niagara Falls. The President had been reliably informed, he con-fided, that this city was rampant with pickpockets. Jokingly he suggested that his fellow excursionists watch their possessions closely during their stay in the city—an admonition which may have recalled to some Chief Bull's earlier warning to Exposition-goers against thievery.

The President's laugh-provoking sallies as the cars sped along had revealed him in one of his lighter moods. Those about him were delighted.

Minutes before noon the cars rolled into the Falls Station at Second and Main Streets, where once again the President found himself confronted with and overwhelmed by blaring bands, cantering horsemen, fluttering flags, cheering citizens, waving handkerchiefs, and ceremonial splendor.

In the past, Niagara Falls had greeted hundreds of illustrious visitors, but the warmth of its welcome and hospitality was in no way diminished because of its familiarity with the great. Before the President's visit to Suspension Bridge the mayor, Major Butler, astride an impressive mount, cantered up at the head of a welcoming delegation to purvey the city's cordial greetings.

Lieutenant G. Barrett Rich, a veteran of the recent Spanish conflict, years later was to recall the flurry of excitement, as well as the conjectures that arose, when the President's carriage entered the famous span. Mounted on a brown mare, Rich cantered along in his assigned position directly back of the left rear wheel of the carriage. As the carriage moved toward the center of the bridge, the President grew increasingly nervous, admonishing the coachman to observe punctiliously a chalk line, which had been drawn some hours in advance to mark precisely the international boundary line.

At the turn of the century American Presidents had not yet started to rove the world. Meticulous care, therefore, had been observed in the President's visit to the bridge, for he intended scrupulously to observe precedent and not venture so much as a foot beyond the line marking the United States boundary.

Indeed, an alert press already had sharply focused attention on a situation as yet hypothetical, dwelling with horror upon the eventualities that could arise should the President, even inadvertently, set foot upon foreign soil.

As a public service to its readers, the *Buffalo Commercial* had dug into the chalk line situation with zeal, emerging from its study with this thought-provoking observation:

"If the coachman on the box of the carriage had been careless or had not been carefully instructed he might have easily created a fine lot of complications."

What would have been the result of such an unthinkable violation? The *Commercial*, too, had the answer, which seemingly boded ill for relations between the two great powers.

"If he had crossed the boundary line, there would have been trouble. The President would have been on Canadian territory."

It was true, the paper forthrightly conceded, that the President of the United States was permitted to enter a foreign country; but such a visit must be only on occasions of utmost formality. Belaboring the situation still further, the paper informed its readers of the proper etiquette involved.

"The visit would be the object of formal correspondence between the American and English governments in advance. He would be received with great ceremony."

On such a great state occasion "probably all the troops in Canada would be turned out to meet him. No uniformed soldiers would be permitted to accompany him from this country. It would be a state occasion, the details of which would be arranged at the seats of both governments."

And this final sally: "So, if the President had visited English territory today, it would have been in the nature of an affront to the British government. It would have been at least a diplomatic impropriety."

Fortunately, none of these direful predictions involving a diplomatic contretemps materialized. The head coachman, properly admonished and as circumspect as a foreign ambassador, wheeled the McKinley victoria about with at least a dozen feet to spare before the danger zone was reached. The name of this coachman who held such awesome power in his hands is not known, but the squeamish *Commercial* representative, as well as many others, must have breathed more easily as the handsome horses started back for the protective shores of the United States, where the President was safe from international involvement, if not an assassin's bullet.

No doubt, President McKinley, despite his momentary nervousness, may have been privately amused at the excessive punctiliousness of the occasion. If he felt any such emotion, the President's face gave no evidence of it as the procession headed back. From his seat he preserved his usual magnificent calm, smiling and waving now and then as the carriage headed back to Prospect Park.

At the turn of the century Niagara Falls was just emerging from the village stage. Only this very year of the President's visit it had been proclaimed a full-grown city of 26,000; yet because of its world-wide fame and its proximity to the source of electric power, it had, four years before, been seriously considered as Buffalo's rival for the Exposition. In fact, in 1897 President McKinley had driven a stake on nearby Cayuga Island, signaling it as the site of the Exposition. However, war had intervened and plans had been changed.

The Niagara describes a sharp bend at the Falls. The area within this crook of the river was crammed with garish bazaar-like shops designed to lure the attention of the million annual visitors away from the evanescent beauty of Nature's wonders to the tawdry trappings of commercialism. Piled helter skelter upon each other, establishments vied among themselves in bewildering displays of Indian moccasins, Iroquois beads, miniature birch bark canoes, shells emblazoned with pictures of the mighty waterfall, cups and saucers, glassware, and enough souvenir pillows to cushion the woes of the entire nation.

The more fastidious often complained of the atmosphere of brash commercialism that dominated the city. There were mutterings too against the city's hack drivers, said to be the most aggressive and obstreperous in the world. The "hackies" bawled the merits of their respective excursions from every street corner, almost kidnapping the inexperienced or unwary visitor.

Since it was first sighted by early French explorers, visitors, and particularly writers, had expounded on the great falls. Awed at first sight by the great crystal body of falling water, the Flemish priest, Father Louis Hennepin, had two centuries before miscalculated its height at six hundred feet. "It is without parallel," recorded Charles Dickens. In different ways and at different times Harriet Martineau, Captain Frederick Marryat, Mrs. Lydia Huntley Sigourney, James Fenimore Cooper, Thomas Moore, and François René de Chateaubriand had come to marvel at its power and beauty.

The waterfall was one of the wonders of the new world, but

Mrs. McKinley, yielding to one of her recurrent weak spells, was to catch only a glimpse of it from the Suspension Bridge. The morning activities had fatigued her, so in obedience to the President's wishes the carriages were headed through densely packed streets to the International Hotel, where rooms on the main floor had been assigned for the President's use. One of the city's most famous hostelries, this imposing white frame building stood amidst shade trees, sweeping lawns, and gardens at Main and Falls Streets.

Here a mass of people thronged before the entrance and cheered lustily as the President, his high silk hat raised, drew within view. It was with difficulty that Welch's mounted escort cleared the street, so that the Chief Executive might conduct the First Lady to her quarters.

The schedule now called for a tour of Goat Island, so named for the herd of goats that portage-master John Stedman had raised there in 1779. Within minutes the President, still acknowledging the plaudits of noisy spectators, was on his way to the small island, which divided Horseshoe Falls on the Canadian side from the American Falls. It was reached by a bridge, from which curving driveways extended in many directions over the wooded island. When Father Hennepin visited the Falls, it had covered an area of 250 acres; but time and erosion had meanwhile reduced it to about one-third that size.

After a whirlwind tour of the island, McKinley returned to the hotel, entering by the back entrance to avoid the people who were massed along the street and on the sidewalks in front of the building.

Photographs of the historic visit reveal the President in a variety of moods. For the most part, he appears brisk and confident. Now he is smiling, perhaps at some sally from a member of his entourage; again, more characteristically, he is serious, a man of statuesque calm. The photographs show the ubiquitous Foster either at the President's side or hovering close by as the party stopped briefly for a view of Prospect Park or mounted the steeply inclined path leading to the American Falls, or later when the Chief Executive alighted at the rear entrance of the International Hotel.

Foster, his derby cocked, his vest buttoned tightly, is on the alert once more, standing behind the President and Milburn as they posed at one o'clock for what is often erroneously claimed as "the last photograph." Once to please a photographer the President removed his lucky carnation. The fresh one that replaced it was given to a young girl at the Temple reception.

A small private luncheon in rooms 8 and 9 was planned in McKinley's honor at the hotel. Since a few minutes intervened before its start, the President after freshening up took advantage of the respite to pace the hotel's shaded porch with Melvin C. Hanna, Senator Hanna's brother. The President was smoking one of his favorite Garcias when Count Quadt of the German embassy was announced. The Count paid his respects, adding that even though the German Court at that moment was in mourning, he had been granted special permission to attend the luncheon.

The noonday repast—served buffet style—was limited to the President's immediate party, plus a few Niagara Falls guests. For this occasion twelve tables, fastooned with autumnal decorations of goldenrod and purple asters, had been set.

By early afternoon, McKinley was ready to resume his sightseeing. As always, he seemed fresh, even eager for the sights ahead; but, characteristically, Mrs. McKinley, despite her rest, seemed fatigued. Since the sultry heat of the day had come, and there appeared to be no possible escape from the noise and the excitement that distraught her, the President decided to drive her back to the excursion train. There she could await the completion of his scheduled tour.

Following brief visits to Luna and Prospect Parks, the President was driven for an inspection to one of the marvels of the dawning electrical age—the Niagara Falls Power House. After an examination of the equipment, buried some 240 feet below the earth's surface, then a novelty of the first degree, the President shook hands with Addison Barker, the elevator boy, and departed for the Fifth Street crossing to board his train.

Had McKinley at this point recapitulated his three-day visit, as well as the result of his personal appearances, he could quite honestly have rated himself high in public esteem. Judging from the mass reaction spontaneously displayed time after time, his popularity was at its crest. The enthusiasm for him, both as a man and as a public figure, was warm and undiminished.

Papers on both sides of the Atlantic were commenting favorably on his speech of the day before. Many predicted that it would rank with Washington's Farewell Address. Reactions from papers of both parties were favorable.

The Republican *Philadelphia Ledger* commented: "Our great problem is that of securing more markets for our increasing surplus of products. One way to accomplish that is by reciprocity treaties, 'sensible trade arrangements which will not interrupt our home production.' Reciprocity on the President's lines should meet with no opposition in the Republican party or from any friend of the protective tariff."

The Democratic *Philadelphia Times* praised the President's honesty:

"With experience and greater opportunities he surveyed a wider field and was honest and manly enough to change his opinions when he was convinced that those which he had formerly held were no longer for his country's highest good."

The New York World proclaimed McKinley's statesmanship and wisdom: "These are the words of a statesman and a wise party leader," commented this Democratic sheet. "They are economically sound as applied to a palpable trade condition. They are politically sagacious in responding to and leading a popular demand which is certain to extend and grow more insistent with the passing of time."

The Associated Press reported heartening responses from London. *The Times* forecast an end of America's isolationism. *The Standard* stated that the speech would excite throughout Europe "as keen interest as it will arouse in the Western Continent." *The St. James Gazette* called the speech "sensational." *The Globe* thought that the President's program forecast "a severe rivalry which Great Britain must expect from the United States, amounting . . . to an abandonment of extreme protection."

By midafternoon Buffalo papers were reporting individual reactions to the McKinley speech. Interviewed on the Exposition grounds, one J. S. Boddy, former warden of the Simcoe County Jail, Ontario, was enthusiastic about the Presidential thinking. "It was the kind of talk that would give all nations a better idea of the great people of a great nation," said Boddy.

But the really sensational local news on this day was the shift-

ing of Captain Michael Regan from the fourth to the first precinct—a fortunate move in view of the events of the next few
hours.

The Buffalo Times was reporting a variety of other events.
From Middelburg, Cape Colony, Lord Kitchener reported a victory over the Boers; a dispatch from London revealed that King
Edward was submitting to the light, water, and massage "cure"
at Homburg; from Pittsburgh it was reported that steel workers
had rejected the latest offer of the Big Steel combine.

The Chicago Automobile Club announced the start of its 20-
car expedition, which optimistically hoped to reach the Exposition grounds later in the fall. "The machines," a dispatch said,
"will carry about fifty persons. In many of the cities which will
be passed public receptions will be tendered the club members.
The trip will occupy about nine days, and the automobiles will
average sixty-four miles a day." A similar expedition from New
York City under the leadership of Colonel John Jacob Astor—
also with the Exposition as its goal—had found the going too
rough; it had bogged down amidst heavy storms and washed out
roads at Rochester.

The climax of McKinley's visit had come. At 3:30 the excursion train ground to a stop at the violet-colored Exposition Station amidst yet another enthusiastic demonstration. The Presi-
den stepped down briskly, showing no fatigue from his crowded
schedule of the past few hours. He had, in fact, spruced up and
changed his collar on the train during the return trip from the
Falls.

Plans now called for the First Lady to return to the Milburn
house while her husband completed his final brief tour of the
Exposition to be concluded by the 4:00 reception. She smiled,
waving farewell to the big crowd as the President gently helped
her into the Hamlin victoria.

A moment later, as the vehicle was about to draw away, the
President gave his wife her smelling salts; then affectionately
squeezing her hand, he said in a low voice, "I hope you enjoy
your ride—good-bye."

He stood, his eyes fixed upon the victoria as it moved away;
then turning to Milburn and Cortelyou, who were at his side, he

remarked, "Well, gentlemen, let's get on with the business at hand."

At this juncture, the "business at hand" entailed the President's calling at the picturesque Mission Building, located at the extreme northeast corner of the grounds. As the President's party moved along slowly through the crowd-packed roads, it passed the famous Sunken Gardens, drawing up before the Mission Building at 3:45.

"I am glad to see you back in Buffalo," said John B. Olmstead, a committee member, who had been selected to welcome the President at this point.

McKinley's reply was prophetic. "Yes," he said jocularly, "I don't know whether I will ever get away."

Once this bit of pleasantry had passed, McKinley began to move through the building, now admiring the wainscoted walls, or again, the bell tower, the tiny marble and mosaic chapel and the Leland Stanford window, then on preview before its permanent installation in the California university.

The President's visit to the building was short—only of five minutes' duration; but it afforded him a welcome respite, during which he smoked a cigar and sipped a cup of chocolate.

A few minutes before four, he stepped into his victoria and, surrounded by a special corporal's guard of the 74th Regiment, began his drive to the Temple of Music.

10

"Go Easy on Him, Boys"

UNDER THE BRILLIANT AFTERNOON SUN the Temple glittered like a giant confection. Since James Parker had arrived and taken up a position behind Czolgosz, the waiting crowd had swelled, beginning in a slender line, then stretching, as the minutes and hours passed, formlessly to the Esplanade beyond.

At five minutes to four a small buckboard clattered to a stop before the building. Harry Hamlin reined his horse to a stop and bounded out, followed quickly by Captain Babcock. The two had driven rapidly across the grounds to catch a glimpse of McKinley at the Mission Building. If Quackenbush's earlier flippant remarks had raised even vague qualms, Babcock's last-minute check now must have dispelled them. Helmeted soldiers of the 65th and 74th National Guard regiments, rifles perched on shoulders, briskly paced before the entrance; mounted police and soldiers loped their horses up and down the Esplanade, shepherding the formless masses into some semblance of order. Captain Wisser's 73rd Coastal Artillerymen, who had trooped in at 3:00 under Corporal Bertschey, had been stationed strategically so that they might command a view of the narrow two-foot aisle along which the line of people would move.

Private Francis O'Brien assumed a position close to the reception area. Private Brooks was placed to O'Brien's left; behind O'Brien stood Privates Louis Neff and Arthur Crosby. Private Ivey Fenenbaugh was stationed across the aisle, so that he could look directly at the President. Nearby stood Privates Maximilian R. Kubatz and William Heiser, both within fifteen feet of the reception area. Although the President would be surrounded by his Secret Service detail and the four detectives who had hovered at his side since his arrival, Babcock, determined to leave no gap open, had augmented the total guard. In the area between the stage and the Temple's grand entrance still more guards and police had been stationed. Now as they gave the protective measures a final check, Babcock and Hamlin saw that at least eighty guards would scrutinize the visitors as they shuffled along from the entrance to the reception area. The protection, it appeared, was so strong that it defied intrusion.

Nevertheless, several cardinal rules of customary procedure would be broken. Foster, for instance, was to forego his usual position out of deference to Milburn. Generally, at affairs of this kind Foster hugged the President's left side, peering into the faces of all who approached. On this afternoon, Milburn would occupy that position, however, so that he might more readily introduce visitors of importance. The screen that Babcock had caused to be erected behind the President and the smallness of the reception area violated a long-standing rule of police protection that a spacious area should be cleared on all sides. Further, the soldiers, unaccustomed and untrained for police work of this kind, were clustered too close together—a confusing disadvantage as it later developed.

There existed, too, a cardinal rule that no one should approach the Chief Executive unless his hands were plainly exposed, but because of the heat and the prevalence of handkerchiefs, this regulation was waived. Indeed, the President himself, before leaving Milburn's that morning, had stuffed three extra handkerchiefs into his own pockets. Thousands of others on the grounds used handkerchiefs not only to wave as symbols of welcome, but to wipe their sweaty hands and faces.

The heat, then, probably accounted for the general indifference this afternoon to the man who stood with hundreds of others a few yards from the Temple entrance, waiting for the reception to begin, and waiting, too, to sacrifice his drab existence in exchange for the President's life.

The long wait had been a very tedious one for James Parker. Naturally gregarious, he would have liked to talk with the man who stood next to him. Once or twice he attempted some small talk, but met with silence.

Czolgosz now was like a man enchanted with his own impending doom. Irrevocably committed to the hideous task ahead, he stood like someone on the brink of a precipice, mesmerized by its yawning depths. At this moment, shortly before 4:00, he might have slipped away unnoticed, for aside from Parker's occasional sallies to which he gave no response, no one had paid him the slightest attention.

His very appearance, as one of the great anonymous army of workingmen, was in his favor. While he stood in line, he heard a great shout from across the Esplanade. The shouting spread and was taken up by those around him. At exactly five minutes to four, the vanguard of the President's mounted escort with plumes bobbing and in full panoply announced the arrival of the Chief Executive himself.

Again, McKinley's popularity was acclaimed in cheers, in fluttering handkerchiefs, in hats sailing into the air; and again the President lifted his own silk topper, nodded and smiled as Milburn helped him to alight. After McKinley entered the Temple, his first reported impression was that of relief from the sweltering heat. Outside, it was 82 degrees. Turning to Milburn, the President remarked, "It's much cooler in here."

Without any explicit directions he moved down the aisle, taking up his position in the area, where he paused momentarily to survey the upper galleries and the stage. Then, W. J. Gomph, the Temple's organist, began to play. A look of pleasure suffused the President's face as he listened to the deep organ tones of Bach's Sonata in F swell and reverberate.

Meanwhile, amidst chatting and laughter, Milburn slipped into his assigned position on the President's left; Cortelyou stationed himself on the President's right. The President nodded pleasantly to Milburn, saying, "Let them come."

As if in answer to this Presidential utterance, the heavy Temple doors swung back and the people began to file in—hot, dusty, and weary, many of them obviously excited at the prospect of meeting the President of the United States. Dr. Clinton Colegrove, of Holland, New York, was the first man to shake the President's hand. As the doctor reached the President, he murmured, "George Washington, Abraham Lincoln, and President McKinley."

"Thank you," responded the President, as he moved the doctor along.

In receptions such as the one in progress the President extended the fingers of his right hand, using his left hand to move the visitor along courteously but quickly—a technique he had learned from President Hayes. Usually he spoke a word or two of greeting, sometimes adding a smile or friendly nod.

Justice Alfred Spring of the New York State Appellate Division was among those in the vanguard of the line; but most of the early arrivals were housewives, many of whom had brought along their youngsters. As always the President was delighted with the children. He patted them affectionately on the head, murmuring a few words to one curly-headed girl who caught his fancy. He was pleased rather than disturbed when a small but aggressive boy broke suddenly from his mother's side and ran up to him. When the distraught mother arrived a second later to apologize, McKinley complimented her on her son's brightness.

Cortelyou, who had never fully overcome his fears about the reception, was fidgety. As he watched its progress, his apprehensions mounted. Within five minutes after its start he moved to stop it. He summoned Edward R. Rice, an Exposition committee member, to his side. "See Babcock and have him end the reception in five minutes," he ordered.

Rice nodded. Thousands were still milling about outside the building, but it was evident that the President could never hope to shake everyone's hand. Rice replied that he would notify Babcock at once. He pushed his way to Babcock, whispering, "Speed up the line. Cortelyou wants the reception ended in five minutes."

Upon receiving these orders, Babcock started at once for the Temple entrance. "Speed up the crowd and shut the doors in five minutes," he ordered the guards.

Meanwhile, Parker was straining at what to him seemed like endless delays. He had been in the line under the hot sun for a long time; beads of sweat glistened on his black face and trickled down his cheeks. As the line inched on, it seemed to Parker that the man in front of him was too slow. Once, Parker demanded, "If you can't go faster, at least let me by."

His protest brought no response. With less than five minutes of the reception remaining, Czolgosz edged his way, step by step, forward. When, at last, he reached the Temple door and had proceeded a few feet within the building, a guard bellowed, "Get in line!"

He had strayed slightly out of line, but he quickly resumed his place. The guard said no more. After that close call Czolgosz trembled. Slipping the handkerchief about his right hand, he moved along, step by step, down the aisle. Soldiers and guards flanked him on either side—so closely that he might have touched them. Ahead he could see the President smiling, shaking hands; but his impressions at this moment were vague and uncertain. He progressed as if on a treadmill, or in a dream. He must go on. There was no retreat. Only a few people remained now; then he would face the President.

Young John D. Wells was noting each detail of the scene now unfolding. Now and then as if recording the events for posterity instead of his own small paper, Wells drew out his open-faced silver watch to check the exact time. He observed, too, the President's easy assurance, his eagerness to meet the people, his engaging smile, and the kindly attention he bestowed on the children, as if he were compensating for his own lack of them.

The assiduous Wells jotted down all the details—the rumbling and swelling of the organ music, the dull shuffling of shoes along the pine floor, the babble of voices, the curious abashed expressions on the spectator's faces, and now and then a peal of laughter.

"To every child, the President bent over, shook hands warmly and said some kind words," Wells recorded. "As each person passed he was viewed critically by the Secret Service men. Their hands were watched; their faces and actions noted."

At this point Wells's attention was drawn to "a man of unusual aspect—short, heavy, and dark with a heavy black mustache. Under his black brows gleamed a pair of black glistening Italian eyes."

Here was a man to arouse suspicions; as he edged his way closer to the President, Foster intercepted him. The Secret Service agent grabbed the man roughly by the shoulder, scrutinized him a moment, then apparently satisfied that no malicious designs lurked behind his dark brows, released him. He was allowed to shake McKinley's hand.

It was 4:07. The punctilious Wells, after noting that, glanced up. As he did so, he saw a youngish man with tousled blond hair had moved into position for the next handshake. The man was neatly dressed. That much caught Wells's observant eye. Wells spotted the bandaged hand, which the man carried uplifted as if supported by a sling beneath his coat.

The man's left hand crossed his right as he extended both to meet the President's outstretched hand.

Ireland, still faintly suspicious of the swart Italian, was pushing him on his way. Organist Gomph was reaching a crescendo movement in the sonata. As Wells watched, the young man "quick as a flash withdrew his right hand, and before anyone knew what was transpiring two shots rang out, one following the other in the briefest portions of a second."

The first shot sounded muffled like a small firecracker exploding. The President rose on his toes, clutching his chest, then started to pitch forward. A mushroom of smoke issued from the handkerchief. Then came the second crackling report.

For one long ghastly second no one moved. The long line froze. Those surrounding the President, so gay and confident a moment before, stood transfixed like the incredulous witnesses to a hideous dream. Smoke was still pluming from the assassin's revolver. A flaming handkerchief was plummeting to the floor. Pale and grim, the assassin crouched before the President. There were no histrionics. No historic utterance fell from his lips such as John Wilkes Booth had spoken as he leaped from the box in Ford's Theater the night Lincoln was shot. Czolgosz was grimly silent and efficient, like a man who had taken his cue, and was now playing a scene he had rehearsed many times. He steadied his revolver at a 45 degree angle, ready to pump a third shot into the President's helpless body. And he might have well succeeded, but for Private O'Brien.

Alone of the artillerymen who guarded the President, O'Brien appeared able to act when action counted. The insane scene which had just flashed before him had paralyzed him, but only for a second. He and Detective Geary acted almost simultaneously. O'Brien dived and brought the assassin crashing to the floor in front of the wounded President. At the same moment, Parker swung his giant fist connecting solidly with the assassin's skull.

At the first shot the President had pitched upward and forward. At the second he fell backward and would have dropped to the floor but for Geary. The detective ran a few steps forward, caught the President, and was supporting him when Cortelyou and Milburn came to his aid.

Privates Brooks and Neff leaped to the assistance of O'Brien. Almost at the same moment the Secret Service agents sprang at the assassin, Foster yelling to Gallaher, "Al, get his gun."

Neff grabbed Czolgosz's hand, but it was O'Brien who managed to wrest the revolver loose. As the wild confusion continued, the President, supported by Cortelyou, Milburn and Geary, was led to a nearby chair. In staggering the last few steps, the President tripped on a piece of bunting. Slumping down, his massive head on Milburn's shoulder, he gasped, "Cortelyou, Cortelyou."

The secretary had turned aside momentarily, his eyes riveted upon the madness in the aisle, but hearing his name, he bent over the President.

"Be careful about my wife—do not tell her." As the President spoke he fumbled with the buttons of his white vest. Blood was oozing from his body, staining his vest with a patch of red.

The President slipped his fingers beneath the opening in his shirt near his heart. As he withdrew his hand, those in the little circle around him saw that his first and second fingers dripped with blood. Even this small effort seemed to expend the President's fast-waning strength. His head dropped wearily on his chest. He was heard to murmur, "This wound—it pains greatly."

Milburn, Scatcherd and the others around the President, realizing their utter impotence, turned away. At this moment a small white-haired man forced his way through the crowd. The man was de Aspiroz, the Mexican diplomat, "Oh, my God!" he cried in English, "Are you shot?"

The excited Latin diplomat threw himself at the President's feet.

"Yes—I believe—I am," the President gasped out the words slowly and disjointedly; and as if the effort had been too great his massive head fell backwards. His eyes closed. He seemed to have lost consciousness.

Seconds after the shots were fired, Quackenbush, frantically tore away the blue bunting and cleared a small space for the

President to rest, then rushed to a telephone to call the doctors and the Exposition Hospital.

Back at the scene of the shooting, he proceeded to mark off the exact area, then post guards. Then he telephoned Superintendent Bull, who promised to rush reinforcements to the Temple at once. Meanwhile, people were herded out of the building; but to do this it was necessary for the artillerymen and guards to draw their sabre bayonets and use extreme force. There was little more that those around the President could do but pray while they waited for the arrival of the ambulance.

One of the wonders of this day was the assassin's escape with his life. Floored by Parker's ponderous fists, tackled viciously by O'Brien, he had collapsed. What followed was very like the Anarchy which he professed to love. The guards had rushed in and were raining blows with their rifles and clubs upon him. The confusion helped to save his life. The guards and soldiers, frantic and bewildered, in trying to get at the assassin, tackled each other; thrashing about on the floor they became entangled in such a melee that their effectiveness was impaired. Several were sent spinning to the ground.

As the flaming handkerchief plummeted downward, Foster sprang forward like a suddenly released animal. By an almost superhuman effort he dragged the Anarchist to his feet. Clutching him by the throat with his left hand, Foster snarled, "You murderous . . !" and he struck the assassin squarely in his already badly battered face. So powerful was the impact of the blow that it sent Czolgosz sprawling to the floor.

As Czolgosz lay bloody and inert, he might not have long survived this brutal punishment but for the President. Half-conscious himself, McKinley fixed his eyes upon his badly drubbed and bloody assailant, then mercifully murmured, "Go easy on him, boys."[1]

The President's admonition came in a faltering gasp, hardly audible, yet it served to halt the beating. The assailant, blood drooling from his eyes and nose, his hair wildly disheveled, his legs like rubber, his clothing rent, and his body pummeled, was hauled to his feet amidst utter bedlam, then dragged to a small room in the northeast part of the Temple.

While this wild scene ensued, O'Brien handed the assassin's

---

1. The President's exact words were variously reported in the press.

weapon to his immediate superior, Corporal Bertschey. When Cortelyou asked to see it, however, the corporal refused to surrender the weapon without Captain Wisser's express order. Babcock, at this point, reminded Bertschey that he (Babcock) was in charge; that the artillery detail, therefore, was technically under his command while in the Temple. The corporal, after this remonstrance, consented to show Cortelyou the revolver, but dispatched Private Heiser for Captain Wisser.

Wisser was in his tent. Upon receiving Babcock's message, he set out at once for the Temple on the double. After he arrived there, he examined the revolver, noting that the hammer was down and "the next chamber being opposite the barrel was not visible." All other chambers were loaded. In his haste Wisser had forgotten his glasses and could not read the numbers on the weapon. A later examination disclosed that the revolver bore the number 463344 and had been manufactured by the Johnson Arms & Cycle Works at Fitchburg, Massachusetts. Later, Wisser placed the weapon in a box, which he tacked and sealed.

After Wisser left, Babcock issued orders that the Temple interior was to remain as it was until District Attorney Thomas Penney arrived.

The guards, after dragging Czolgosz to the room off the Temple stage, slammed the door behind them with a resounding bang. They dumped the assassin unceremoniously upon a small table and searched him. But his possessions were inconsequential—only $1.54 in cash, inexplicably a rubber nipple from a baby's bottle, a pencil, and a letter certifying his paid-up membership in a fraternal order known as The Knights of the Golden Eagle. Police conjectured—lacking any other plausible explanation—that the nipple was used as a protective covering for the muzzle of the revolver.

Along the Midway and the Esplanade word of the tragedy began to trickle through. People were stunned. Manager Frederick Cummins, upon receiving the word, strode to the stage of the Indian Congress where 2500 eager spectators were awaiting the afternoon performance. His face ashen, Cummins held up his hand, "The President has been shot!" Tickets, he said, would be refunded, but no one claimed the offer. Those in the audience silently with heads bowed streamed towards the entrance.

At the Streets of Mexico a bullfight was about to start. Unwittingly, President McGuire of the Pan-American Association of Concessionaires blurted out the news to the Mexican bullfighters. After a horrified look at McGuire, they hurdled the arena fence and fled. On stage, McGuire held up his hand, "Ladies and gentlemen," he proclaimed, "it is my painful duty to tell you that our President has been shot by an assassin."

A hush fell over the audience. "There will be no more entertainment today," continued McGuire.

One tightly corseted woman fainted. As the crowd began to leave, a Western cowboy, flourishing his Stetson, dashed to the door, yelling, "What are we going to do about it?"

Elsewhere all along the Midway others were asking the same question. The shows disgorged. People began pouring along the narrow Midway lane, all headed for the ornate red building on the Esplanade.

Great pains had been taken to conceal the prisoner's whereabouts. But people were constantly shuttling in and out of the Temple, and before the Temple doors had been bolted, the word had passed through the environs to the Esplanade. There scores had mounted lofty perches on the flower jardinieres; scores more had clung to precarious perches atop fountains or on tree limbs. An old man wearing a G.A.R. button on his coat lapel shook his head in sorrow. Around him cries were rising in a mounting angry chorus, "Kill the assassin! Hang him! Kill the bastard!"

At this moment a mail wagon with only its top visible above the dense masses of people was pushing its way slowly toward the Government Building. Eager to vent their rage upon any object, the mob moved menacingly toward the vehicle. It was thought the wagon was removing the assassin. "Stop that wagon!" yelled a big man. The cry was repeated, echoing like a chant over the Esplanade. Fortunately, the driver, spurring his horses, moved away before the mob could attack. Meanwhile, a band of Indians, gaudy in head feathers and war paint, galloped up to the Temple door. "Big White Feather has been killed!" they cried.

By the time the box-like electric ambulance sped across the grounds, the vast throng had turned into a sullen mob, which beat against the Temple doors and walls with such fury that both threatened to collapse. After tearing up stanchions and ropes surrounding the building, the vengeful crowd next threatened to push into the Temple itself—and might have succeeded, but for a thin line of Marines and 73rd Coastal Artillerymen. Brandishing loaded Lee-Mitford rifles, the hastily formed line managed to beat back the vanguard of the onrushing mob. But the situation was growing worse by the minute. Wild demands for the assassin's life filled the air as the ambulance wheeled to the Temple entrance. The vehicle had barely stopped before hospital attendants leaped out and rushed into the Temple. They found the President slumped in a chair.

When the President saw the stretcher that they had brought, he tried valiantly to raise himself; but his effort proved too great for his waning strength. He fell back. The attendants lifted him tenderly on to the pillow-lined litter.

A reporter who watched the scene observed. "There was no moaning, no outcry, no sign of suffering except spasmodic twitching and tightening of the features and occasionally a quivering and writhing of the shoulders."

No fewer than twenty men picked up the stretcher and carried it toward the west aisle, then up three steps to the southwest door. The crowd was hushed at the sight of the prostrate President being borne from the building. At first, the President's eyes were closed, but he opened them as he saw the vast throng surrounding the building. He half raised his great head "as if in appreciation of the silence and the sorrow."

It was exactly 4:14.

The people looked on, silent for the moment, benumbed with grief, as the stretcher was slowly, carefully lifted aboard, then fell back to permit Colonel Chapin's mounted detail to form a protective rectangle about the ambulance. Cortelyou, Milburn, Scatcherd, and Foster scrambled into the vehicle to accompany the President. The door banged shut behind them.

The ambulance moved slowly, then more swiftly as it crossed through the packed Court of Fountains amidst cries of "Keep back. Make way." But, for the most part, the admonitions were unnecessary. The people fell back reverentially before the electric car with its surrounding mounted detail, which was heading toward the Exposition hospital at the Elmwood Avenue gate.

In his record of the case, Dr. Nelson W. Wilson praised the skill of young Ellis in his handling of the ambulance: "The dash to the hospital was thrilling and sensational. Mr. T. F. Ellis handled the steering bar with the utmost skill. No chauffeur could have driven with more speed or more wisdom."

At the *Buffalo Enquirer* office, 250 Main Street, a 19-year-old cub reporter, John L. Lynch, was just leaving for the day when the city room telephone rang. Young Lynch could scarcely believe what he had heard as reporter Richard Silver excitedly shouted at the other end of the line. Lynch turned to relay the news to the City Editor, Eli Fouts. "It's Silver on the phone! The President has been shot!"

As reporter Richard Barry dashed, pad in hand, to replace Lynch at the telephone, Fouts yelled to young Lynch, "Get down to the composing room. Tell Eddie Fitzpatrick to hold up that last edition. We're getting out an extra!"

11

"Is He Alive?"

MINUTES AFTER THE PRESIDENT'S REMOVAL to the hospital the mob's pent-up fury began to vent itself, breaking like an angry surf around the Temple. It was, said a *Buffalo Enquirer* reporter who looked on, "a scene of wild rage."

Those in the room where the assassin had been dragged until some course of action could be devised listened with fear and misgivings to the ominous sounds from without. The mob battered and pounded against the walls with a fury that shook the building. Even more terrifying were the cries for vengeance and for the assailant's life. The peaceful excursion-going crowd had, within minutes, been lashed into a frenzied mob, now bent on one objective—hanging or lynching Czolgosz.

"Don't let him get away. Kill him! Hang him! Get the rope! Hang him on the arch and burn him. Kill the son of a bitch!"

Meanwhile, a detachment of fifteen police and a detail of Wisser's 73rd, and Marines under Captain Leonard, had managed to surround the Temple's main entrance.

"Load rifles," barked Captain Leonard.

The *Enquirer* man who watched this scene recorded:

"The breeches clicked and the men held up to plain view the hard steel and the encasing brass as they filled their Lee-Mitfords with cartridges. The effect was obvious, for the women started the movement to draw back. Men and women who had been dry-eyed began to cry. The lips of the policemen and soldiers were twitching."

The people, bent on vengeance, gave ground slowly, sullenly. Within the now beleaguered Temple, Guards McCauley and James peered through the chink-like windows at the mob of some hundred thousand which blackened the vast Esplanade.

101

Colonel Byrne, commandant of the Exposition police, and others in the small room huddled together in a group conferring.

"There's only one way," cried Byrne. "We must get him to Police Headquarters. And for that we need a wagon."

Agent Ireland doubted the feasibility of such a plan. First of all, where was the wagon? And if one were obtained how could it ever be driven through that wild mob to the Temple?

At this crucial moment Guard James shouted that he had sighted a leather-topped carriage drawn by a team of horses about fifty yards away, engulfed in the crowd. Only its top was visible. Earlier the vehicle had been used to carry Exposition committee members to the grounds.

After a discussion of some minutes, it was decided that a messenger should slip from the south entrance and work his way to the carriage. There were many in the room who doubted that this plan would work. However, a messenger was dispatched; but when he reached the carriage the coachman shook his head.

"I can't get through that mob," he protested.

"You must," cried the messenger.

"All right. I'll try," and a moment later as the signal was given, he whipped his team and headed for the southwest entrance.

The crowd quickly sensed the purpose of the move. As the carriage drew near the Temple, the surge of people turned away from the other entrances. "Here he comes. At this door," some one cried.

However, plans had been hastily improvised against such a contingency. The entrance already was roped off and surrounded by police, soldiers and Marines. The prisoner was to be thrown into the vehicle as it reached the door.

The cries grew more clamorous—"Here he is! Kill him! Lynch him! Don't let that carriage get away!"

The line of guards swayed.

The carriage reached the door. Byrne raised his right hand. At the signal Guards James and McCauley clutched the assassin by the shoulders. The Marines stood with bayonets fixed. The guards, picking up the assassin, hurled him like a piece of baggage into the carriage.

Meanwhile, bedlam broke loose. People were shouting, yelling and shaking their fists. "The roar of the crowd," said an observer, "was never to be forgotten by anyone who heard it."

Captain James F. Vallely, chief of the Exposition detectives, was caught up in the swirling mob. Only by the greatest effort did he manage to extricate himself and jump up beside the driver as the carriage headed through the crowd.

At first the carriage tottered precariously, but then it righted itself and moved forward along the Esplanade. Time after time, the mob threatened to overturn the vehicle, which moved on with excruciating slowness. People tugged at its fenders and at the horses' reins.

Several times the vehicle threatened to capsize like a tiny ship battling a heavy surf, but the Irish coachman proved equal to each crisis. He arose, unleashing his whip so savagely that, for the moment, the crowd broke. The carriage crunched ahead a few feet; but again it slowed to a standstill as it neared the Triumphal Causeway, where "the crush of humanity was so dense that it seemed impossible to force a passageway."

The smooth-surfaced, polished carriage fenders helped, for as men tugged frantically to hold back the carriage, they slipped and at times were almost trampled beneath the plunging horses. Time after time, the coachman's long whip sailed through the air and over the crowd.

By the time the carriage reached the Causeway the battle had been won. The crowd, for the most part, had been left behind. A gentle slope, as well as the increasing narrowness of the road at this point, enabled the carriage to outdistance its pursuers except for a cluster of persistent bicyclists, who pedaled behind the carriage's rear wheels, yelling curses at the assassin.

Among the cyclists was young Dick Carr, a Postal Telegraph messenger, who began to follow the carriage as it dashed through the Lincoln gate. Carr was to recall over a half century later that three gray-uniformed Pan-American policemen guarded the assassin while a driver and another Exposition guard were on the high front seat.

Only the alertness of an attendant saved the carriage. He thrust open the gate, then slammed it shut in the face of the advancing mob. The carriage raced down Lincoln Parkway, careening into

Delaware Avenue. A few blocks beyond Milburn's it passed another swiftly moving carriage traveling north toward the Exposition grounds. This was carrying Superintendent Bull. Bull's carriage whirled about, pursuing the vehicle to Police Headquarters. Czolgosz was dragged from the carriage and hauled to Bull's second floor office.

Within seconds people were roaring out of nearby saloons, warehouses and flour mills. They were all heading for the police station.

The small gray hospital, Spanish Renaissance in style, was wedged into the northeast corner of the Exposition grounds. It had been built for emergencies, but never such an emergency as this.

The distance from the Temple was short, hardly more than a quarter of a mile. As the electric ambulance sped toward the hospital, the crowd—heretofore so insistently demonstrative—gave way without direction. "There was no need for the police to ask the crowd to move back," *The Buffalo Commercial* reported. "The crowd itself cleared a pathway along the Court of Fountains and through the Mall, shouting ahead, 'Keep back! Keep back! Make way! Make way!' "

Inside the ambulance McKinley's head rested upon Foster's knee. As the ambulance was passing the Amherst Gate the President fumbled at his blood-stained shirt. Foster bent over him. Then he heard the President say quietly, "Foster, doesn't that feel like a bullet?"

The Secret Service man pressed his fingers against the flesh near the President's breastbone. He could feel something hard and oblong under the skin. "Yes, it does, Mr. President," Foster replied.

"Well, we have got one of them anyway," McKinley said, and smiling faintly he closed his eyes.

The small hospital where the President was to fight for his life throbbed with excitement. Nurses and internes under Superintendent Walters's direction scurried about the operating room readying it for his arrival.

Outside, the Mall was thickening with people. Then from

across the Mall there sounded the clatter of hoofs. The crowd parted to clear a passage for the cavalrymen, and presently the ambulance swung up to the hospital door. In silence the throng watched the President being lifted from the ambulance and borne into the hospital. Exactly eighteen minutes after the shooting he was carried through the small rotunda to the operating room in the rear wing. He was placed on an operating table, disrobed, then given a hypodermic injection of morphine and strychnine to ease the pain of his wounds. Foster and his assistants guarded the outside door while Cortelyou and Milburn remained with the President.

Members of the Presidential entourage—Scatcherd, Hamlin, Melvin C. Hanna and others—gathered in the hallway, talking excitedly and ready, if needed, to help.

The greatest need at this critical moment was doctors—doctors capable of diagnosing and treating the President's wounds. Frenzied telephone calls went out. Messengers rushed about the grounds, buttonholing physicians wherever they could be found, on the Esplanade, in the Midway, on the Mall.

Even Dr. Rixey was temporarily out of reach. After taking Mrs. McKinley back to the Milburn house, he had returned with his wife to tour the Exposition grounds. His itinerary was known, and at this moment W. V. Cox, superintendent of the United States Government building, was trying frantically to locate him. Most sought of all—because of his position as Exposition medical director, his reputation, and his knowledge of gunshot wounds— was Dr. Park. But at this moment, entirely ignorant of the tragedy in Buffalo, Park was performing a lymphoma operation in Niagara Falls upon a Mr. Ransom of Ransomville. When Charles W. Goodyear, an Exposition director, rushed to Park's home, the doctor's maid, hoping to expedite the President's treatment in any way she could, thoughtfully thrust her employer's instrument case into his hands. The next problem was to speed Park's return to Buffalo. For this, Harry Parry, New York Central's general agent, went into action at once, communicating with his Niagara Falls office to arrange for a special train.

Meanwhile, Dr. Edgar Wallace Lee had been shaking hands with Buffalo Bill when a messenger informed him of the tragedy. A visitor from St. Louis and former medical director of the

Omaha Exposition, Lee dashed off and was one of the first to reach the President's bedside. For a few brief moments Lee assumed charge of the hospital, but his aggressive conduct aroused resentment among the Buffalo doctors.

Another, though less aggressive, early arrival was Dr. Peter W. Van Peyma, a Buffalo obstetrician. Van Peyma was chatting with J. N. Adam, a prominent downtown merchant, near the Temple of Music when the Exposition ambulance passed them. The fact that it was surrounded by a mounted escort piqued their curiosity. Just then a man, hatless and agitated, rushed up to them, screaming, "What shall we do now?"

Adam replied composedly, "Oh, we shall do as we have been doing."

As soon as the two men had learned the cause of the man's excitement, they set out rapidly for the hospital. When they reached the hospital they found it surrounded by mounted police. Adam went in at once but soon returned to invite Van Peyma to enter also, stating that he might be of assistance. When he reached the main hall, Van Peyma saw no one he knew, so he stood by "quietly." Presently, a man stepped up to him, and, he recounts, ". . . looking at me fixedly and sternly for some time, inquired who I was. I informed him, and returned the question, and was informed that he was Mr. Cortelyou, private secretary to the President."

At that moment, young Mann appeared and asked the doctor to enter the operating room to see the President. Van Peyma continues, "I found him lying upon the operating table undressed and lightly covered. I was shown the wound and finding that it had been carefully and aseptically dressed, advised the reapplication of the dressing. At this time the only physician who had seen the President was Dr. G. McK. Hall, an interne."

Introduced to the President, Van Peyma was impressed by "his calm and dignified manner," reassuring him about his regular and strong pulse. By way of response: "He looked at me with his dark, inquiring eyes and said, 'Poor fellow, why did he do it?'" Since at this time no one knew who the "poor fellow" was, there was no answer to this question, if there ever would be.

Van Peyma stayed at the President's side for some time and introduced the surgeons who were now arriving. "One of these gentlemen spoke of having shaken hands with him at a reception the day before and reminded him of something he had said to the President. The President looked up, and considerately said, 'Yes, I think I remember.' "

This was obviously a reference to the President's brief exchange of pleasantries with Dr. Herman Mynter the afternoon before at the Government Building. Mynter was the first surgeon to make a thorough examination of McKinley's wounds.

One bullet, Mynter saw, had struck the sternum on the left side between the second and third ribs. This shot had glanced off the skin. The second bullet had pierced the abdomen about two and one half inches to the left of the median line, at a level of one and one half inches above the umbilicus. Mynter's experienced eye saw at a glance that the abdominal wound might prove fatal. Surgery would be imperative.

As those in charge were doing what they could to give him temporary relief, the President motioned Cortelyou to his side.

"Be careful about the doctors. I leave all that to you," he warned.

In this admonition it is likely that McKinley was recalling the Garfield case, the details of which he well knew. An intimate of President and Mrs. Garfield, he was aware of the long, tortuous weeks in 1881 when the former President lay dying without faith in the treatment he was receiving.

By now, doctors were piling into the hospital and milling about the hall. The problem was no longer a shortage of physicians, but which of them should take charge.

In the absence of Mrs. McKinley and Dr. Rixey the decision fell squarely upon Cortelyou. In desperation, the secretary turned to Milburn. "You know these men," he said, "when the right one arrives tell me."

Milburn, nodding, may well have wished for Park's presence; but a moment later his decision was made. "There's your man!" said Milburn, pointing to a physician who had just arrived.

The physician was 56-year-old Dr. Matthew D. Mann, who at the moment was shaking hands with Scatcherd. He was a small, gray-bearded man. Deep circles rimmed his gray eyes. He had established a world wide reputation in gynecology and had authored a standard textbook on the subject. Born in Utica and trained in the United States as well as in Europe, Mann had served on the staff of the Yale Medical School before accepting a call to the chair of obstetrics and gynecology at the University of Buffalo. Although an expert in his field, he had done only a limited amount of upper abdominal surgery.

Doctors Mann, Mynter, and Lee were joined in consultation by Dr. Eugene Wasdin, surgeon of the Marine Hospital service and an authority on Yellow Fever. Dr. John Parmenter was invited to join the group. Parmenter, professor of anatomy and clinical surgery at the University of Buffalo's Medical School, found that the physicians had already agreed to treat the President as they would a person of less exalted position. "In other words," he recorded, "the personality of the patient was not to weigh in the scientific treatment of the case."

There were two courses open—neither of them bright. One was to operate on the President at once. The other was to remove him post haste to the recently completed Buffalo General Hospital's operating amphitheater, there to await Park's return to the city— a course which might involve a gamble on a concealed hemorrhage or increase the odds on post operational peritonitis.

The theory of the day called for immediate treatment. This undoubtedly influenced the physicians to begin the operation at once despite the far from ideal situation at hand. Cortelyou, Milburn, and Scatcherd were now called in and told that an immediate operation would be necessary. Mann, it was agreed, should be in charge and would perform the operation. Mann now informed the President of the decision to operate. The President's courage and calmness in hearing the decision made a deep and lasting impression on Dr. Van Peyma. "Gentlemen," the President told the doctors, "I am in your hands."

Was it professional jealousy or a genuine fear for the President's life—or perhaps elements of both—that motivated Mann and his colleagues to rush into the operation at once?

By 5:20 the doctors had taken the positions assigned them by Mann, Dr. Mynter was opposite to Mann, ready to act as his chief assistant. Beside Dr. Mynter was Dr. Lee, and next to Dr. Mann was Dr. Parmenter. Young Mann and Simpson were placed in charge of the sutures and instrument tray. Wilson was to keep the records. Miss A. P. Barnes and Miss M. C. Morris were to act as sterile nurses; Miss Rose Barron, Miss Mary A. Shannon, and Miss L. E. Dorchester, as general assistants. Dr. Hall would assist Dr. Zittel meanwhile in the general care of the hospital during the operation.

Dr. Mann had responded to the summons to the Exposition hospital precipitately without knowing why he was wanted. One newspaper account even had him jumping out of the barber's chair. Now he found himself chosen to perform a life-and-death operation on the President of the United States without his surgical instruments. Apparently the person or persons who knew of Dr. Park's instrument case being in the hospital office were unaware of Mann's predicament. Here Dr. Mynter stepped in and gave Dr. Mann his own large pocket case, which contained most of the necessary instruments.

An egregious omission—also attributable to haste, no doubt— is pointed out in Dr. Park's notes: "I do not recall anyone in the room wore caps or gauze."

Inadequate lighting presented a severe obstacle. The sunlight, upon which the surgeons evidently intended to rely, was waning and filtered through awninged windows.

Without the very properties which to the modern TV viewer symbolize surgery, the operation upon the Chief Executive of the United States was begun this September afternoon in 1901 at 5:20.

Dr. Wasdin, aided by Nurse Catherine Simmons, administered the ether so skillfully that the patient suffered no "unpleasant symptoms." Murmuring the Lord's Prayer as he lost consciousness, the President was completely under the anesthetic in nine minutes.

Mann now began to cut a three-inch incision along the line of the entrance of the bullet. Since a deep layer of fat encased the President's stomach, the physician found it necessary to lengthen the incision an inch before he reached the peritoneum. At the bottom of the incision and in the bullet wound he found a small circular bit of cloth, evidently a piece of undershirt, which had been carried in by the bullet. This he removed. After opening the peritoneum, he found the intestines uninjured—a happy discovery, since at first it had been thought that the bullet had perforated them. When Mann had been so informed upon his arrival, he had exclaimed, "My God—then nothing can be done for him!"

Using fine black silk, Mann sutured the jagged wound that

perforated the anterior wall of the stomach. Then the incision was lengthened two inches so that the stomach's posterior wall might be examined. A second wound following the course of the bullet was somewhat larger and more jagged. This Mann sutured as he had the first.

By this time Rixey had reached the operating room, where, noting the weak light he attempted to repair it by reflecting the sun's rays with a mirror, later abandoning this in favor of a movable electric light bulb equipped with a reflector. Even with improved light Mann was experiencing great difficulty. The three-inch roll of fat encasing the President's abdomen made the surgeon feel at times as though he were operating at the end of a long, darkened hole and restricted further search for the bullet, whose full course could not be traced. It was thought to be lodged somewhere in the lumbar muscles, where it would become encysted; so search for it was abandoned.

"Is he alive?" That was the question which leaped from lip to lip in the throng massed along the Mall. When a guard at the door nodded in assent, the crowd, records Dr. Wilson, "swayed backward and forward with a rustling noise, as the word passed along in whispers, like a wheatfield dipping to a summer breeze."

The *Buffalo Enquirer* reporter described the crowd as the "quietest . . . ever seen on an Exposition ground."

"A cordon of Exposition police and city mounted police," he continued, "held the public back at a respectful distance, keeping clear a space about 150 feet square immediately in front of the hospital. Within this space were local newspapermen, outside correspondents, secret service men and others whose positions gave them a right to the first news from within, waiting to pounce on whoever might come out of the building."

At last the news began to trickle through to the crowd thronging the Mall that Park was momentarily expected. The word spread like flames licking a sun-dried prairie. The people wanted Park. Now he was on his way. But the doctor was having his troubles. The operation he was performing was a difficult one, "requiring careful dissection." He had just finished the critical stage when a messenger entered and whispered, "Doctor, you are wanted in Buffalo."

Park without turning replied, "Don't you see I can't leave—even for the President of the United States."

"It is for the President," was the astonishing reply.

Later, recalling this dramatic scene, Park said, "As soon as I had recovered my equanimity, I turned to Doctor Campbell, who knew all the railroad people at the station, and asked him to go at once and make the necessary arrangements for a special engine or train, saying that Doctor Chapin and I would finish the operation and be at the station by the time things could be readied."

When Park arrived at the Niagara Falls station, he found everyone, including the station master, upset and confused by the news from Buffalo.

Park recalled, "It has always seemed to me that an engine might have been speedily detached or furnished for the emergency, but I was told that a Michigan Central through train would be along shortly, and that I should be sent up on that, while a special engine would be waiting at the Black Rock junction to take me round on the Belt Line and down upon the special tracks which had been laid into the exposition grounds."

At a little after 6:00 an automobile noiselessly sped down the Mall. "That's Park!" one man exclaimed, and shouts of "There's Park," reverberated through the crowd.

Park hurried into the hospital, was quickly introduced to Cortelyou, and informed that the operation was then in progress with Dr. Mann in charge. After hastily preparing himself Park entered the room.

Park's initial impression was unfavorable: ". . . the first incident which attracted my attention was Dr. Mann rapping Dr. Mynter's fingers with one of the instruments because said fingers were apparently in his way. This was but a sample of Dr. Mann's petulance when excited during an operation, nevertheless it was an unfortunate time at which to make such an exhibition of annoyance."

Park went directly to Dr. Mann, saying, "Hello, do you want me to get my hand in?"

"No, it's practically finished." Mann shot back, at the same time complaining of the lack of a certain needle-holder and needles which he wished to use.

Park had evidently been informed of the presence of his own

instrument case in the building, for he left the room and secured the desired items. After seeing that they were properly sterilized by an alcohol flame, he handed them to Dr. Mann.

Park was given a rundown on what had happened. All that remained, he saw, was to flush the abdominal cavity with a saline solution, then sew up the abdominal wound.

Dr. Mynter had emphatically advised drainage of the wound. The question—a crucial one—was put to the breathless Park. Though later he was to be critical of the procedure taken, he deferred perhaps out of professional courtesy, to Mann's judgment. After the other doctors had outvoted Mynter, the incision was closed without drainage. At 6:50 the anesthetic was stopped and the bandages applied. The President's pulse was 122 and his respiration, 32.

When Park entered, Dr. Rixey had approached him and asked him about the qualifications and experience of the surgeon doing the operation. Reassured by Park, Rixey nevertheless insisted, "Well, you are the only one here that I know anything about, and I want you to take charge of the case." Since at the moment such a take-over would be impossible, Park stated simply that the whole matter could be arranged later and went about plans for the care of the patient subsequent to the operation.

It was obvious that the little hospital did not have the facilities for this purpose. Park joined the group of men outside the operating room, who at 5:30 had been joined by Secretary Wilson. Milburn and Cortelyou quickly informed Park that they had already promised the President that he would be removed to the Milburn house as soon as possible after the operation.

Accordingly, Park conferred with Miss Walters about the necessary details for the President's removal. Miss Simmons and Miss Barnes were sent on to the Milburn house along with a surgical bed, an ample supply of bedding, as well as other medical equipment needed for the President's treatment. These were placed in a police patrol wagon, which started for its destination at once.

"To illustrate the rapidity and perfection of the arrangements," Park later recalled, "Mr. Huntley, of the General Electric Co. had run in a special wire, and installed electric fans, with possibilities for anything else needed in this direction and the fans were actually in operation by the time we reached the house."

Park then gathered together in his office all the doctors involved in the operation, including Dr. Van Peyma, and explained that they were "practically under a sort of military discipline, if not martial law;" hence, no information was to be given out except that which passed through Cortelyou's hands. The dissidence that had marked the Garfield case was to be avoided at all costs.

Park had scarcely finished his admonition when Mynter objected to the President's removal to Milburn's. Park quashed any further argument on this subject by stating that plans were already under way. Then the delicate matter of who should be in charge of the case arose. Park said that he felt that Rixey should make the choice. Rixey then repeated his request in the presence of the group that he wished Park to take charge. "I replied," said Park, "that that was hardly fair to Dr. Mann, but that I was sure that both Dr. Mann and the others would cheerfully join in rendering all possible service in any desired way."

Further selection Rixey left to the physicians themselves—which resulted in the choice of Drs. Mann, Mynter, and Wasdin, with the others to be available if needed.

12

"This Can't Be So"

AT ONE MINUTE TO FIVE a two-seated open carriage raced along Lincoln Parkway headed south in the direction of Milburn's. The man who sat beside the driver looked as if he had seen a ghost. Indeed he had seen worse.

Director Buchanan, his face ashen, his eyes riveted straight ahead, pressed the driver to greater speed. The carriage had barely reached the Milburn hitching post when Buchanan leaped to the curb and ran along the driveway to the house. His vague forebodings of the early morning seemed now like an ugly dream materializing. He had been standing near the President: there had been laughter and gaiety—then two flashes, two crackling reports. As the melee raged on the Temple floor, Cortelyou had called him aside. "You had better go to Milburn's. Keep the news from her for now."

Keep the news from the First Lady! Just how would he accomplish that? Cortelyou's request might not be easy to carry out. What if he encountered her before he had a chance to inform the others in the house? What if she learned of his arrival before he had told the rest of the household the whole dreadful story of the afternoon's tragedy? Fortunately, neither of these situations arose. A maid who answered the doorbell told him that Mrs. McKinley was at that moment still asleep in her bedroom on the second floor.

"Get the servants quickly," Buchanan told the maid.

When everyone in the house was assembled in the living room, Buchanan told them, "The President has been shot. We must keep the news from Mrs. McKinley as long as possible."

The McKinleys' nieces were aghast. Hardly two hours had elapsed since their return from Niagara Falls. They pressed around Buchanan asking questions, but other than the grim truth of the act itself there was little that Buchanan could tell them. The Presi-

114

dent had been rushed to the Exposition hospital. Even now doctors were probably operating upon him.

By this time a new problem presented itself. Along the avenue carriages with members of the diplomatic corps and others who were calling to pay their respects had pulled to the curb. Already a cluster of people, moved by natural, if morbid, curiosity, was gathering on the sidewalk and lawn outside the house. To forestall mob scenes like those around the Temple and the hospital, Police Captain Cable from the nearby precinct rushed a detail under Sergeant Conners's command to the area. The block from Cleveland Avenue to Ferry Street on Delaware Avenue was closed to all traffic. In order to isolate the house more completely, telephone service was suspended.

As twilight came, a string of carriage lamps glittered along Ferry Street. The crowd was swelling, and at times Conners and his men had to swing their clubs to keep unruly spectators from breaking through the rope barriers.

At 6:30 the First Lady awoke. Her nieces gathered about her in the sitting room of her suite, trying to divert her. For awhile they were successful—chatting with her as she crocheted. Suddenly, noting that it had grown dark, she remarked, "I wonder why he doesn't come."

At two minutes to seven Dr. Rixey arrived from the Exposition hospital with the news that the President would be brought to the house within the hour. "Where is Mrs. McKinley?" he asked. "We must tell her."

Buchanan and the doctor mounted the stairs. When they reached the doorway of Mrs. McKinley's room, she looked up from her needlework. She must have guessed something was wrong, for there was alarm in her voice as she asked, "Where is Mr. McKinley? Why doesn't he come?"

The doctor was hesitant, but only for a moment. The time had come. There could be no more delay or subterfuge. "I have bad news for you, Mrs. McKinley," he said in a low voice.

She stood up, dropping her needlework, and took a step toward the two men. "What is it?" she demanded. "Is anything wrong? Has he been hurt?"

"Yes, he has been hurt," the doctor replied. "He has been shot."

"I must go to him," she cried.

"No," said the doctor, "we are going to bring him here. Everything now depends on you—maybe his life. We look to you to help us."

The doctor led her to a chair, then quickly related the events of the past few hours. Haunting him was the fear that the First Lady might succumb. She had in the past been reduced by far lesser shocks. Evidently realizing that much of the success of her husband's battle for his life might depend on her, she bore up stoically.

"Those who had anticipated a painful scene and a possible collapse on the part of Mrs. McKinley were most agreeably disappointed," *The Buffalo Enquirer* observed.

At 7:30, after what had seemed to the anxious crowd like an interminable wait, the hospital doors swung back. Everyone sensed what this meant. The same ambulance that had moved the President to the hospital was now backing up to the entrance. Dr. Park, bareheaded, in his shirtsleeves, appeared in the doorway. Behind four doctors bore a stretcher upon which lay the President, his face as white as the pillow under his massive head. His eyes were open. Slowly, gently, the stretcher was slid into the back of the ambulance. Park and Wasdin stepped aboard, taking positions at the President's head and feet. Young Simpson with one bound leaped in front beside driver Ellis. General Welch and Chapin drew up their mounted soldiers around the ambulance, in the same manner in which they had guarded the President's victoria a few hours before. The ambulance moved away, slowly at first, followed by two automobiles. The first contained Cortelyou, Wilson, Milburn, and Dr. Mann; the second, the other surgeons and members of the President's party.

The little procession, Park recorded, "passed no faster than men could easily walk, this partly because many of the escort were on foot, and because although the streets were very smooth, we did not want to jostle the patient any more than was necessary.

"The passage . . . through the crowd and down Delaware Ave. was one of the most dramatic incidents I have ever witnessed. The fairgrounds were crowded that day, and it seemed as though the entire crowd had gathered to witness this event. Every man's hat was in his hands, and there were handkerchiefs at many eyes. I never saw a large crowd so quiet."

When the ambulance reached the rope barriers on Delaware Avenue near Cleveland, the crowd was so dense that the Exposition bicycle guards preceding the ambulance had difficulty in clearing a path.

Once this was accomplished, the ambulance moved to the curb before Milburn's. Dr. Park, Simpson, and Ellis carefully drew the stretcher from the ambulance and moved slowly up the walk. The President's groans could be heard. Those who formed an aisle through which the stretcher bearers moved saw that he was wrapped in a blanket. A white towel concealed his face. He was borne up the front steps, through the hallway, and taken to his bedroom. The room, as Park describes it was "a large rear one, connecting with an equally large front room." The doctor noted, ". . . everything was ready down to the smallest detail."

Once the President's bandages had been examined, Mrs. McKinley was brought into the room. Dr. Rixey held her arm as she walked slowly to the bedside. She dabbed her eyes, then leaned over to kiss her stricken husband. They talked in whispers.

At 9:00 P.M. the President's physicians issued the following bulletin:

The President was shot about 4:00 P.M. One bullet struck him on the upper portion of the breastbone and did not penetrate.

The second bullet penetrated 5 inches below the left nipple and 1½ inches to the left of the median line. The abdomen was penetrated through the line of the bullet wound. It was found that the bullet had penetrated the stomach. The opening in the front wall of the stomach was carefully closed with sutures, after which a search was made for the hole in the back wall of the stomach. This was found and also closed in the same way. The further course of the bullet could not be discovered, although careful search was made.

The abdominal wound was closed without drainage. No injury to the intestines or other abdominal organs was discovered.

The patient stood the operation well. Pulse of good quality; rate of 130. His condition at the conclusion of the operation was gratifying.

The result can not be foretold. The condition at present justifies hope of recovery.

The bulletin bore the signatures of Drs. Rixey, Mann, Wasdin, Park, Mynter, and that of Cortelyou.

"What's in the bundle?" one of the newsmen asked Foster, as he, Gallaher, and Ireland pulled up before the house in an automobile.

That, Foster explained, contained the President's clothing—his high silk hat, his frock coat, two cigars, a silver pocket piece and a few dollars in cash. The cigars and other petty possessions, which might have been those of an eight dollar a week clerk, somehow seemed to suggest the human frailty and vulnerability of a President.

What attracted the newsmen even more was the bullet, which Foster held in the palm of his hand. It was the one that had struck McKinley's breast, a memento that Foster would keep for the rest of his life.

As reporters scribbled feverishly the Secret Service man gave them more details on the shooting and the ambulance drive across the Mall. "After we had Czolgosz on the floor, I kneeling with one knee on each arm, he made a desperate effort to shoot again, and struggling fiercely, raised one hand and tried to pull the trigger.

"President McKinley did not fall. He stood on his feet for three minutes after being shot, and opened his vest himself."

Gallaher, frozen-faced, stood by silently; but within a few hours he too was to give his version of the assassination attempt. The President, he said, had never entertained the slightest fear of an assault. Indeed, since the Spanish-American War he had traveled all over the country, meeting people everywhere. In Canton the President walked the streets alone; he attended church alone or with the First Lady, but never with an escort. While in Washington he showed the same complete disregard for danger.

On this afternoon, said Gallaher, at the reception there had been a deviation from the usual plan at Cortelyou's request. "It had been my custom to stand back of the President so I could see the right hand of any person approaching, but Secretary Cortelyou requested that I stand opposite the President so that Mr. Milburn could stand to the left and introduce people who approached."

News of the assassination attempt had spread with lightning speed. Young Lieutenant Rich, who had acted as one of McKinley's mounted escorts at Niagara Falls earlier in the day, was busy in his downtown office when the report reached him. "Why, I just left the President," he protested. "This can't be so."

Thousands like Rich thought the report must be some kind of cruel hoax.

The assassin had escaped the fury of the mob on the Exposition grounds, but it had been a miracle. Would he be so lucky again? Within fifteen minutes after his arrival at Police Headquarters a mob of one thousand, the vanguard of thousands to come, advanced menacingly against the police station, shouting angry threats.

Trembling, the assassin peered out of Superintendent Bull's second-floor office window. Upon their arrival at the Police Headquarters, Detectives Solomon and Geary had dragged Czolgosz from the carriage to the detectives' room. He was jammed into a chair to await the arrival of Bull and a representative of District Attorney Thomas Penney's staff. He was so shaken that many around him thought he would surely succumb.

After one of the Exposition guards had handed him a glass of water, he seemed, however, to revive. He settled back, his eyes intent upon the crowd outside. After the arrival of Bull, Assistant District Attorney Haller and County Court stenographer Frank T. Haggerty, he was removed to Bull's private office.

Meanwhile, hysteria was sweeping the downtown area with its vortex at the Iroquois Hotel. By 8:00 P.M. a small army of people, including some of the city's foremost citizens, had begun to gather there and at Main and Swan Streets. Moving down Swan Street toward Police Headquarters, they shouted ominous threats: "Hang him to the first pole!" and "We'll lynch him!"

As the mob surged on, a rope dangling suggestively from a window overhead lashed them into a fresh fury; but at the Pearl Street intersection a triple line of policemen stationed behind a rope barrier blocked their progress. The ropes swayed. A few heads were bashed, and the rioters halted, still muttering threats and cries for vengeance.

But thousands more jammed Main Street. For over a mile they surged backward and forward, stopping now and then before the newspaper offices to read the latest bulletins, but pushing inevitably toward Police Headquarters.

In his earlier shakeup of police captains, Superintendent Bull had never anticipated violence like this; but the shift, which had moved Captain "Big Mike" Regan to Headquarters that day, was a fortunate one. No one but Regan could have coped with the mob's fury that night. He had come on duty at 6:00 and his first move was to order reinforcements from the city's outlying precincts. Then fearing that even this move might not meet the situation, he summoned members of the 65th and 74th National Guard regiments to their armories to stand by.

Regan, a burly man well over six feet, swung his club furiously as, time after time, he and his men sallied out to beat back the mob.

One enraged man mounted the steps of the Columbia Bank at Pearl and Church Streets and began to harangue those around him. "To No. 1 and lynch him!" he shouted, and was soon drowned out by a chorus of approval.

"This way," the would-be leader cried, as he leaped from the bank steps and started toward Niagara Street with the mob in full pursuit. Some wielded clubs. Others carried ropes.

At Franklin Street Regan met them head on. Clubs were raised. Heads were bashed. The mob fell back slowly, sullenly, still muttering angry threats.

To a *Buffalo Enquirer* reporter the scene was an unforgettable one. Peering from a window in Police Headquarters, he saw the mob surge back and forth. It was like an angry breaking surf.

Until now the information on the assassination attempt had been meager. Police flashed message after message to the outlying precincts, and patrolmen passed the word along as they paced their beats. The reports, at first, were vague, little beyond the fact that the President had been shot.

How? Why? What was his condition? Who had shot him? From far and wide frenzied people sought more specific information on why the shooting had taken place and how seriously the President had been wounded. The cyclists who had pursued the carriage carrying the assassin spread the report as they pedaled along the street; those boarding street cars at the Exposition repeated the news all along the line. Slowly, two or three indisputable facts emerged from a welter of confusion and misinformation; McKinley had been shot, his condition was serious, he might die. The assassin was an Anarchist. He had given his name as Fred Nieman.

By 9:00 a cordon of foot patrolmen, reinforced by a detail of mounted police, completely encircled Headquarters. Blocked in one direction, the growing mob, like water surging through a breached dyke, broke loose in others. One contingent stopped as it reached the Terrace, pouring around the west side of the station, while another mob pushed its way along the Terrace, roaring as it went.

Regan's men met the onrushing mob. Checked for an instant, the crowd broke loose into Erie Street. At that moment a mounted patrol and a dozen foot policemen led by Commissioner Rupp moved in and charged. There was a momentary lull. Rupp walked to the center of the street. Holding up his hand he shouted, "Go home—New York State will take of the prisoner."

Rupp's appeal made a slight impression. A few left, but half an hour later another mob began to pour into Swan Street, shouting wildly as it advanced. It lacked a leader although two men trying to assume that role were arrested. W. A. Dwyer, of 141 Court Street, and Benjamin H. Downer, of Plymouth Avenue, were hauled into custody as they exhorted the crowd to action. Later they denied any attempt to incite riots.

"Didn't you say to me in Swan Street that two hundred men ought to get together and lynch this man?" Regan asked Downer at Headquarters.

"I don't believe I said that," Downer replied; "but, by God, that's what I think."

As midnight approached, thousands still jammed the downtown sidewalks, spilling into the streets. An electric sign which flashed in glowing letters the message "Teddy is disappointed" was greeted with hisses and jeers.

Under a sputtering gas lamp Court Stenographer Haggerty scratched hieroglyphics on a small brown pad. Around him in the hazily lighted room huddled Superintendent Bull, District Attorney Penney, his assistant, Haller, and Detectives Geary and Solomon. As the prisoner's confession fell from his lips, Haggerty recorded it word by word. Those in Bull's office who watched the prisoner as he spoke could scarcely believe that he alone had carried out a crime of such enormity, apparently with the purpose of setting loose Anarchy's chaotic forces.

At first, the assassin gave his name as Fred Nieman. He was 28, although his slender boyish figure, innocent air, and almost handsome face made him look younger.

Bit by bit, slowly and reluctantly, his story and confession emerged. Along with biographical details, he revealed some of the forces that had impelled him to his inexplicable crime. He had read books on Socialism and met many Socialists. He was "pretty well known as a Socialist in the West," he boasted.

He supposed he had become bitter. He had never had much luck and this fact preyed upon him. Apparently the doctrine of Anarchy had offered some hope, not only for himself but for the whole stratum of American working people.

In Cleveland he had listened to Emma Goldman preach her subverting doctrines. Her words set him "on fire" and he determined to do something big for the cause he loved.

Eight days before, while in Chicago, he had picked up a newspaper that recounted the details of President McKinley's proposed visit to the Buffalo Exposition.

It was at this point that he decided to go to Buffalo. Out of the scores of boarding houses in that city, he had picked Nowak's because John Nowak was a politician and known leader of the Polish people of the locality. At Nowak's he asked questions about the President's visit—how long he intended to stay in the city and whether people would be able to see him. Nowak told him what he knew of the President's plans, but of course had no idea of his guest's as yet nebulous purpose.

"Not until Tuesday," Czolgosz revealed, "did the resolution to shoot the President take hold of me. It was in my heart—there was no escape for me. I could not have conquered it had my life been at stake."

The prisoner briefly outlined his three attempts and failures to get close enough to the President to carry out his mission.

He had been among the first to arrive at the Temple of Music and had waited at the spot for the afternoon reception to begin.

"Then he came, the President—the ruler—and I got in line and trembled until I got right up to him and then I shot twice through my white handkerchief. I would have fired more but I was stunned by a blow in the face—a frightful blow that knocked me down—and then everybody jumped on me. I thought I would be killed and was surprised the way they treated me."

He denied that he had any accomplices or that he was connected with the Paterson radicals. "I had no confidants—no one to help me. I was alone absolutely."

Steadfastly his blue eyes were fixed upon a point in space. There were no remorse, little or no emotion.

District Attorney Penney rapped the table with his knuckles. "Did you really intend to kill the President?" It was a question which seemed superfluous in view of the confession.

"Yes, I did," replied the prisoner.

"What was your motive?"

The prisoner explained this simply. "I am an Anarchist—a disciple of Emma Goldman. Her words set me on fire."

13

"What Will Happen to the Stock Market?"

THE MIRACLE of rapid communication that McKinley had praised at the Exposition now proved its efficacy. As the news reached them, McKinley's friends were grief-stricken; his enemies, stunned into silence.

When Theodore Roosevelt heard the reports, his reaction was characteristically vehement. Clapping his hand to his head, he cried, "My God!"

The Vice President was concluding a speech before the Fish & Game League at Isle La Motte, Vermont, and was about to enter the nearby home of his host, former Lt. Governer Fisk, when a messenger handed him a telegram. Roosevelt's mouth set grimly as he passed the wire to Fisk. Then the Vice President gestured with his hand to detain the crowd, which was breaking up. Senator Redfield Proctor was asked to make the announcement.

Raising his hand for silence, the Vermont Senator told his audience, "Friends, it is my sad duty to inform you that President McKinley, while in the Temple of Music at Buffalo, was shot twice this afternoon by an Anarchist, two bullets having taken effect. His condition is said to be serious, but we hope that later intelligence may prove that statement to be exaggerated."

A moan swept over the grounds. For once, Roosevelt, renowned for his vocal prowess, found himself almost speechless. "I am so shocked and grieved that I can not make a statement," he managed finally to stammer to reporters.

Plans were swiftly improvised for the Vice President's departure for Buffalo. Newsmen would not accompany him. That, said the ordinarily publicity-conscious Roosevelt, would be "a desecration."

Within minutes Roosevelt, aboard the *Elfreda*, W. Seward

Webb's private yacht, was speeding across Lake Champlain. At Proctor, a village in Vermont, the Vice President boarded a special Rutland Railroad train.

First reports of the shooting reached New York shortly after it happened. Within three minutes after the first news flash from Buffalo, bulletins were pasted along Park Row, where throngs of anxious people milled about, waiting hungrily and half-incredulously for further developments. The first flash to reach *The New York Times* stated tersely that the President had been shot twice. No further details were disclosed—not even the assassin's name.

Thousands of office workers, disgorged from the downtown buildings, joined the crowds already in the streets. A sea of eyes from upturned faces riveted upon the crayon-lettered bulletins that appeared every few seconds and relayed fresh scraps of information.

"Half of New York was homeward bound," reported *The New York Times,* adding, "The news traveled with lightning-like rapidity, creating an air of suppressed excitement and heartfelt mourning which the city had not experienced since President Garfield's assassination twenty years before."

Swarms of newsboys soon were hawking extras. Thousands first learned of the assassination attempt when conductors, motormen, and passengers on the city's trolley cars shouted to pedestrians. Elevated guards took up the cry, shouting the news to stationmen as the cars shot northward.

There was a feeling of awe and grief among the swirling crowds. Mixed with the grief were frequent expressions of sympathy for Mrs. McKinley. Would her delicate health withstand the shock, many wondered.

But, at best, the news was meagre, giving rise to all sorts of wild versions of the tragedy. One reported that the President had been stabbed to death; another circulating widely was that the assassin had been torn limb from limb—the latter probably an evidence of wishful thinking.

Downtown saloon owners and cafe proprietors sent messengers scurrying to the newspaper offices to copy down the bulletins.

Would the President live?—that was the question which crackled through the great throngs. Rivaling this for interest and asked only with slightly less frequency was, "What will happen to the stock market?"

The ticker tapes had stopped when the first flashes reached Wall Street. Since it was Friday afternoon and the weather summery, Wall Street brokers, for the most part, had left by Long Branch boats, yachts, and suburban trains for a country weekend.

In a speculation-crazed age when everyone from bakers and brokers to servants and men of the cloth pursued the rewards of Wall Street, the possible effect on the money marts seemed paramount. By evening all sorts of wild speculations were spreading. J. P. Morgan, rumor had it, had already boarded his private yacht along with a small powerful clique of New York City bankers with whom he would confer about ways and means to meet an anticipated crisis. Other wild tales were circulating about the financier's whereabouts: he was at the Fifth Avenue Hotel, at Delmonico's, at the New York Yacht Club, and at the Buckingham. A check of these various places, however, failed to disclose his presence. Lights in his Wall Street office burned brightly on into the night, but the titan of Wall Street was reported as "not there."

Fresh from his most recent financial coup, the formation of the Great Northern Securities Company, Morgan, however, was on the point of leaving his office for the day. Outside the Morgan offices at 23 Wall Street a carriage awaited the tycoon. Morgan had put on his high silk hat. Cane in hand, he was glancing at a ledger on a clerk's desk when a *New York Times* reporter rushed in with the first reports. Morgan, attracted by the reporter's haste, turned to him and asked brusquely, "Well?"

"We have a dispatch, Mr. Morgan, that states an attempt has been made upon the life of the President at Buffalo."

"What?" broke in Morgan, grasping the newsman's arm and looking him intently in the eye.

"When did it happen? Where and how? Are you sure the news is authentic?"

Assured the report was true, Morgan was "for a moment utterly overwhelmed."

He tossed his cane on a desk, then took several rapid strides to his own desk. He whispered to one of his confidential representatives, who immediately retired to the rear of the office where a telephone was situated. Fifteen minutes later, the man returned to the financier with confirmation of the press reports.

Morgan was dumbfounded. His hat still on his head, he sat staring at the carpeted floor, then read and reread the confirmation.

"This is sad, sad, very sad news. I don't want to say anything," he told the *Times* man. "There is nothing I can say now."

He picked up his cane, and a moment later he drove off.

Quickly gaining momentum was a rumor that all bank presidents of the city were holding a secret session in the Metropolitan Club. Actually, James Stillman, taciturn president of the National City Bank, and Charles M. Schwab, president of the United States Steel Corporation, were discovered dining at Delmonico's. When queried for his opinion on the possible effect of the assassination attempt, Schwab asserted, "Should the President die it would certainly have a most depressing effect upon business and industry."

Stillman assured *The New York Times* that the country's prosperous condition and stability would prevent panic, adding that the clearing house banks "would take care of the money market as they always have."

"There is nothing to fear," the great banker concluded.

Despite Stillman's confidence, betting was rampant. Odds were offered that certain stocks would break. "Bets were taken not singly but by the scores," reported *The New York Times*.

All over the city rage swelled against the Anarchists, with feelings highest in Harlem. On 125th Street a well-dressed young man created a sensation when he called for volunteers to follow him to Paterson. "If President McKinley dies," he shouted, "there will be 10,000 Anarchists killed in Paterson to avenge his death."

As crowds swarmed around him, he yelled, "All those who want to go to Paterson with me, come on!"

With this parting shot, he began to mount the elevated railway steps, with a mob of about 100 boys and men at his heels.

A *New York Times* reporter calling at Schwab's saloon found that Anarchists' haunt quiet. Mrs. Schwab was at the bar.

"Ever hear of this man Czolgosz?" the reporter asked.

"No," blurted out Mrs. Schwab's son who was standing nearby.

"Isn't it possible one of your members assumed the name?" Mrs. Schwab laughed. When asked about Goldman's whereabouts, she replied, "Why ask me where Emma is?"

Reactions in other parts of the country rivaled those in the nation's largest city. A pall of gloom descended over gay Newport; social events and other late summer parties were cancelled as residents besieged the telephone and newspaper offices.

In Pittsburgh thousands milled about the bulletin boards outside the newspaper offices. When the excitement reached its height, a man brazenly yelled, "Hurrah for the man who killed McKinley!" The words had barely left his lips when he was knocked down and battered with blows and kicks. By dint of hard running, he managed to escape down Diamond Alley with the mob at his heels. Fortunately a trolley was passing by and he leaped aboard.

In Paterson's Bartholdy Hall, members of the Right to Existence group toasted the assassin so frequently that they were "in a fair way to getting drunk" said a *New York Times* reporter. Every few minutes a member arose and proposed a toast to the assassin. Although they claimed not to know Czolgosz, they honored him, whoever he was, for having done his duty. Some felt, nevertheless, that he might more advantageously have expended his effort upon one of the European rulers. They conceded that there had been a plot afoot to assassinate European heads of state; but, they protested, McKinley had never been one of their intended victims. Pedro Esteve, a radical leader, loudly denied that Czolgosz was an Anarchist. "I never heard of him. He is probably some German lunatic—or fool."

The blow struck with terrific impact in the national capital. Reports filtered through to the streets just as government employees were pouring out of their offices and making their way home. Throngs began to jam the White House sidewalks and swarm over the lawn.

Charles G. Dawes, one of the few high officials in the capital, was about to leave his Treasury Department office when correspondent Sam Small, Jr., rushed in with a telegram. Dawes' hand shook as he read it. After hurrying home to inform his wife,

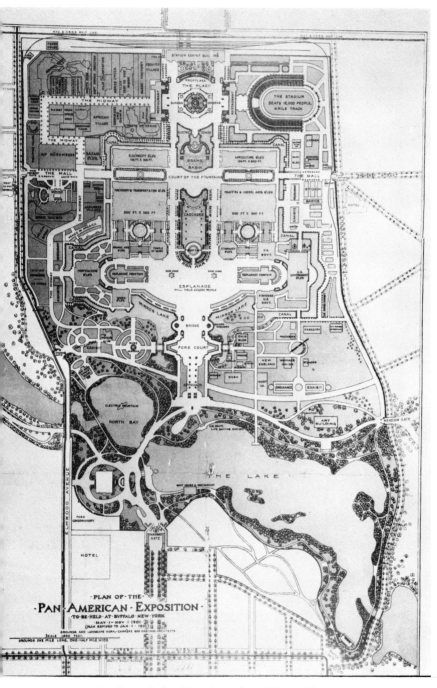

A plan of the Pan-American Exposition.

President McKinley.

A view of the Midway of the Pan-American Exposition.

On the west side of the Esplanade was the Temple of Music and the Machinery and Transportation Buildings. To the north was the Electric Tower and the Propylaea.

September 5, 1901: President McKinley delivers what proved to be
his last speech on the Esplanade of the Pan-American Exposition.

Some of the many onlookers who heard the President's address of
September 5.

The Electric Tower of the Pan-American Exposition by day . . .

and by night.

The Pan-American Exposition: The Machinery and Transportation Building and the Temple of Music as seen from the Electric Tower. (The Roy W. Nagle Collection)

September 6, 1901: President McKinley leaves the Milburn home for the trip to Niagara Falls.

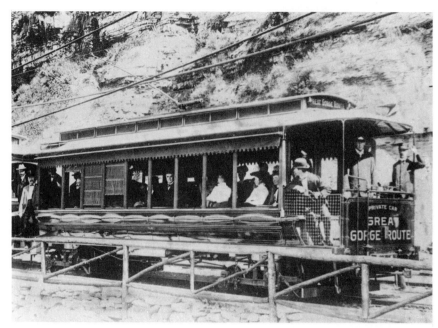

President McKinley (in dark suit, in window) tours the Great Gorge Route.

The President tours Niagara Falls.

The infamous Temple of Music, the building in which McKinley was shot.

An interior view of the Temple of Music.

The President's last posed picture, inside the U.S. Government Building. Left to right: Mrs. John Miller Horton (with parasol), John G. Milburn (rear), Mexican Ambassador Aspiroz, McKinley, George B. Cortelyou, Col. John H. Brigham and his son.

This picture was taken only minutes before the President was shot while greeting well-wishers on a reception line at the Temple of Music.

This electric ambulance carried the wounded President from the Temple of Music to the hospital on Exposition grounds.

People waiting outside Milburn House, Buffalo, for news of the President's condition.

The Ansley Wilcox home, where Theodore Roosevelt took the oath of office, September 14, 1901.

September 15, 1901: Funeral procession leaves Milburn home.

The funeral procession approaching Shelton Square, Buffalo.

Assassin Leon Czolgosz, who was executed for his crime October 29, 1901.

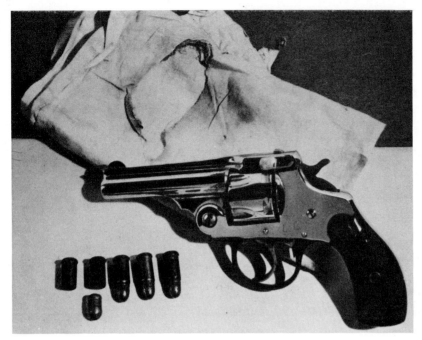

The evidence: A .32 caliber Johnson automatic pistol, and the handkerchief in which Czolgosz concealed it.

Mark Hanna at the head of the table at his Cleveland home. The McKinleys are in the right foreground.

Theodore Roosevelt posed at his desk.

Theodore Roosevelt (far left) walks with Mark Hanna (wearing fedora).

he sped to the White House war room, deserted at this hour except for John Barber, the First Lady's nephew, and Major Rand, who were in touch with Milburn's by wire. The first reports were meager: the assassin's name was Nieman; one bullet had struck McKinley's chest; the other had ripped into his abdomen.

At 7:15 Dawes leaped aboard a Buffalo-bound train. His depressed spirits were buoyed somewhat at York, Pennsylvania, when he was handed an encouraging dispatch from H. C. Briggs of the *Chicago Tribune*. Later, as the train was speeding northward, a White House telegram gave him further grounds for hope.

This once tranquil day found the cabinet members scattered through the country, beguiling the last precious hours of summer. Frantic telegrams summoned them to the President's bedside, and all except Secretary of the Navy John D. Long and Secretary of State John Hay responded at once. Postmaster Charles Emory Smith swung aboard a train at Philadelphia. Within a few hours Secretary of the Interior Ethan Allen Hitchcock was speeding toward Buffalo from Dublin, New Hampshire. At the same time, Secretary of the Treasury Lyman J. Gage departed from Chicago, and Attorney General Philander Knox left Pittsburgh. The ailing Hay was to arrive later; he was gloomy and haunted by the past, conditioned no doubt by the fact that he had previously served under both martyred Presidents—Garfield and Lincoln.

In no place was the grief more poignant than in Canton. The first reports spread quickly with frequent bulletins channeled into the home of the First Lady's sister, Mrs. M. C. Barber. By nightfall sidewalks surrounding the President's home were jammed. There was a general feeling that if the President died his wife would survive him for only a brief time.

In European chancellories and palaces, where assassinations were dreaded, the murderous attempt on McKinley's life, following on the heels of King Humbert's murder and the even more recent attempt upon Kaiser Wilhelm's life, caused monarchs to quake. Was it a part of an international plot by radicals to topple all heads of state?

Reports reached Czar Nicholas II and the Russian royal family as they cruised off the Danish coast. Badly shaken, they continued their voyage, meeting the German royal yacht *Hohenzollern* with Kaiser Wilhelm II aboard. With the spectre of this latest horror before them the monarchs watched a series of grand maneuvers, which culminated in a sham attack on the fortified shores of Danzig.

Protective measures were redoubled as the Czar proceeded to Kiel. The Russian monarch, after passing through the North Sea canal, was greeted at the French port of Dunkirk by President Emile Loubet. In France every conceivable measure was taken to safeguard the royal family; even the railroad track area was guarded by French infantry reinforced by a second line of cavalry.

14

"Doctors Speak Encouragingly"

IN AN UPPER ROOM in Milburn's, only half-conscious, his body wracked with pain and mutilated by the assassin's bullet, the President was waging his fight against death.

The odds were against him. He was 58, badly overweight, weakened by the rigors of office and still further by the strain of the war.

The night had passed and the dawn of September 7 had come. At this hour, an Army officer hurriedly left Milburn's and rushed to the carriage house. This was Major Thomas W. Symons, who, at this moment was sending a message to General Gillespie in Washington. The President still lived—he was resting comfortably, had suffered no unfavorable symptoms and no pain "except when he breathes deeply."

"Doctors speak encouragingly," the message concluded.

At 6:00 A.M. a bulletin signed by Drs. Rixey and Park confirmed the Symons report. The President had spent a good night.

During the night just passed trains had roared toward Buffalo; Cabinet members Root, Smith, and others were on their way. From Cleveland, in a train flagged down at 5:24, shocked and speechless, his ugly premonitions of the past haunting him, came Hanna. The Republican boss had been seated in his club when the news broke. At first he refused to believe it. Crowds swarmed around him as he pushed his way out of the club.

Myron Herrick, stunned, started for Buffalo in his private car with Mrs. William Duncan, the President's sister, and her husband aboard.

The world, shocked and benumbed by the brutal shooting, looked to the day ahead with trepidation.

Milburn's had been transformed into a military camp. Since

131

the early morning hours, and now as the city stirred to life, sentries with rifles glistening paced the walk; across the avenue the press corps, on the alert after a sleepless night, dashed to and fro as telegraphers ticked out the bulletins that told with medical brevity the news an anxious world awaited.

The President still lived.

All morning visitors arrived. Horses and cabs clacked down the avenue but were stopped by the police and soldiers who manned the rope barriers fencing off the big house a block's distance in each direction.

Behind the barriers stood the curious, many red-eyed and jaded after an all-night vigil, eyeing the house, the arriving automobiles, the elegantly caparisoned carriages, the nationally known figures like Hanna and Dawes, drawing from each some conjecture which was speedily relayed along the line. A rumor started and spread that McKinley had already undergone a second operation. A harried Milburn promptly denied it. The President's close relatives shuttled in and out, among them Mrs. Duncan; another sister, Helen McKinley; and John Barber, the First Lady's nephew.

Bit by bit, good news trickled from the house. The First Lady, after breakfasting in her room, had visited the President briefly. The President was taking food hypodermically.

Even the weather seemed to favor the President's improvement. It was warm, but not oppressive; and as the day advanced, a little breeze from the lake sprang up.

All night news correspondents had been pouring into the city. They took up hastily improvised quarters in tents across from Milburn's, waylaying visitors as they entered and left the house. Among their number were the famous correspondents Max Ihmsen and James Creelman. The latter had stopped work on a book he was writing to speed to Buffalo. Before the week was out, newsmen would number 250, making it the largest corps ever to cover a major event up to that time.

As the crowds outside the house grew and noises increased, the President's physicians issued an order for "more absolute quiet." The doctors' request was obeyed so punctiliously that a *Buffalo Times* reporter noted ". . . now one may hear distinctly the wings of a hummingbird among the honeysuckle bushes nearby."

As the day wore on, spirits rose. The midafternoon bulletins held out a faint ray of hope. There was no change for the worse, they stated. The late afternoon bulletin described the President's condition as much the same, noting that he was responding well to medicine.

Upon a table in the Milburn living room, helter-skelter, lay stacks of still unanswered cablegrams and wires from monarchs in Europe, from Governors, from Senators, from Congressmen, from McKinley's friends, from his G.A.R. comrades.

Upstairs, the doctors and nurses were preparing for the night ahead.

News of Leon's horrible crime reached the Czolgoszes' Cleveland home during the morning and left the family aghast. Jake, one of Leon's older brothers, ran to the grocery store for a paper.

"My God!" he cried, scanning the front page. "That's Leon, all right. Yes, that's him."

After Jake had translated the news to the elder Czolgosz, the old man started to pace the living room floor. "I can't think it of Leon," he kept mumbling.

Of the entire family Jake was the most talkative. After recovering from the initial shock, he told a *Plain Dealer* reporter, "I don't know what to say—we haven't seen Leon in several months."

He described his brother as timid, adding, "We never would have suspected him of doing anything like this. I suppose people think we had something to do with it. But they surely can't blame us. Leon never acted like an Anarchist. He never talked to us about such things."

The reporter asked Jake if he thought Leon was crazy.

"Oh, no!" Jake said. "No more than I am. Peculiar maybe in many ways but not crazy. He never mingled much, and never talked of such things."

Leon's stepmother thought differently. "I always thought Leon was crazy," she cried. "He was never like an ordinary boy. He was timid, a regular coward. He must have been crazy or he never would have tried anything like this."

Friends and neighbors could hardly imagine Leon summoning enough courage for his murderous act. They recalled his timidity —how he would catch flies, then release them. How could such a man kill anyone?

Gory memories of the shooting, visions of the hangman's noose, remorseful thoughts which may have lurked in his mind failed to affect the prisoner's appetite. At lunch, he outate his jailors and fellow prisoners, disposing of generous portions of roast beef, roast lamb and sliced tomatoes, along with bread and coffee.

After eating ample portions of cold roast pork, fried potatoes, bread and tea for his dinner, he asked for a cigar. When the request was relayed to Captain Regan he exploded, "That son-of-a-bitch gets no cigar from me."

At 1:00 the eastbound New York Central train clanged into the Exchange Street depot. As the car *Grand Isle* was still rolling abreast the covered railroad shed, a man in a badly rumpled suit leaped from the car and started on a run through the station with reporters in hot pursuit. Only the Associated Press man managed to reach the Vice President, but even he had no luck. He was shunted aside.

Reaching Exchange Street, the Vice President bounded into a carriage. As the carriage moved away he shouted back to reporters, "I have nothing to say."

Five minutes later in front of the Iroquois Hotel the carriage wedged its way through a cheering throng of people, jostling each other and standing on tiptoe to catch a glimpse of the hero of San Juan Hill. Theodore Roosevelt looked fatigued and travel-worn—hardly heroic. His one idea had been to reach the city as soon as possible. Now his hastily improvised plan was to engage a top floor room at the Iroquois, where he might be removed if possible, from interruptions and noise.

"Almost by chance" in front of the hotel he met his friend, Ansley Wilcox, who offered to play his host during his Buffalo sojourn. Georgia-born, Yale- and Oxford-educated, Wilcox was now a prominent attorney in the city. The two had become friends during the 1880s when Roosevelt was an Assemblyman in Albany, and Wilcox had been seeking to persuade the state to appropriate $1.5 million for the Niagara Reservation.

Although, as Wilcox explained, the rest of his family and most of the household were still in the country and the house was partially dismantled, it would offer him a quiet place to sleep and eat. Roosevelt readily changed his original plan and accepted his friend's invitation.

The Wilcox Mansion, atop a sloping terrace at Delaware Avenue and North Street, was spacious, imposing, and already replete with historical background. Of post-Colonial design, it was fronted by six sturdy fluted pillars, its most impressive feature. More than 60 years before it had served as the Army officers' quarters for the more extensive Poinsett Barracks, named for President Martin Van Buren's Secretary of War, Joel Roberts Poinsett (also responsible for giving his name to the Christmas flower, poinsettia). During the Patriots War in Upper Canada, when a detachment of the Army was in residence here, the house had been the scene of many a gay soiree, as dashing young officers entertained Buffalo belles. Living in one wing, the post surgeon, Robert Crooke Wood, had on one occasion entertained his father-in-law and the future President, Zachary Taylor.

After a brief stop at Wilcox's, the Vice President was driven up the avenue to the Milburn house. For the first time since arriving he smiled as, enroute to Milburn's, he listened to encouraging reports on the President's condition.

"Glad to hear that," was his comment.

His stay at Milburn's was short. Accompanied by his friend Elihu Root he emerged from the house at 2:00; arm in arm, the two strolled down the shade-mottled sidewalk to Ferry Street, where they turned west. Again, reporters dogged him—but with no success. "I don't care to make a statement now," snapped the Vice President.

Police doubted Czolgosz's story. Trying to skein together his shadowy movements before the shooting, they picked up saloon-keeper Nowak, his clerk Walkowiak, and also one of their roomers, Alphonse Stutz. Antoni Kazmarek, a Lake Shore railroad section hand who had boarded Czolgosz earlier in the summer, also was grilled.

Kazmarek was stunned by his sudden notoriety, but managed to recall that about six weeks before the shooting, Czolgosz had arrived at his small home about 6:00 one evening and asked his wife for lodging. Kazmarek said he had been at work at the time, but his wife, after some haggling, agreed to board Czolgosz.

Czolgosz proved to be a rather vague boarder. Indeed Kazmarek had never learned his full name.

"He went by the name of Frank. He went to Buffalo, and two

or three times told me he was going to the Pan-American. I asked him if he was working and he said, 'No, it is too hot.' He left my place about a week ago. He was owing me $1.75, and for that he left a revolver which is broken."

John Nowak recalled that Czolgosz had arrived at his Broadway saloon at 9:00 P.M., August 31. Czolgosz, he said, hadn't aroused his suspicions.

"I make it a practice to observe clearly," Nowak stated. "I take in only good people. He seemed a fair sort of man. I took him to be a clerk, bartender, or writer. He spoke Polish fairly well for an American but English better. His conversation showed him of more intelligence than ordinary."

The saloonkeeper explained that he had conducted his drinkery for seven years and had six rooms for guests. "He asked for a room. I said I could let him have one for $2 a week. I give him a receipt."

Nowak added that Czolgosz bought his cigars at the saloon but no meals and that he had had little to say. "Except only one night. I and Walkowiak were playing cards. He looked on, and he said that on Sunday he'd attended St. Casimir's church."

On the night of September 5, Czolgosz had returned to the saloon-hotel at 10 o'clock carrying a bundle of papers. On the morning of September 6, he had bought a cigar and left early, as usual.

Frank Walkowiak, the law student who served as Nowak's clerk, remembered Czolgosz's arrival and his giving Doe as his name. "I asked Czolgosz about Doe," the clerk related, then quoted the prisoner's explanation: " 'Well, I'll tell you. I'm a Polish Jew and I didn't like to tell him or he wouldn't keep me in the house.' I then asked him his true name. He said it was Nieman. I asked him what he intended to do, and he said he thought he would make some money and was going to sell souvenirs."

Walkowiak also recalled Czolgosz's looking in on the card game. "He said he had been to church and that he had heard a sermon which was that if God did not care for the world for five minutes that everything would go to damnation."

John W. Romantowski, a 31-year-old widower living on Buffalo's East Side at 1044 Sycamore Street, told of walking one day in the vicinity of Fillmore Avenue and Broadway when he struck up a conversation with Czolgosz. "He asked me to have a drink. We went to Gressner's saloon at the corner."

The two men drank their schupers of beer, smoked cigars, then Czolgosz suggested a trip to Niagara Falls. "He showed me a roll of bills," Romantowski recounted. "One bill was $50." Nonetheless, before the men parted Czolgosz boasted that he never worked. As for the trip to the Falls—that never materialized.

A barber who had shaved Czolgosz while he was at Nowak's characterized him as "very quiet." To Joseph Rutkowski of 940 Broadway the prisoner had seemed "rational, and a cigar smoker who was always sober and spoke intelligently. He never gave his name, but he asked me about socialists in Buffalo. He said he didn't believe in Socialism."

Alphonse Stutz, a Nowak roomer and retired German army officer, recalled Czolgosz as "a pest" who awakened him one morning to borrow a pitcher of water.

The most sought after woman in the world on the morning of September 7 was Emma Goldman. A police net had been spread coast to coast to capture the woman who had inspired Czolgosz.

On this morning millions of Americans were trying to pronounce Czolgosz's name, were figuring the odds on McKinley's chances of survival, and attempting to solve Emma Goldman's part in the crime. Was Czolgosz merely a cat's-paw? Was his murder attempt part of a vast conspiracy aimed not only against McKinley but against other heads of state and finance as well? Red Emma, police believed, might answer these questions.

Her Rochester relatives were placed under surveillance. Her haunts in New York, Chicago, and elsewhere were checked, but without success. She was believed to be in the Midwest, possibly in Chicago or St. Louis; but in neither of these cities were police able to locate her although she had actually been in the latter city since September 2.

Late on the afternoon of September 6 Emma was about to board a St. Louis streetcar when she heard newsboys shouting, "Extra! Extra! President McKinley shot!"

She plucked an extra from a newsboy, tucked it under her arm, and jumped aboard the car. It was so crowded that she found it impossible to read; but as she was jostled about she heard the other passengers heatedly discussing the attempted murder. When she reached her temporary St. Louis home, she met Carl Nold, one of the comrades formerly associated with Berkman in the Frick affair.

"Carl had arrived . . . before me. He had already read the account," Emma later recounted. "The President had been shot at the Exposition grounds in Buffalo by a young man by the name of Leon Czolgosz. 'I never heard the name,' Carl said; 'Have you?' 'No, never,' I replied."

Carl went on to say that it was fortunate that she was then in St. Louis and not in Buffalo; otherwise "the papers will connect you with this act."

Emma replied that she thought that nonsense, adding that although the American press was fantastic it was not crazy enough to "concoct such a crazy story."

But on September 7 she was bug-eyed as she read the headlines in a St. Louis paper: "Assassin of President McKinley an Anarchist. Confesses to Having Been Incited by Emma Goldman. Woman Anarchist Wanted."

She bought several papers, which she took into a restaurant. Turning to an inside page of one, she spied a picture of the McKinley assassin. "Why that's Nieman!" she gasped.

When she read that the home of her friends, the Isaaks, had been raided and that several of her associates in Chicago were being held without bail, she decided that she must go at once to their relief.

Although this quixotic design appeared fantastic to Nold and her St. Louis friends, they gave her a rousing sendoff, including a "Lucullan" feast, and later accompanied her to the Wabash station, where she boarded a Pullman car in a Chicago-bound train.

Next morning she awoke to blistering invective directed against her and Czolgosz. Someone regretted that she hadn't been locked up long before. "Locked up nothing!" another retorted, "she should have been strung up to the first lamp-post."

"I listened to the good Christians while resting in my berth. I chuckled to myself at the thought of how they would look if I were to step out and announce: 'Here, ladies and gentlemen, true followers of the gentle Jesus, here is Emma Goldman!' But I did not have the heart to cause them such a shock and I remained behind my curtain."

When calling at Milburn's, Root had managed to repress his rising temper. In 1906, however, in a Utica speech he exploded in an angry outburst against Hearst and his yellow journals. "What wonder that the weak and excitable Czolgosz answered to such impulses as these," Root inveighed. "He never knew McKinley; he had no real or fancied wrongs of his own to avenge against McKinley or McKinley's government—he was answering to the lessons that it was a service to mankind to rid the earth of a monster and the foremost of the teachers of these lessons to him and his kind was and is William Randolph Hearst, with his yellow journals."

When the shooting occurred, Hearst had been working in his Chicago office. With a sudden premonition of the storm breaking about his head, he turned to Charles Edward Russell, his Chicago publisher, and said, "Things are going to be very bad."

He could hardly have assessed the situation more accurately. To forestall the rising tide of fury, he dispatched policy telegrams to his *New York Journal,* as well as to the *San Francisco Examiner,* counseling a delicate course of sorrow and hope. Homer Davenport, whose cartoons had once whittled McKinley down to pygmy size, was ordered to execute immediately a sympathetic captionless drawing which depicted Uncle Sam holding the beloved President's hand.

Three days after the shooting an Exposition visitor offered the *Journal* a foggy photograph of what purported to be the act itself. The amateur photographer was rewarded with $50, and the picture was published as another Hearst scoop.

Hearst editors like Arthur Brisbane, who had once described McKinley as "the most hated creature on the American continent," now did an abrupt switch. The stream of vituperation ceased, and in its place a hymn of praise arose. In a magical reversal of form Hearst hoped that "the President may not leave his much loved wife behind . . . that he may devote his days and strength to the program of national duty and national prosperity which his latest speech outlined. . . ."

Hearst's mealy-mouthed utterances served only to arouse a vengeful public, and no less the rival press, which, gleefully capitalizing on the situation, fell upon the king of yellow journalism like a swarm of angry hornets. Too many were aware of Hearst's philosophy that "an ideal morning edition . . . would have been one in which the Prince of Wales had gone into vaudeville, Queen Victoria had married her cook, the Pope had issued an encyclical favoring free love . . . France had declared war on Germany, the President of the United States had secured a divorce to marry the Dowager Empress of China . . . the Sultan of Turkey had been converted to Christianity—all of these being 'scoops' in the form of 'signed statements.'"

Fearful, Hearst began to pack a revolver.

With a clairvoyance smacking of fiction and characteristic reckless disregard of facts, the Hearst press boasted of a "notable scoop" in breaking the assassination story at 3:30—some forty odd minutes before it had occurred.

A Hearst reporter later vividly recalled the hectic scene in the *New York Journal* office. The paper's head copyboy, Peter Campbell, took the flash from Buffalo over the telephone. He swung back the telephone booth door, and shouted to Foster Coates, the managing editor, "McKinley shot at Buffalo by a crank!"

Coates blasted back an order to verify the flash, then dictated a bulletin and story.

The electrifying scoop on an otherwise dull afternoon had come from John Tremain, Hearst Albany correspondent, who was covering the President's Buffalo visit. Tremain grabbed the only available phone, which he had spotted shortly before the shooting. After his flash from Buffalo, Tremain's phone went dead, so that the initial flash could not be confirmed for an hour.

Part III

THE DAYS AFTER

Part III

THE DAYS AFTER

15

"He Is First Rate"

SUNDAY, SEPTEMBER 8, was a day of rising hopes, tinged only by a gloomy sky. The first tipoff on the President's condition came at 9:00 A.M. as Dr. Mynter, wearing a jaunty air, emerged from Milburn's to report that the President's progress was encouraging. Dr. Park, leaving the house at the same time, verified his colleague's report, adding, "He is first rate."

These verbal reports were confirmed at 9:20 when the eagerly awaited morning bulletin was issued, disclosing that the President had passed a good night. His condition was quite encouraging. "His mind is clear," read the bulletin. "Resting well. Wound dressed at 8:30 and found to be in a very satisfactory condition."

Meanwhile, the arrival of an X-Ray machine from New York City caused a flurry of excitement. At 11:30 reporters questioned Dr. H. A. Knoll, the X-Ray expert, who said he did not believe the machine would be used in an attempt to locate the bullet, at least not for the present.

From dawn on, across the nation, from humble chapels and lofty cathedrals alike, prayers for the President arose in a steady heavenward stream. Roosevelt attended services in Buffalo's First Presbyterian Church. Seated beside Ansley Wilcox, his jaw set grimly, the Vice President listened intently while the Rev. Dr. Smith of Indianapolis expatiated on the theme of self-sacrifice.

After the services Roosevelt walked the two miles from church to Milburn's. Following a brief call he made no effort to conceal his optimism. Senator Hanna, who had joined the Vice President in chatting with newsmen, tempered the Rooseveltian optimism to a degree. Complications, he said, might arise; but conditions could hardly be more favorable at that time. Both men wished to emphasize one point—the bulletins were not colored.

"Physicians," said Hanna, "are giving the facts to the public."

Taking the Senator's arm, Roosevelt added, "Senator, let me put it this way. The doctors' bulletins are made with scrupulous understatement."

"Yes, scrupulous understatement," echoed Hanna, who went on to clarify another point—it would be 48 to 72 hours before physicians could reach a conclusion. It was impossible for any doctor to state the final outcome until such a period had passed.

As the Senator and the man he had once branded a "madman" boarded the Hanna carriage, arm in arm, photographers clamored for a picture. Roosevelt, grinning, waved them back. "No, no—not at a time like this," he said.

The Vice President, who in a moment of pique had once compared McKinley's backbone with that of a chocolate eclair, was moved on this Sabbath day to a more kindly appraisal. "McKinley," he said, "was such a lovable and gentle, as well as a great, man, that I can't understand how any man can do this."

With the exception of Secretaries Hay and Long, cabinet members were now in the city, most of them being quartered at the exclusive Buffalo Club in Delaware Avenue. As yet no formal meeting had been announced, but there was some discussion on the eventuality of Roosevelt's acting as Chief Executive. No precedent for such a move existed, but it was recalled that Vice President Chester Arthur had not assumed office until after President Garfield's death, some two months after he was shot.

A call by Dr. Charles McBurney, well-known New York City specialist, may have allayed doubts of metropolitan physicians and the press of that city that the President was not receiving the ultimate in care from the local doctors. Dr. McBurney had nothing but admiration for the operation upon the President, describing it as "the epoch of the century." He added, "The judgement of Dr. Mann in operating as he did within an hour after the shooting in all probability saved the life of McKinley." At the time of this glowing pronouncement he could not have foreseen the controversy that would later arise over the so-called epochal treatment.

By midafternoon the avenue swarmed with carriages and automobiles laden with callers, among them Robert T. Lincoln, president of the Pullman Co., who had been traveling with his family in his private railway car. Some 36 years before he had stood with John Hay at the bedside of his father, likewise the victim of an assassin's bullet. Lincoln said he felt reassured by his visit to Milburn's.

On September 9 confidence outweighed the haunting fears of the hectic sixty or more hours since the assassination attempt. After a quarter hour's consultation with Secretary Cortelyou and the President's physicians, Roosevelt summarized the situation: "I am absolutely certain everything is coming out all right."

McKinley was stronger. He was showing an interest in national affairs; and, perhaps most indicative of improvement, he was able to turn himself in bed. The President's pulse at 112 was nearer to normal, having receded eight beats to the minute since 6:00 A.M. He was relatively free from pain. The physicians, barely able to conceal their cheerful frame of mind, did not hold their usual noon consultation. Another evidence of the President's continued improvement was his keen anticipation of Mrs. McKinley's forenoon visit. When she entered the sickroom, the President took her hand, saying: "I'm feeling much better. In a few days more we can talk all we wish."

Both confident of McKinley's full recovery, Secretary Gage and Attorney-General Philander Knox had left the city.

Twice during the day Roosevelt, preferring, as he said, to stretch his legs, walked from Wilcox's to Milburn's.

Of all the visitors Senator Hanna was the most optimistic, describing McKinley's condition as "just glorious." "He wants to talk," Hanna told newsmen. "Why, he'll be ready for a cigar soon."

Joshing with photographers, Hanna, who seemed vastly relieved at the President's improvement, revealed that he had experienced a chilling dream the previous night. "You know," he told reporters, "dreams go by contraries. Well, sir, in the dream I was up at the Milburn house waiting to hear how the President was getting along and everybody was feeling good.

"We thought the danger was past. I was talking with General Brooke and Mr. Cortelyou, and we were felicitating ourselves on how well the physicians had been carrying the case. Suddenly, in my dream, Dr. McBurney entered the room through the door leading to the sickroom with a look of utmost horror and distress upon his face. I rushed up to him and putting a hand on either shoulder, said, 'What is it, doctor? What is it? Let us know the worst.'

"Dr. McBurney replied, 'My dear Senator, it is absolutely the worst that could happen. The President has had a tremendous change for the worse: his temperature is now 440 degrees.' I fell back in my chair in utter collapse."

As he finished Hanna laughed heartily and said, "But do you know, I couldn't rest easy until I saw the early bulletins this morning?"

While police from coast to coast tightened their dragnet around Emma Goldman, eleven of her Anarchist friends, including the Isaaks, who were accused of complicity in the attempt on McKinley's life, were brought before Magistrate Prindville in Chicago's Harrison Street jail.

Protesting bitterly, Abraham Isaak told the magistrate, ". . . we are herded together like cattle."

Magistrate Prindville denied Attorney Leonard Saltiel's request for their release and set bail at $3,000 each for Julia Mechtlanic, Maria Isaak, Maria Isaak, Jr., Michael Roz, Martin Rozinick, Morris Fox, Isaak and his son, Abraham, Jr., Henry Travegelino, Hippolyte Havel, and Alfred Schneider.

In court Julia Mechtlanic carried a red rose and a copy of Leo Tolstoy's *The Slavery of Our Times* while Miss Isaak read from the same author's *Resurrection*. After a hearing was scheduled for ten days later, the prisoners were taken to their cells overlooking the site where the Haymarket rioters had gone to the gibbet.

The 1886 riots now came into sharper focus since, as *The Buffalo Express* reminded its readers, their case had a direct bearing on the state's rights to punish Czolgosz's possible accomplices for the attack upon McKinley. None of the four Chicago rioters who had gone to the gallows was "even alleged to have been guilty of throwing the deadly bomb" and neither were the two condemned to life imprisonment by Governor John P. Altgeld of Illinois. The actual bomb-thrower had never been caught; but as *The Express* pointed out "The men who were punished were those who by their anarchial declamations had incited the crime."

Fog swirled about the Milburn house early on September 10. The President had passed a somewhat restless night and had slept "only fairly well."

Secretary Hay and his fellow cabinet members Root, Hitchcock, Wilson, and Smith left the house at noon after meeting with Roosevelt. Brimming with confidence, despite the restless night report, Roosevelt told the press that he expected to leave for Oyster Bay that night since the President was completely out of danger.

Reminded that Garfield's progress had been satisfactory for ten days after Guiteau had shot him, Roosevelt was ready with an answer: "Ah! but we forget twenty years of modern surgery!"

The Vice President conceded that amidst the tremendous excitement of the past few days he had given little thought to legislation to curb the Anarchists. What disturbed him, he said, was why even an Anarchist would make an attempt on McKinley's life. "The President had no fortune . . . he was a self-made man, a kindly Christian gentleman."

The hero of San Juan hill shooed away a Secret Service man who hovered close by. "I don't need anyone," he announced. ". . . the Oyster Bay police force isn't large enough to permit assignment of a guard to me, and if I get used to it here they might have to increase the force at the expense of the poor taxpayer of which I am one."

After the laughter had subsided, Roosevelt vetoed a suggested visit to the Exposition grounds. "I came here as a matter of duty," he said, "not for pleasure."

Lunching an hour later with Dawes and Wilcox at the latter's mansion, the Vice President, however, consented for a brief period to gauge his chances as a 1904 Presidential candidate. Dawes informed him that his prospects in Illinois were good.

Later, Mrs. McKinley summoned Dawes to her apartment at Milburn's. Dawes found the First Lady weeping but still confident of her husband's recovery. Dawes told her that her optimism was not misplaced; in fact, he was so certain now that the critical stage of the President's convalescence had passed that he was preparing to leave for Washington that very night.

As McKinley's condition appeared to be improving, Emma Goldman in Chicago barely escaped being arrested in the nude.

Upon her arrival in that city she had been faced with the problem of where to stay since all of her associates would obviously be under surveillance. Finally, a Mr. and Mrs. J. Norris were selected as being the least liable to suspicion. Mr. N. (as Emma refers to him in her autobiography) was the son of a well-to-do minister.

At the end of her first day in Chicago Mr. N. returned home with the news that the *Chicago Tribune* had offered $5,000 for an interview with her. Although bitterly opposed to the profit system, she recognized that the sum might be necessary in the legal ordeal she anticipated; so she consented. The next morning after her hostess had departed for work and her host for the *Tribune* office, Emma was in her bath when she heard the splinter of glass.

Hastily donning a kimono, she rushed into an adjoining room, where she spied a policeman on one of the window ledges. Soon the room was packed with policemen under the command of the massive Captain Schuettler. Trying to pass herself off as a Swedish maid unable to speak English, she protested that her name was Lena Larson and that she did not know Emma Goldman.

After ransacking the apartment, Captain Schuettler, according to Emma, "walked over to the book-shelves. 'Hell, this is a reg'lar preacher's house,' he remarked: 'Look at them books. I don't think Emma Goldman would be here.' They were about to leave when one of the detectives suddenly called: 'Here, Captain Schuettler, what about this?'"

The detective held up a fountain pen with Emma Goldman's name inscribed upon it.

" 'By Golly, that's a find.' cried the Captain. 'She must have been here and she may come back.' He ordered two of his men to remain behind."

Emma "saw that the game was up," and admitted her identity. Captain Schuettler and his men "stood there as if petrified. Then the Captain roared: 'Well, I'll be damned! You're the shrewdest crook I ever met! Take her, quick!'"

Emma was whisked off to Police Headquarters, where she was kept in a stifling room while police grilled her for over eight hours. At least fifty detectives passed before her. Attempting to get a confession, the detectives shook their fists in her face. One shouted, "You was with Czolgosz in Buffalo! I saw you myself, right in front of Convention Hall. Better confess, d'you hear?"

Another yelled, "Look here, Goldman, I seen you with that son of a bitch at the fair! Don't you lie now—I seen you, I tell you!"

A third cried, "You've faked enough—you keep this up and sure's you're born you'll get the chair. Your lover has confessed. He said it was your speech made him shoot the President."

Schuettler, his massive bulk towering above her, bellowed, "If you don't confess, you'll go the way of those bastard Haymarket Anarchists."

Although she had been arrested a number of times since serving a year in Blackwell's Island penitentiary in 1893, Emma had never been subjected to such abuse and bullying. Her head throbbed. Her lips were parched. When she stretched out her hand for a pitcher of water which stood on the table before her, a detective yelled, "You can drink all you want, but first answer me. Where were you with Czolgosz the day he shot the President?"

After hours of torturous treatment she was removed to the Harrison Street police station and locked up in a barred enclosure which exposed her to view from every side.

A grilling by Chief O'Neill failed to shake Emma's story. "Do you know that your words are what Czolgosz claims stirred him to shoot the President?" demanded O'Neill.

"No," she cried, "I never advise violence." She had apparently forgotten for the moment her part in Berkman's attempt on the life of industrialist Frick when the Homestead strike raged in 1892. "I scarcely know Czolgosz. I was leaving for Rochester via Buffalo, when Czolgosz had a few words with me. He said he'd heard me lecture in some memorial hall in Cleveland, last May. I scarcely remembered anything about him save that his complexion was light."

"Then," demanded O'Neill, "you do know him?"

She shrugged her shoulders.

"What did you think when you heard an attempt had been made to kill the President?"

"Oh! the fool!" she cried, then launched into a discourse on Anarchism.

"We are opposed to violence. Education is our watchword," she declared.

Bit by bit, the shadowy outlines of her movements in the past two months began to emerge. She had arrived in Chicago in early July to visit the Isaak family. On the night of July 12, she answered the doorbell.

"Czolgosz stood there," she recalled. "I was about to catch the Nickel Plate train. Isaak's daughter and I were to go to Rochester. He [Czolgosz] went with us to the Rock Island depot. That's all there was between us. I am an Anarchist but nothing I said knowingly would have led him to act."

"Not even your lectures?" asked O'Neill.

"Am I accountable because some crackbrain person puts the wrong construction on my words?"

Held incommunicado she was flooded with scurrilous letters, many of which were unsigned.

" 'You damn bitch of an Anarchist,' one of them read, 'I wish I could get you. I would tear your heart out and feed it to my dog.' 'Murderous Emma Goldman,' another wrote, 'you will burn in hell-fire for your treachery to our country.' A third cheerfully promised' 'We will cut your tongue out, soak your carcass in oil, and burn you alive.' The description of some of the anonymous writers of what they would do to me sexually offered studies in perversion that would have astounded authorities on the subject. The authors of the letters nevertheless seemed to me less contemptible than the police officials. Daily I was handed stacks of letters that had been opened and read by the guardians of American decency and morality. At the same time messages from my friends were withheld from me. It was evident that my spirit was to be broken by such methods. I decided to put a stop to it. The next time I was given one of the open envelopes, I tore it up and threw the pieces into the detective's face."

While Emma defied Chicago authorities, Buffalo reporters found Czolgosz, his hair matted, his face thick with stubble, his shirt limp and blood-splotched, pacing his cell.

In a sly attempt to find out whether the President had died he asked one of the newsmen, "Think they'll let me go?"

That subject was taboo—his query met with stony silence. The prisoner proved quite loquacious, freely discussing the jail food which was "good," but he craved a good cigar. "I'm a great smoker, you know. Someone offered me a cigarette, but I don't smoke 'em."

"Heard anything from your mother or brothers?" he was asked. "No, I suppose they're afraid."

Cecil Hooke, a member of the Pan-American Exhibitors Club, after viewing the prisoner averred that during the summer Czolgosz had for a brief time worked for him. "I found out very quickly he wasn't a carpenter," said Hooke. "My little son identified him from a picture in the paper. He's the man who worked for me two or three weeks, then disappeared."

By this time Hearst's enemies had descended upon him like a swarm of hornets. The publisher was flayed as a demagogue, as a wily capitalist who posed as labor's friend, as an inciter of malcontents like Leon Czolgosz. His enemies, comprising virtually the entire Fourth Estate, worked night and day, vying with each other in their campaign to hatchet the publisher and scuttle his papers. Hearst still was packing his revolver against any eventuality, but what he really needed was a battery of howitzers to ward off the storm of abuse. The *Journal*'s editorial, attributed to Hearst's star writer and editor, Arthur Brisbane, was reprinted. In retrospect, its words "killing must be done" took on a macabre significance that had been lost at the time of its original printing five months before.

Although a fabrication, the story circulated that Czolgosz had a copy of the *New York Journal* in his pocket when he shot McKinley. Czolgosz himself, unaware of the delicious comfort he was bringing to Hearst's legion of enemies, denied he was a Hearst reader. Although a rumor persisted that he had been offered $10,000 for his family if only he would confess that he was a *Journal* reader, Czolgosz was uncooperative. He repeated as if by rote that Goldman's lectures had provoked his act. His stolid lack of interest in the inciting possibilities of journalism was small comfort to Hearst's enemies.

Nevertheless, cries of rage against Hearst publications sounded north, south, east, and west; and bales of Hearst papers were seized and burned. Hotels, cafes, bars, clubs, and barbershops threw out Hearst papers or were boycotted. The Grand Army of the Republic at its encampment in Cleveland resolved that "every member exclude from his household the *New York Journal, a teacher of Anarchism and a vile sheet."*

A ban on Hearst publications in San Francisco's Bohemian Club caused Edward Hamilton, Ashton Stevens, Jake Dressler, and other San Francisco staff members to stalk out of the club in a body.

Hearst himself was faring badly. Effigies of him, hung ignominiously beside those of Emma Goldman and Czolgosz, were pelted and burned amidst uproar and abuse. Threats against his life mounted. The publisher, fearful of bombs, refused to open any packages addressed to him which arrived by mail.

The sorely beset publisher replied by editorial: "From coast to coast this newspaper has been attacked and is being attacked with savage ferocity by the incompetents, the failures of journalism, by the kept organs of plutocracy, heading the mob."

Hearst conceded that one of his paper's offenses was that it fought for the people "against privilege and class distinction, class greed, and class stupidity and heartlessness."

"Note the thrift of the parasitic press," retaliated Hearst, "It would draw profit from the terrible deed of the wretch who shot down the President."

On September 11, rumors spread that the President would be removed to Washington by Thursday or Friday in a Pennsylvania Railroad car fitted up like an ambulance, also that he had undergone a second abdominal operation the day before.

In denying the latter, Dr. Park strongly objected to the use of the word operation. "It should not be dignified by such a term," he told newsmen. "We merely cut the stitches—took them out. The President is doing nicely. What he eats and drinks is passing through his stomach in the natural, normal way."

Dr. Mynter contributed to the growing optimism by reporting that he was more confident than ever of the President's recovery. He revealed that McKinley had taken beef broth, also water. He vetoed, however, any suggestion that the President might leave Buffalo, at least during the next few weeks.

Something of Emma Goldman's movements during the summer were gradually coming to light. She had actually been in Buffalo, it was discovered, on two different occasions. After leaving Chicago on July 12 in the company of Miss Isaak, she had arrived in Buffalo the next day, staying with a Hattie Lang, who recalled that Emma had made trips to the Exposition grounds with a Dr. Kaplin and a Mr. Saylin. Two days later she had gone on to Rochester. She and Miss Isaak had remained in that city for five weeks, then returned to Buffalo on August 13. Again they "did" the Exposition. Her stay in Buffalo this time was brief, for she moved on to Pittsburgh, then St. Louis, where she arrived on September 2.

It is possible, though never substantiated, that during her August visit she may have met another Exposition-goer, one Leon F. Czolgosz, then making frequent sallies to the Buffalo fair from his West Seneca boarding place.

Now in the Chicago Harrison Street jail she vehemently denied any complicity in the crime. She was puzzled herself by Czolgosz's act. Why, she asked herself, had he chosen McKinley "rather than some more direct representative of the system of economic oppression and misery. Was it because he saw in McKinley the willing tool of Wall Street and of the new American imperialism. . . ?"

McKinley she regarded as a hopeless reactionary in his attitude toward labor. "He had repeatedly sided with the masters by sending troops to strike regions. All these circumstances . . . must have exercised a decisive influence upon the impressionable Leon," she concluded, "culminating in his act of violence."

As she paced her cell, an image of Czolgosz recurred to her. He was very young, very erect, a man of handsome face. She recalled too Isaak's piece in *Free Society,* branding Nieman as a possible spy. At the time she had thought it flimsy, even fatuous.

16

Change for the Worse

A *BUFFALO TIMES* MAN pacing the Milburn walk in a downpour of rain on the morning of September 12, noted that within the house ". . . lights burned dimly . . . all seemed well."

At 7:20 Dr. Rixey, who alone had attended the President through the night, reported that his patient had slept almost continuously.

Emboldened by the fact that he had taken beef juice by mouth the day before, on this morning he asked for toast and coffee. Since the beef juice on Wednesday was the first food he had received naturally since his operation, his request occasioned a consultation of his doctors. When he learned that their decision was favorable, his face lighted up.

After receiving a small quantity of his desired breakfast, he turned on his side and slept for several hours.

On this morning he was also given a small amount of beef juice. One of his nurses reported, "This he relished greatly and smacked his lips and asked if he couldn't have some more."

His request was denied at the time, but twenty minutes later he was given more. "He took considerable," the nurse continued. Then he was quiet, "apparently satisfied."

The same nurse also later recalled that on this day her famous patient evinced his first interest in how the press was treating his case. "He was seeking information," said the nurse, "but his questions were circumvented."

The doctors' off-the-cuff comments were glowing.

Pausing briefly as newsmen swarmed around him, Dr. Mynter described the President's condition as "eminently satisfactory."

"The patient could not be doing better," was Dr. Mann's contribution. "Why he even asked for a cigar."

"Did he get it?" asked one of the reporters.

"Well, hardly," replied Dr. Mann, smiling.

Dr. McBurney was elated, especially that the President had been able to take coffee, toast, and broth. "We are looking for an egg, fresh-laid for invalids," he wisecracked. In fact, the President's condition appeared to be so improved that Dr. McBurney returned to New York City, leaving on the same train as Secretary Root.

But later in the day a negative reaction set in. The President complained of fatigue. In the afternoon bulletin the physicians disclosed the fact but with no suggestion of deep concern. Their gathering an hour earlier than usual for their evening consultation was in itself not reassuring. The 6:00 bulletin was delivered to newsmen by Cortelyou in person. The President's condition was admittedly "not so good."

Their explanation was plausible. The reason for the first oral feeding the day before had been the failure of the artificial means of supplying nourishment by injection. This had been accomplished through the rectum, which by Wednesday had become irritated and rejected the enemas. The stomach, the doctors felt, had not yet been ready to perform its normal functions properly. The problem now facing the medical men was the disposal of the food taken in the morning.

Dr. Charles G. Stockton, highly regarded in the area as a stomach specialist, was summoned into the consultation. Under his direction calomel and oil were administered. Heart stimulants were also given.

At 9:35, Secretaries Hitchcock and Wilson, anxious for personal assurances of the President's condition, hurried into Milburn's, where Dr. Mann told them and Abner McKinley that the undigested food in the President's stomach would undoubtedly pass away during the night and he would be improved by morning.

But for hours McKinley failed to respond to treatment to relieve the troubles caused by failures of his organs of digestion and assimilation. The failure added to the depression that existed until midnight when the desired relief came with two movements of the bowels. The physicians felt that these would allay the wild heart pulsations. To a limited degree such was the case, for the

President's pulse decreased from 128 to 120. But this was still too rapid for a temperature of 100.2.

The news was nevertheless encouraging enough that Abner McKinley, Colonel Brown, his business partner, and the President's nephew, Lt. James McKinley, left the house. At midnight Secretary Cortelyou crossed the avenue to deliver the midnight bulletin to scores of newsmen who had been eagerly awaiting it. In the misty gloom under the flickering lights the harried Secretary, with Milburn at his side, announced, "The President has responded to medical treatment and is better. . . . He is resting nicely now . . ."

17

"The President Has Passed Away"

A DAY OF SHATTERED HOPES lay ahead. As if to augur the arrival of Friday the 13th, at midnight peals of thunder rumbled across the heavens, and a blustery wind blew in from the west.

Despite the momentary encouragement felt earlier and Cortelyou's reassuring statement, shortly after 2:00 A.M. the President's condition became grave. His heart action weakened so perceptibly that doctors and nurses feared the end was near. They hurriedly administered digitalis and strychnine and injected a saline solution intravenously. When these restoratives failed, telephone calls summoned the rest of the consulting physicians back to the house. Telephone messages went out and telegrams were dispatched to relatives, close friends, and officials. Amidst rolls of thunder and flashes of lightning messengers darted to and from waiting vehicles in the stormswept street.

At 2:50 A.M. Dr. Park bounded from his carriage and dashed up the front walk. The doctor, aroused from his sleep with the news of McKinley's sinking spell, arrived only minutes after the President's brother, Abner. Both Mynter and Mann were grim-faced, refusing any comment as they made for the house.

In his mansion a few blocks south on Delaware Avenue Ansley Wilcox was also awakened in the early morning hours. Would he be able to contact the Vice President? Wilcox said he would try; he immediately telephoned Roosevelt's secretary, William Loeb, in Albany, who took over the task of locating his superior. But it would not be easy. Satisfied that McKinley would recover and perhaps to demonstrate to the country his assurance of the fact, Roosevelt had embarked upon a camping and mountain-climbing expedition in the Adirondacks and was at that moment remote from communication by telephone or telegraph.

In his Washington home Dawes was awakened at 4:00 A.M. by the jangling of his telephone. From the White House Captain Montgomery relayed the news, which had just come over the wires from Buffalo. Dawes rushed to the Executive Mansion, where Montgomery was in communication with Cortelyou. At 5:30 Secretary Gage arrived. Together he and Dawes bent over the messages as they came through from Milburn's.

By 6:00 Dawes was on his way to Buffalo.

For some reason Hanna could not be reached at his Cleveland home by telephone from Buffalo or locally by Col. Herrick, to whom Cortelyou had left the task of notifying him. Herrick was able to arouse a neighbor of Hanna, named Perkins, who had to shout under a window of the great magnate's home in order to attract anyone's attention.

In less than two hours a special train was speeding over the Lake Shore railroad tracks, bringing Hanna and several of Mc-Kinley's relatives and friends, among them Hanna's house guests attending the G.A.R. Encampment—Senator Charles Fairbanks of Indiana, and Judge William R. Day of Canton, former Secretary of State. The trip usually clocked at four hours and thirty minutes was accomplished on this sad occasion in three hours and eleven minutes.

Day dawned in a downpour of rain. Sodden newsmen and soldiers paced their beats before the ivy-clad house. News of the President's sinking spell had spread and by now hundreds of men, women, and even children were massed along the rope barrier, their anxious faces turned toward the house as they waited for fresh bulletins.

When the rain had abated somewhat, a flock of crows flapped over the housetop. The appearance of these birds of ill-omen on this dismal morning—added to the inauspiciousness of the date, Friday the thirteenth—sent shudders through the crowd of faithful onlookers.

After their all-night vigil, which had left them limp and dismayed, Cortelyou, Milburn, and Wilson paced the Milburn porch. "Tama Jim" said he had not yet abandoned hope, but his bearded Scottish face was sad and he seemed to lack his usual conviction as he spoke the words.

At 7:30 spirits were momentarily buoyed up when word came

from the sickroom that the President had rallied slightly. As Dr. Mann and Dr. Mynter left they assured reporters that they had not yet given up hope.

Newspapermen, mystified by the abrupt change of tone in the reports they were receiving, tried unsatisfactorily to pierce the ambiguity of statements. For a week they had been turning out optimistic stories for their papers—now, suddenly, the President was said to be dying. A group of them intercepted Dr. Wasdin as he was leaving the house.

"I cannot reiterate too often that the President is holding his own," stated the Marine Hospital surgeon.

Holding his own? There had been no such suggestive phrasing as this before.

"Has he rallied perceptibly?" a voice demanded.

"Yes—and no."

"What does that mean?" queried a reporter, unable to fathom the paradoxical retort.

The physician then explained that there had been fluctuations in McKinley's condition. "One moment he appears to revive . . . the next a depression sets in."

During the morning, as had been her daily custom, Mrs. McKinley visited her husband. Before she came into the sickroom, the President, well aware of his condition, summoned Dr. Wasdin, asking that the truth be concealed from her. But this was difficult, for she had watched him so closely that she could easily detect the most insignificant change. Tears welled up in her eyes as the President with his usual concern tried to reassure her. When she left he relapsed into a kind of stupor although he was able to recognize those around him.

Behind the ropes the lines of people thickened. Carriages and automobiles milled about the street. Cabs discharged passengers, only to take on new ones. Among those arriving were Major Symons and Secretary Hitchcock. Mayor Diehl, after a conference with Dr. Mann, emerged from the house to state that if the President survived the day there might be hope. A buzz of conjecture moved through the crowd when the Rev. Arthur O. Sykes, Navy chaplain, arrived. It was feared that the end might be near and that the clergyman had come to offer the President final consolation. Sykes, however, newsmen learned, was only delivering a resolution of sympathy from the residents of Portsmouth, Virginia.

Callers continued to stream in: Hanna, breathless and pale; Dr. and Mrs. Herman Baer, the latter Abner McKinley's daughter; Governor Richard Yates of Illinois; the President's friend, the Rev. Dr. Corwin Wilson, formerly of the Canton First Methodist Church.

At 2:30 P.M. came a clear tipoff from Cortelyou. The haggard secretary, after releasing a statement, rushed back to the press tents, to request that the words "he is better than yesterday at this time" be stricken out.

At 4:00 the President's pulsations grew so alarming that saline injections were resorted to. At this hour he was in a stupor. A nurse pressed water to his lips but there was no response.

At 5:00 the President suffered a heart attack. Later, amidst the growing gloom of evening, Harry Hamlin dashed into one of the press tents. His voice quavered as he told the correspondents, "Mr. Cortelyou says he can't come out. Tell the boys that the President is dying. They might as well know."

Of course, "the boys" did know already, but this was the official confirmation and they scurried to dash off new leads before the next bulletin—perhaps the last—would be ready.

At 7:45 Dr. McBurney jumped from a carriage, only to encounter saddened faces all about him. The doctor had barely reached the house before Elmer Dover, Hanna's secretary, emerged to tell newsmen, "The President has asked for Mrs. McKinley. He is very low and cannot live. He groans feebly but continually."

Early in the evening the administration of oxygen aroused the President from a semiconscious condition. He opened his eyes, looking about him with that kindly, gentle expression which had so endeared him to all who were attending him.

His lips moved. Those around the bedside saw that he was trying to say something. They bent over him and heard him whisper in a voice barely audible, "Mrs. McKinley." Then he closed his eyes. The time for farewell had come. The First Lady was brought to her dying husband's side, but by the time she reached it with Mrs. McWilliams's help the President had lost consciousness. After waiting a few moments she was led back to her room.

At 8:00 the President again gained consciousness; again he whispered his wife's name and again she was brought to him. Seating herself beside him, she took his outstretched hand in hers. His eyes opened; he mumbled several sentences half audibly. Those nearby thought they caught the words of his favorite hymn, "Nearer, My God, to Thee." His face lighted up with a faint smile as he clasped Mrs. McKinley's hand. The end could not be far away, and as she sat there, her face white, her hand enfolding his, Ida McKinley must have recalled the early days of their marriage and their happiness, and too, his habitual forbearance, and his gallantry over the three decades of their life together.

Dawes arrived in time to see this touching scene. When his cab had pulled up before Milburn's he was met by a tearful Latta. "Hurry, or you'll be too late," urged the White House secretary.

It was 8:00 as Dawes quickly ascended the stairs and entered the sick chamber. Mrs. McKinley was seated beside the bed, her face near her husband's. "He had one arm around her and was smiling at her," Dawes recorded in his journal. "He looked up at me in the kindly way which was so natural to him." As Dawes neared the bedside, Abner McKinley took his hand and they stood silently with the President's sisters and the McKinley's nieces and nephews. The faithful Cortelyou was at the foot of the bed.

Again the pampered Ida McKinley showed that remarkable fortitude of which she was capable when extreme circumstances demanded it. "Mrs. McKinley made no outcry," wrote Dawes; "her grief was past words. She was led away to see him no more alive. Before she went she was told the President would not awaken in this world."

Without him life would be empty and she longed to have the Lord take her with her husband.

But the President was not to die for several hours. The suspense, in view of the certain eventuality, must have been harrowing for those in the death chamber, and, no less for those waiting in the Milburn living room. Now and then, one of them waylaid one of the physicians for a word of encouragement—but none came. Now that hope had been abandoned, those who had kept up the long vigil in the living room were permitted to mount the stairs one by one and stand in the bedroom doorway and look for a moment upon their dying Chief Executive.

Hanna's farewell was in its way as poignant as the First Lady's.

There lay, unconscious and dying, not only his dear and intimate friend, but the summation of all his political hopes and ambitions. "William, William, don't you know me?" he sobbed, but there was no response to his anguished query.

Secretary Wilson, who had so faithfully dogged the President during the Pan-American visit and followed the course of his illness during the past week, now held back from a final visit. He could not bear to see the President in his death agony.

But as Dawes described him, "The President did not seem like a dying man. He moved his limbs freely and did not seem to breathe with difficulty." From time to time he would reach out like a child to clutch the hand of Dr. Rixey, who had taken Mrs. McKinley's place at the bedside. Once he seemed to murmur, "Oh, dear," as if in some distress.

Like many other prominent figures of history McKinley has been credited with several last words. Most of them are rather stilted and moralistic sentences like, "Good-bye, all, good-bye. It is God's way; not our will, but Thine be done." While both Mrs. McKinley and Dawes refer to his speaking the words of the hymn, "Nearer, My God, to Thee," other farewell messages are no doubt apocryphal. Not that McKinley was not capable of the highest form of Christian sentiments.

Cynics could easily attribute the regularity of his church-going, his strict Sabbath observance, even his unfailing courtliness to good policy; but generally the politic façade crumbles in the presence of pain and imminent death. In characterizing his famous patient Dr. Park was later to confess: "Up to this time I had never really believed that a man could be a good Christian and a good politician.

"His public acts showed him to be the latter, while the evidences of his real Christian spirit were most impressive during his last days. His treatment of Mrs. McKinley during the many trying experiences which he had with her fortified a gentleness in his manly character, while the few remarks or expressions which escaped from him during his last hours stamped him as essentially a Christian in the highest and most lovable degree."

While the death watch went on, avid newsmen in front of the house continued to jot down the names of the notables arriving and leaving and to buttonhole anyone willing to make a statement.

Shortly after 9:00 P.M. the Rev. C. B. Wilson, the President's former pastor, now of North Tonawanda, a Buffalo suburb, forecast wrongly, "He will not live till midnight."

Senator Chauncey M. Depew was in tears. "The President can't live," he sobbed.

At 11:11 Dr. Mynter disclosed, "The President practically has no pulse; it is just a flutter."

Shortly before midnight an exhausted horse drawing a rig with two occupants staggered to the curb. George Urban had driven the animal so hard that it was near collapse. The passenger whom Urban had picked up at the railroad station was Dr. Edward Janeway of New York City, who with Dr. W. W. Johnson of Washington, another heart specialist, had been summoned the day before.

As Dr. Janeway joined in conference with his medical colleagues, Secretary Long drew before the house, accompanied by an escort of U.S. Marines.

Word came through that *The Buffalo Commercial* already had an extra on the downtown streets, its headline—*"He Is Dead."* Although Milburn himself appeared in front of the house to deny the report, by 1:00 A.M. the other papers in the city had taken up the cry and were hawking extras announcing the President's death.

Through the gloom an automobile chugged and came to a squeaky stop while newsmen swarmed around it. Out stepped Erie County Coroner Wilson. "I got a call from District Attorney Penney," he explained.

The correspondents didn't wait for more. "The President is dead," someone yelled and the others took up the cry as they dashed for telephones and telegraphs.

Meanwhile Coroner Wilson was being met at the Milburn front door by Cortelyou. "I am the Coroner," announced Wilson. "I have come to take charge of the body."

"Please leave the house," said Cortelyou. "We will send for you when we want you."

At 1:44 A.M. Dr. McBurney, minus his usual jauntiness, left the death watch. The President lay at this moment as if dead. His heart was still beating, yet there was no pulse.

Of McKinley's last moments Dawes recorded: "The President

was breathing mechanically and audibly. Finally he ceased to breathe and it seemed he was gone. Then he drew another breath after a time. Then all was still."

At 2:10, Dr. Rixey placed his stethoscope to the President's chest, paused, then said in a low voice, "The President is dead."

Cortelyou, who had hardly slept since the shooting, was the first to move. The secretary's face was ashen and haggard as he moved to the hall and down the stairs to the livingroom. A hush pervaded the room. Everyone knew why he had come, but waited for him to speak. "Gentlemen," he said, "the President has passed away."

At Police Headquarters Chief Bull, mindful of the riots that had raged on September 6, alerted the city's 750 policemen for duty. Ropes were stretched in front of the entrance. Precautions at Headquarters savored of military defense. Doors were locked and back of each stood four to six police, each with a loaded revolver and nightstick.

A dozen men were detailed north of the main entrance while 50 more were held in the reserve room. Since the day before there had been ominous rumblings of trouble to come if McKinley died.

"When the President dies look out for trouble at Police Headquarters," read one threat. "Czolgosz will be mobbed and lynched or shot."

At 8:00 P.M., 300 police reserves, called into action earlier by Chief Bull, reported to Captain Regan. Regan posted them in strategic positions along Main Street to keep the crowd moving and to direct it away from Headquarters. Despite these measures people began to gather several rows deep at the rope barriers. There were ugly mutterings and threats.

One group headed down Main Street and spilled into Franklin Street. Half a dozen patrolmen in front of St. Stephen's Hall at Erie and Franklin Streets waited behind the ropes. Men swung their canes and waved their hats as they rushed the barrier. Shouts and shrill police whistles filled the air. Within seconds Assistant Police Superintendent Patrick Cusack, followed by 100 policemen made a wild rush on the approaching mob.

At sight of the advancing police reinforcements the mob leaders concluded it was time to stop. The mob turned tail and fled down Franklin Street with police in hot pursuit. Thus ended an abortive uprising, which might have reached dangerous proportions had it not been for police vigilance.

At 10:00 P.M. some 500 people were still milling about, but now they were intent upon the bulletins, which disclosed that McKinley's death was near. At this critical hour, General Welch telephoned Headquarters to inquire about the general situation and informed Bull that the 65th and 74th National Guard and regulars from Fort Porter stood ready to help quell any further outbreaks.

An hour later Bull confidently announced, "I don't believe there will be any attempt to take Czolgosz from us. If there is we are prepared."

18
"Now That the End Has Come"

TO ALL FOREIGN GOVERNMENTS Secretary Hay sent copies of the following official notice:

Department of State
Washington, September 14, 1901.
Sir:
It is my painful duty to announce to you the death of William McKinley, President of the United States, in the city of Buffalo, at fifteen minutes past two in the morning of today, September 14th.

Laid low by the act of an assassin, the week-long struggle to save his life has been watched with keen solicitude not only by the people of this country, who raised him from their own ranks to the high office he filled, but by the people of all friendly nations, whose messages of sympathy, and hope, while hope was possible, have been most consolatory in this time of sore trial.

Now that the end has come, I request you to be the medium of communicating the sad tidings to the government of the honored nation you so worthily represent, and to announce that, in obedience to the prescription of the Constitution the office of President has devolved upon Theodore Roosevelt, Vice-President of the United States.

Accept, sir, the renewed assurance of my highest consideration.

John Hay

Shaken by the earlier news of the assassination attempt, then encouraged like the American people by the sanguinary reports of the President's recovery, the rulers of Europe received the news with horror mingled with sorrow. Deeply affected, the German Kaiser at Danzig hastily ordered the German royal navy at half-mast, then cabled Secretary Hay expressing the deepest sympathy of the German people. In a more intimate message to the bereaved First Lady the Kaiser joined with the Kaiserin in an expression of sorrow "which you have suffered by the death of your beloved husband, felled by the ruthless hand of a murderer."

Across the channel, the London papers, reflecting the grief of the masses, bordered their editions in black; the English court by royal edict was swathed in mourning for seven days; the buildings and churches were hung in crepe; the Archbishop of Canterbury, the Lord Mayor of London, the Lord Chief Justice expressed the grief of a nation only then emerging from their own sorrow at Queen Victoria's death.

As the British navy was ordered at half-mast, King Edward VII, then at Fredemborg, Denmark, cabled his sympathy to the President's widow.

In Rome, still saddened by the untimely death of King Humbert, the Pope, after suspending all audiences, knelt in prayer while the Dowager Queen Margherita confessed that Mrs. McKinley was "constantly in my thoughts and prayers."

No less stricken was France, whose President Emile Loubet conceded the "deep pain" he felt at McKinley's succumbing. In a cable to the First Lady he sympathized "in the calamity which thus strikes at your deepest affection, and which bereaves the great American nation of a President so justly respected and loved."

In an age unabashedly sentimental McKinley's own countrymen, forgetful of his shortcomings and failures, wept openly in the streets as bells tolled the sad news across rivers, farmlands, mountains, and prairies.

At about 12:00 noon after Coroner Wilson had granted permission officially, Dr. Harvey B. Gaylord and Dr. Herman G. Matzinger of the State Pathological Laboratory began work on the autopsy in the presence of the district attorney and the doctors who had attended the President—to determine, if possible, the cause of death so entirely unexpected up to a few hours of its occurrence.

Between two and three hours of probing failed to disclose the second bullet. Further search was halted at the request of the McKinley family, who wished there to be no undue mutilation of the President's body. Its location, however, was still considered unimportant.

The official report states:

"The bullet which struck over the breastbone did not pass through the skin, and did little harm.

"The other bullet passed through both walls of the stomach near its lower border. Both holes were found to be perfectly closed by the stitches, but the tissues around each hole had become gangrenous. After passing through the stomach the bullet passed into the back walls of the abdomen, hitting and tearing the upper end of the kidney. This portion of the bullet track was also gangrenous, the gangrene involving the pancreas. The bullet has not been found.

"There was no sign of peritonitis or disease of other organs. The heart walls were very thin, and there was no evidence of any attempt at repair on the part of nature, and death resulted from the gangrene, which affected the stomach around the bullet wounds as well as the tissues around the further course of the bullet. Death was unavoidable by any surgical or medical treatment, and was the direct result of the bullet wound."

The report bore the signatures of Drs. Gaylord, Matzinger, Rixey, Mann, Mynter, Park, Wasdin, as well as Dr. Charles G. Stockton, who had been added to the staff on Thursday, and Dr. Edward G. Janeway, of New York, and Dr. W. W. Johnson of Washington, who had been sent for on Friday. Other witnesses who signed the report were Dr. Charles Carey, Dr. W. P. Kendall, Dr. Edward L. Munson, and Dr. Hermanus L. Baer, Abner McKinley's son-in-law.

19

"For the Peace and Prosperity and Honor

of Our Beloved Country"

FOG CLUNG TO THE MOUNTAIN RAVINES, rolling up and obliterating the narrow passes, obscuring vision and making travel a hazard that only a daring or foolhardy man would attempt. Rain and wind swept down in mad gusts along the mountains, pelting the two-seated surrey that plunged forward, almost capsizing as it whirled through mud and water. The big black carriage horses, as though conscious of the drama of this night, strained and headed for North Creek, 16 miles down the half-inundated road. A snap of the whip. Another. Driver Mike Cronin wasn't sparing the horses tonight. As they hurtled along the precipitous road, the driver shouted to the passenger, only half visible in the seat beside him, "Shall I slow up?"

Cronin heard his passenger, Vice President Roosevelt, shout back, "Not at all; push ahead. If you are not afraid I am not."

This was the last leg of Roosevelt's wild all-night ride to North Creek on the night of September 13, 1901. Satisfied that the President was on the way to recovery, Roosevelt had left Buffalo on September 12 and embarked on a mountain-climbing expedition. September 13 dawned dark and bleak with a murky drizzle wreathing Lake Colden, where the Roosevelt party was camping in preparation for its ascent that day of Mount Marcy. The day was foul. Even Roosevelt conceded that.

"I hate to drag you out in this weather," the Vice President told Guides Noah La Casse and Edward Dimmick.

The grizzled guides smiled. What was bad weather to them! Besides they knew that Roosevelt aspired on that day to reach at least the timberline, a point to which General U. S. Grant had

169

once climbed. Roosevelt, who years before had mastered the Matterhorn, found the going rough and the underfooting treacherous. However, three hours from the start he and his guides saw Lake Champlain and the St. Lawrence stretching beyond in the distance—cold, blue patches behind the lifting misty wreaths.

"Bully," was the Vice President's comment as he stood surveying the magnificent prospect before him. Minutes later his party started back, intending to lunch at Lake Tear of the Clouds, a small mountain lake that nestled dark and deep between Mounts Skylight and Marcy. The mountain-climbers were munching sandwiches when they saw Harrison Hall, a guide from the Tahawus Club, struggling his way up along the mountainside.

When Hall arrived he handed the Vice President a slip of paper. Those around Roosevelt stood silent as he read the message. Presently they heard him murmur, "Complicated, complicated," and then add, "I don't want to be President through a graveyard."

Was the impossible materializing? Were the vague premonitions that had haunted Hanna becoming a reality? There could be no doubt of the message; it was brief and clear. The President was dying. Roosevelt was summoned to Buffalo.

Three hours and fifteen minutes later the Vice President and his party tramped wearily into the Tahawus clubhouse. There Roosevelt crammed a few clothes into a valise, jumped aboard a buggy hitched to a big workhouse, and with David Hunter the club superintendent driving, he started out for the Tahawus Lower Works, ten miles away.

Besplattered with mud, the big bay pulled up to the Lower Works two hours later. Here, Orin Kellogg, a driver for the club, was waiting with a team hitched to a surrey for the second leg of the wild night ride. The men spoke little. Kellogg cracked the whip over the horses' flanks. The surrey creaked. Once as Kellogg urged the horses he heard Roosevelt mutter through his teeth, "If it had been I, he wouldn't have gotten away so easily. I think I'd have guzzled him."

At 2:15 the surrey splashed through the mud and water to Aiden Lair, where Cronin waited with a second surrey and a handsome pair of black Morgan carriage horses. North Creek lay sixteen miles away over tortuous back country roads, but Cronin and the horses had traveled them often and knew every inch of the way. As they roared into their destination at 4:45, the Vice President bounded from the still moving surrey onto the steps of a waiting Delaware & Hudson train. The tracks were cleared. The train sped on through heavy veils of fog, switching at 7:56 in Albany to a New York Central track. Loeb was waiting. He handed Roosevelt a sheaf of telegrams.

Engine 908, piloted by Engineer Frank Bishop, raced through Amsterdam at 8:45, Utica at 9:41, Rome fifteen minutes later, reaching Syracuse at 10:40.

Enroute, Roosevelt refused to see any visitors.

During the morning of September 14 Buffalo police, as well as railroad authorities, were trying to shroud in secrecy the time and place of the Vice-President's arrival. The first tipoff came shortly after 1:00 P.M. when a squad of police was detailed to keep the crowds moving along Franklin and Erie Streets. This move, however, did not excite undue suspicion at first since it was thought that the police were apprehensive about protecting Czolgosz, who was thought to be at Police Headquarters nearby.

At 1:20 the detail was increased. At the same time Colonel Chapin appeared in full regalia; he stood in front of Headquarters, talking with General Welch and Bull. Presently Ansley Wilcox and George L. Williams drew up in their carriages. They were followed by a detail of mounted police.

Police pushed back the crowd around Headquarters, then cleared an area at the nearby small Terrace railroad station, so that the Wilcox and Williams carriages and an automobile could swing into position near the railroad tracks.

The area had hardly been cleared before puffs of smoke and a shrill locomotive whistle proclaimed the arrival of a train, and the crowd buzzed with conjecture as it chugged slowly into the station. The train consisted of a day coach, a Pullman car inscribed *Oldenburg*, and a third coach marked 200. As it rolled to a clanking stop, a New York Central detective appeared on the rear platform. Behind him was a muscular, broad-shouldered man weighing about 200 pounds. He wore a wrinkled gray overcoat and looked tired and careworn. His usual smile and ebullience were gone. He glanced along the tracks, paused a moment, then rapidly descended from the train, followed closely by his private secretary, William Loeb, and the detectives. The crowd needed no introduction. That face and the man behind it were famous. The crowd whooped, "Hurrah for Teddy Roosevelt!"

Roosevelt swung about, fixing the crowd with a stern eye. The cheering stopped. He walked rapidly to the carriages. Two boys were brushed aside as Roosevelt entered the Williams carriage with its owner and Wilcox. "Now which is the closest way?" he asked Wilcox.

"Straight ahead to my house," Wilcox replied.

The carriages, the second carrying the detectives and Loeb, were about to swing down the street when Patrolman Anthony Gavin, a former Rough Rider, stuck his hand through the open carriage window. "Mr. Roosevelt, will you shake hands with me?"

"Why, hello, Tony—glad to see you," answered Roosevelt, extending his hand.

Reporters were brushed off with the terse comment, "Nothing to say!" And the carriages were off at such a smart clip that the cavalry escort had to gallop to catch up.

Along Delaware Avenue near North Street throngs had gathered until approximately 5000 were milling about the Wilcox house as the small cavalcade pulled up.

At Wilcox's Roosevelt was to be served lunch, then wait there for further suggestions. However, he waited for neither, but decided to go at once to Milburn's and convey his sympathy to Mrs. McKinley.

Roosevelt had left the Adirondacks so precipitately that he had forgotten his hat; he was able to borrow a silk hat from Scatcherd. Wearing the borrowed hat and a coat lent him by Wilcox, Roosevelt was about to depart for Milburn's when he spotted the Signal Corpsmen forming a cordon through which his carriage was to pass. He called to Colonel Chapin, "Colonel, tell your men that I don't want an escort. I only need two men—two policemen will do. I desire the military escort to remain here."

Brushing aside any further formality, Roosevelt leaned from the carriage window and ordered the coachman, "Go ahead!" The coachman flicked his whip. The carriage lurched forward a few feet; then Roosevelt again poked his head from the window. He had heard the rattle of hoofs. This time it was a detail of mounted police.

"Hold on!" he ordered the coachman. Then he summoned the police sergeant in charge of the mounted escort. "Sergeant," snapped Roosevelt, "I don't want an escort." The sergeant saluted as the carriage moved away.

It was at first thought that Roosevelt might take the Presidential oath at Milburn's, but a consultation of cabinet members, following his brief call upon the First Lady, resulted in the choice of the Wilcox house as a more appropriate setting under the circumstances. Emerging from Milburn's, Roosevelt touched Root's arm. "Let's take a walk. It will do us both good," he suggested to his friend.

Noting plain clothesmen in their wake, the Vice President told Root to dismiss them. "We don't need any protection."

The question now arose as to the protocol to be followed in administering the Presidential oath. Root suggested that two decades before some one must have looked up the procedure when Arthur was sworn in after Garfield's assassination. Accordingly, Milburn sent Captain Babcock to the Buffalo library to check the files of the *New York Herald* for 1881, and, as Babcock later recalled, "I imagine that procedure was followed."

By 3:00 P.M. Roosevelt was back at the home of his host. Presently, the members of the cabinet began to arrive and congregate in the library, where the Vice President chatted with them informally. There had been no time to issue invitations, so that besides the half-dozen cabinet members then in the city and members of the Wilcox family, there were present only a few close associates. Wilcox later recalled that the library where the ceremony took place was not large and that it was far from full, so at the last moment all of the newspapermen who wished to attend were allowed to do so. However, no photographs were permitted.

At 3:30 P.M. a hush fell over the book-lined, low-ceilinged room where 43 persons now waited breathlessly for the 26th President of the United States to be inducted into office. Roosevelt was pale. His powerful shoulders were thrust back and his head was held erect. Some who stood close by thought they detected that his eyes were misty behind his gold-rimmed spectacles. He wore Wilcox's gray frock coat, and gray pin-striped trousers. He toyed nervously with his gold watch chain.

At exactly 3:32 Secretary of War Root began the solemn ceremony. "Mr. Vice President, I——," he began, but here the Secretary's voice faltered and tears began to trickle down his face. His lips quivered. He paused for fully two minutes—overcome by emotion.

With obvious effort he regained his composure and began again: "I have been requested on behalf of the cabinet of the late President, at least those who are present in Buffalo, all except two, to request that for reasons of weight affecting the affairs of government, you should proceed to take the constitutional oath of office of President of the United States."

Root had been selected to present the formal request because he was the ranking cabinet member then in the city in the absence of Secretaries Hay and Gage. Also, he was an old and intimate friend of Roosevelt and one of his chief advisors.

Roosevelt was extremely nervous. He tugged at the lapel of his coat. His voice quavered, but then grew firmer as he replied, "I shall take the oath at once in accordance with your request and in this hour of deep and terrible bereavement I wish to state it shall be my aim to continue absolutely unbroken the policy of President McKinley for the peace and prosperity and honor of our beloved country."

Roosevelt moved a few steps toward the bay window on the south side of the room. United States District Judge John R. Hazel asked Roosevelt to raise his right hand. As the jurist read the oath, Roosevelt repeated it after him a few words at a time, ending, ". . . and this I swear."

The President, the youngest ever to take office, then signed the oath which was typewritten on a sheet of ordinary legal cap. He then announced that the present cabinet members were to remain in office and shook hands with those in the room, including the United States Senator from New York State, Chauncey M. Depew.

Just as the ceremony ended Senator Hanna entered the house. He showed the effects of great strain and suffering. His face was gray and deeply furrowed. He leaned heavily on his cane.

The President extended his hand, and said, "How do you do, Senator?"

Hanna's voice shook. "Mr. President, I wish you success and a prosperous administration. I trust you will command me if I can be of service."

The whole ceremony had lasted only half an hour. The small company then dispersed, leaving the cabinet officers with Roosevelt, who held an informal session in the library.

Later, Wilcox was to recall, "I was asked to produce the 'Letters and Speeches of the Presidents'—the volume containing a proclamation by President Arthur of the death of President Garfield, and did so. This was considered in the cabinet meeting, which only lasted a few minutes.

"After this meeting, the President took a walk with Mr. Root and then returned to the house, drafted his proclamation of the death of President McKinley, and appointed Thursday, September 19, a day of national mourning. This was issued to the press that evening."

Roosevelt drafted his proclamation in the Wilcox morning room, which he used as an office during his stay. The original copy on yellow legal cap was written in pencil. A few lines were rewritten and some words crossed out, but generally it remained as first composed. Loeb made a clean copy and sent it to Cortelyou at the Milburn house. The original draft, retrieved from the wastebasket, was presented to Wilcox.

The ceremony, so hastily improvised, had gone off smoothly with one possible exception. Unaccountably, some of the newspaper accounts had omitted the word "honor" from the phrase "for the peace, prosperity, and honor of our beloved country" in Roosevelt's brief acceptance speech. This caused him much concern. He had, he told Wilcox, intended to give that word special emphasis.

Later, H. H. Kohlsaat, the Chicago publisher, claimed to have discussed with the new Chief Executive a possible cabinet shakeup, despite earlier promises to the contrary.

"I am going to let John Hay go and appoint Elihu Root as Secretary of State," Kohlsaat quoted Roosevelt as saying. "I am going to ask Lyman Gage for his resignation."

The publisher objected, "John Hay is a warm friend of mine. . . . What have you got against Lyman Gage?"

Kohlsaat further reminded the new President of his recent statement that he would keep the McKinley cabinet intact. "Saturday, the stock exchanges of the country closed when the news came of McKinley's death. Today's papers report there is a great uneasiness as to what will happen when they open tomorrow. Why? Because you are considered a bucking bronco in finance and now you propose to let Gage out of the Treasury Department and Heaven knows whom you will appoint. It will probably cause a panic, and it will be known for all times as the 'Roosevelt panic.' "

Roosevelt promised to reconsider his decision. "Old man," Roosevelt later confided to the publisher, "I'm going to keep both of them."

20

"We Mourn Our Loss"

ON THE MORNING of September 15 companies of the 65th and 74th National Guard, a platoon of Marines, sailors from the U.S. Frigate *Michigan*, and a company of 14th regulars from Ft. Porter wheeled into position opposite the Milburn house, ready to march in the first of three funeral ceremonies, which were to be conducted in Buffalo, Washington, and Canton, for the martyred President.

Shortly before 11:00 A.M. a heavily fringed hearse, draped with black hammercloth, equipped with silver-plated carriage lamps and drawn by four coal black Flemish horses, came to a halt before the house. An armed escort of soldiers and sailors, as well as five members of the U.S. Hospital Corps, surrounded the hearse.

The scene was one of gloom. Sorrow was etched upon the faces of cabinet members as they stepped from carriages and entered the house. Secretary Long, as if he had forgotten the date, was wearing a straw hat. Root looked careworn.

Presently, a carriage drew to the curb, and General Dan Sickles, who had lost a leg at the battle of Gettysburg, hobbled up the walk on crutches. A group, including the Governor of New York State, Benjamin B. Odell, stood on the lawn talking in whispers when at two minutes to eleven the Wilcox carriage arrived. The new President, who had spent the night at Wilcox's, stepped out, raising his high silk hat as he moved briskly to the ivy-covered front porch. As he reached the house, Roosevelt turned to his right and entered a large hall leading to the spacious oblong-shaped drawing room where McKinley lay. The upper part of the massive mahogany coffin (one selected by Senator Hanna) had been removed; an American flag was draped over the lower part, on which rested masses of white and purple asters inter-

177

mingled with roses. The President's head rested upon a pillow of tufted white satin; his left hand lay across his breast; his features were shrunken, yellowish and parchment-like and bore the signs of suffering. He was dressed in black and a small G.A.R. button gleamed from his coat lapel.

Senator Hanna and members of the McKinley cabinet were clustered about the casket when Roosevelt entered the room at one minute to eleven. The new President's face was grim. His mouth twitched nervously as he stood for a long moment looking at the body of his martyred predecessor. Then he whispered to Secretary Long, apparently asking that proper cabinet procedure be followed. Root stepped forward to replace Long. Back of Root, Smith took up his position to be followed by Long, Knox, Hitchcock, and Wilson.

As soon as these arrangements had been completed, the Rev. Dr. Charles Edmund Locke of the Delaware Avenue Methodist Episcopal Church of Buffalo, the son of McKinley's former pastor in Canton, entered the room. Dr. Locke took a position near a door leading to the outer hall, so his voice might be heard distinctly by the First Lady, who along with Dr. Rixey, Mrs. Barber, Miss Barber, and Mrs. Garret A. Hobart, was seated at the head of the stairs leading into the hall.

As the First Presbyterian Church quartet from the Milburn living room began to sing softly the verses of "Lead, Kindly Light," emotion overcame most of those in the room, for it was known to be one of McKinley's favorite hymns.

Dr. Locke then read the entire 15th chapter of I Corinthians. The quartet sang a second favorite hymn, "Nearer, My God, to Thee," even more intimately associated with the late President. A prayer and the benediction by Dr. Locke closed the 25-minute service.

During the moment's lull that followed, while President Roosevelt and the cabinet still stood beside the coffin, the tall man next to Governor Odell arose and walked slowly across the room. Senator Hanna seemed suddenly to have grown old as with bowed head and hands clasped behind his back, he gazed silently and tearfully at his dead friend. He had not been able to do so before; now it was time for a farewell. After he had resumed his seat, soldiers and sailors raised the coffin gently and carried it outside to the waiting hearse. They were followed by President Roosevelt and the cabinet. As the coffin was lifted into the hearse, the 65th band, stationed across the avenue, began softly to play "Nearer, My God, to Thee."

Roosevelt, along with Root, Smith, and Knox, entered the first carriage; Wilson, Hitchcock, Long, and Cortelyou took seats in the second; General Brooke entered the third carriage and Dr. Locke and his wife the fourth.

The hearse, next in line, was surrounded by a detail of G.A.R. veterans and followed by units of soldiers, sailors, and marines.

Mrs. McKinley had granted permission for the President's body to lie in state in the concourse of the City Hall during the day, but had exacted the promise that it be returned to Milburn's by 6:00 P.M.

Overnight thousands had poured into the city; now they swelled the throngs that swarmed about City Hall and lined Delaware Avenue, seven, eight, and ten deep. Some of the crowd wore badges bearing the President's picture and the inscription "We mourn our loss." Fortunately, it was Sunday, so that no vendors could mar the dignity of the occasion by hawking more such baubles along the line of march.

The procession began to move slowly from the area in front of the Milburn house along Delaware Avenue toward the downtown section of the city two miles to the south. As the cortege inched its way down the avenue at a mile-an-hour pace, clouds thickened overhead and a few drops of rain began to fall.

Black, white, and purple crepe streamers and "washed out" Exposition flags, limp from earlier rains, hung disconsolately from many of the downtown buildings. Decorators had toiled for hours to drape black bunting about the outside as well as the inside of City Hall. However, during the night the rain had swept loose much of the outside drapery. By an odd circumstance a part of it had become enmeshed in one of the faces of the tower clock, causing its hands to stop at 2:15, the same time that the President had died on the previous day.

Before dawn long lines had started to queue up in front of the gray stone City Hall, which covered an entire block between lower Delaware Avenue and Franklin Street. By the time of the arrival of the hearse the crowd, packed solidly behind the rope barriers, numbered some 150,000 persons. At 1:00 the strains of Chopin's Funeral March heralded the approach of the cortege. At Eagle Street the procession turned left off Delaware Avenue, then right into Franklin Street, halting before the city hall's main entrance.

At this moment masses of clouds, which had hitherto given only tentative suggestions of a shower, opened and gusts of torrential rain swept the large square. Among the crowd there was no wavering. Umbrellas by the hundreds arose like glistening black mushrooms. Thousands, unprotected, were waiting, drenched to the skin and shivering, but held there transfixed by the mournful obsequies.

Along the line, here and there, stood men with empty sleeves and others who hobbled on crutches or canes—veterans of the days of the Civil War. They remembered the death of Lincoln, the days of sorrow which then had gripped the war-sated nation. They, and others too, could recall that day in 1865 when the Engine *Dean Richmond* had pulled into Buffalo, its headlights swathed in flags, its cowcatcher adorned with two large portraits of the martyred Abe. The city had been jammed then as it was now. One of the reception committee, ex-President Millard Fillmore, had been jeered for his failure to drape his house in mourning. Lincoln's body, enroute to his Illinois home, had lain in state in St. James' Hall, the light from a giant chandelier playing over the dead man's rugged features. On that occasion ladies had entered one door and gentlemen the other to file past Lincoln's coffin in separate lines.

Nine years later in 1874, Fillmore himself lay in state in St. Paul's Episcopal Cathedral, just around the corner from City Hall.

In considering parallel cases, historians exhumed another strange coincidence regarding the three assassinated Presidents; namely that Friday had been a black day for all of them. Lincoln had been shot on Good Friday in 1865; McKinley on Friday, September 6, 1901; and Garfield had died on Friday, September 19, 1881.

As the carriage carrying Theodore Roosevelt pulled into Franklin Street, the horses reared up and might have plunged into the crowd, but for an alert policeman who caught the bridles and steadied them.

Once the excitement subsided the military bearers lifted the coffin and bore it up the steps of City Hall. Roosevelt, under an umbrella held by Secret Service man Foster and followed by members of the cabinet, proceeded to the rotunda, which like every other part of the building was draped in black and white bunting.

Inside, the broad hall running east and west is intersected by a narrower corridor which runs north and south, thus forming a cross. At the point of intersection, the coffin was now placed upon a low sloping black-draped platform and was raised at its upper end to face the east. Thick masses of flowers banked the corridors; from the dome overhead four American flags were suspended to form a cross above the coffin.

Roosevelt and the members of the cabinet took up a position to the coffin's right. To Roosevelt's left stood Knox, Long, and Wilson and across from him stood Root, Hitchcock, and Cortelyou.

No sooner had Roosevelt and his cabinet reached their positions than the bearers lowered McKinley's coffin and removed its lid.

Then the new President and his cabinet filed past, departing by the west entrance. They were followed by Senators Hanna and Fairbanks and other high ranking officials. A moment later began the steady, monotonous shuffling of feet along the marble floor of the corridor. Two lines of people approached, one from Eagle Street on the north, and the other from Church Street on the south. Mounting the steps, they passed through the two front entrances, converging upon the coffin two abreast, then moved out of the building, as had President Roosevelt, at the west entrance.

Sobs rose from the passing lines. Some spoke to the corpse. Still others muttered curses and imprecations upon the assassin's head. Small children were lifted up to view what was meant to become a life-time memory—a dead President lying in state. Toward late afternoon a giant Negro paused before the corpse. James B. Parker, who had done his mightiest to save McKinley's life, took a long look, then moved along, followed by other mourners— clerks, teamsters, high officials and Indians in full regalia, looking especially mournful in their sodden blankets and bedraggled feathers.

At sunset the sky cleared. Hours later the mourners were still filing past. Yielding to public demand, the First Lady had consented to permit the President's body to remain at City Hall.

Like wax figures in a tableau four guards stood inert and unflinching—at the head of the coffin, with rifle at attention, Sergeant Galway of the Seventh Infantry Regiment; at the foot, Chief Master-at-Arms Luze of the U.S. *Indiana,* his cutlass drawn and on his shoulder; on the right and left sides, A. D. Coburn, also from the *Indiana,* and Sergeant Gunther of the Fourteenth Infantry Regiment.

Within view of City Hall was the Terrace Station, scene of the ill-timed welcoming gun salute, which had, some felt, been a presage of the tragedy now consummated.

The funeral train moved out of Buffalo bound for Washington at 8:30 the following morning. A pilot engine preceded the train by 15 minutes in order to clear the tracks and avoid any delays. Favored by a bright, pleasant day, thousands banked the tracks, gazing in silence as the sable-draped chain of cars drawn by locomotives 27 and 408 moved southward. The President's casket rested within plain view in the observation car *Pacific.*

In its course through Western New York the train slackened speed at East Aurora in deference to a delegation of school children and G.A.R. veterans, then again at Arcade and Olean. At Port Allegany, Pennsylvania, townsfolk sought points of vantage on housetops, barn tops and tree tops. After a laborious climb up Keating's Ridge the train changed engines at Emporium Junction, then continued southward past villages and farmhouses many of them draped in black.

Within the train Dawes, like his fellow passengers, heard singing and the tolling of bells. "Poor Mrs. McKinley," Dawes wrote later, "was so bowed with grief that she could not bear to look out of her car window."

"Before the day was over everyone in the train was in a highly strained condition," Kohlsaat recalled. "Tears came easily. At Harrisburg, thousands of people in the depot shed were singing McKinley's last words. As we neared Washington darkness came on; the Negroes in Maryland lighted fires near the track. As the train passed we could see their dark forms in the glare of the burning brush."

As if the nation had not been drained of enough sorrow, it prepared for another day of obsequies. The capital city, which had twice cheered McKinley's triumphs, now prepared to take its leave of a Chief Executive beloved as no President since Lincoln.

Overnight the casket had rested in the center of the White House East room, guarded by a succession of Marines, soldiers, and sailors who stood watch over their martyred chief until dawn.

As day broke over the grief-stricken capital, rain poured from the skies, whipped across the city by an angry wind. The trees dripped with water. Rivulets ran along the glistening streets. Crowds massing behind the cables along Pennsylvania Avenue huddled under a sea of umbrellas. Sable streamers, limp and sodden, hung from buildings and down the gloomy vista of Pennsylvania Avenue. Above, swathed in mist, rose the dome of the Capitol. Again, bells knelled. Again, the strains of "Nearer, My God, to Thee," swelled in mournful cadences as the casket was borne from the White House to the glass-encased hearse. Six coal black horses, netted in black, and each held by a silk hatted Negro groom awaited as Major General John R. Brooke reigned up before the hearse. Then the procession began to advance slowly toward the Capitol, a mile and a half through the misty gloom.

Colorfully accoutred contingents of servicemen streamed from the cross streets to join the line of march—cavalrymen with sabres upraised; field artillerymen, mounted or astride their horse-drawn guns; engineers; hospital corpsmen; Marines; and plumed naval officers. Down the broad avenue swept the cavalcade, plumes sodden in the rain, bayonets and sabres glistening. Legislators, justices, and diplomats mingled with others who had helped to make the country's history during the decades of the past, in politics, in business, in war—among them, former President Cleveland, Senators Cullom, Depew, and Platt, Admiral Dewey, Congressman Cannon, J. P. Morgan, Generals Longstreet and Fitzhugh Lee.

At 10:12 the procession reached the undraped Capitol. The casket was carried to the rotunda and placed upon the catafalque, which stood within a circle of 700 seats, widening out like ripples in a pool. At 11:00 A.M., the same hour when the Buffalo services had begun, a hush fell over the room. Then the choir softly sang "Lead, Kindly Light," while all stood. At the conclusion of the hymn the Rev. Dr. Henry R. Naylor, presiding elder of the Washington District M.E. Church, delivered the invocation. Bishop Edward G. Andrews, of the Methodist Episcopal Church, had come from Ohio to say the last words over the remains of his lifelong friend and parishioner. As the bishop concluded, those in the vast rotunda joined the choir in "Nearer, My God, to Thee," after which the Rev. Dr. W. H. Chapman, acting pastor of the Metropolitan Church, pronounced the benediction. The service now over, thousands outside who had waited for hours rushed for the door, brushing aside police. Horses and cabs were caught in the rush; women fainted; scores were trampled underfoot; several people who had suffered broken arms or other injuries were rushed to a hastily improvised hospital in the rotunda basement.

Once order was restored, the bronze doors swung back and crowds poured in, filing past the flag-draped casket until evening came.

Abraham Lincoln's body, 36 years before, had been placed aboard a train containing eight coaches, six reserved for mourners, one for the guard of honor and one for the casket. Drawn by the engine, *Edward J. Jones*, the train rolled out of the capital bound for Baltimore, lumbering through York, Harrisburg, Philadelphia, New York City, Albany and half a score of other cities before it reached Springfield. The progress of McKinley's body to its final resting place was somewhat less morbidly prolonged, yet the route planned would touch some of the same cities. Despite the outpouring of grief, despite the hymns of sorrow that swelled the length and breadth of the land, despite the millions who had prayed and thousands who had already viewed the corpse, there remained thousands more who wished to pay final homage to the President's body as it was borne back to Canton.

A light rain was still falling as the hearse with the 11th Cavalry escorting it wound through the silent streets of the capital to the station. The casket was again placed abroad the observation car, now illuminated so that it could be clearly visible for those who stood along the tracks waiting in the darkness.

Far into the Washington suburbs crowds flanked the tracks to glimpse the illuminated casket as ghostlike it moved by. At Baltimore crowds swarmed the Union Station and spilled over onto the tracks. The train reached York, Pennsylvania, at 11:30 P.M., and changed its crew and engine at Harrisburg, then moved on to Altoona, Pittsburgh, and Allegheny. Dawn revealed mourners half hidden in the mist as the procession crossed the line into the President's home state, where even the humblest dwelling was draped in black.

The funeral train arrived in Canton shortly before noon on Wednesday, September 18, two weeks after the President in the full vigor of life had departed for Buffalo. Many who had cheered his departure now stood silently, appalled at the unbelievable conclusion to the excursion.

Thousands massed around the railroad station. Troop A of Cleveland, which had twice escorted McKinley from the White House to the Capitol, was drawn up, erect and motionless, outside the station. As the reception committee headed by Judge William R. Day, the late President's lifelong friend, looked on, the casket was removed from the funeral car. Then it was carried to the main corridor of the Stark County courthouse and placed so that the President's head faced the south entrance. The black cloth covering the courthouse walls and ceiling gave the interior of the building the appearance of an immense dimly lit vault. Again the casket rested upon a plain black catafalque surrounded by military guardsmen standing at attention while streams of visitors filed past.

As had been the case in Buffalo and in Washington, when the time came for the doors to be closed, a line blocks long was still waiting to enter. Before the coffin was removed to the McKinley residence it was closed for the last time.

At Mrs. McKinley's request the body was to remain in the North Market Street home until the final rites took place in the Methodist Church the next afternoon.

It was said that not even Queen Victoria's funeral in London a few months before had exceeded in impressiveness that of Mc-

Kinley's final rites in Canton. During the rain-drenched night 100,000 mourners poured into the city. Flowers from the crowned heads of Europe, as well as from every state in the union, were unloaded—eleven carloads in all. Confusion amidst sorrow reigned in the streets. As many as four bands gathered at one street corner; vendors swarmed the sidewalks, hawking their badges of mourning.

The morning dawned ominously, but as the day advanced the sun broke through promising more pleasant weather.

Many old friends of "The Major" and Mrs. McKinley gathered before the President's home. While no one was admitted inside, they were satisfied, it seemed, to gaze at the house, where crossed palm leaves held together by black and white ribbons were fastened to the right of the front door.

At 1:00 Cleveland's Troop A in black hussar uniforms, astride black horses, their flags bound in crepe, the insignia of mourning fluttering from their sabre hilts, swung into battalion formation facing the President's home. As the troop neared the house, President Roosevelt and his party moved up the walk to the entrance. Roosevelt was grave-faced and silent. Around him clustered cabinet members Gage, Root, Wilson, Hitchcock, and Smith, also Cortelyou and Assistant Secretary of State Hill, who represented Secretary Hay.

Ranged along the walk were the Army's high ranking generals: Lieutenant General Miles, Major Generals Brooke, Otis, and MacArthur, and Brigadier General Gillespie—and the Navy's chief figures: Rear Admiral Farquahar (representing Admiral Dewey, ranking head of the Navy), Rear Admirals Crowinshield and O'Neil.

Within the picket gate before the house stood a group of civilians: Governor Nash of Ohio, Henry B. MacFarland, president of the Commissioners of the District of Columbia, Mayor Diehl of Buffalo, Judge Day, and Milburn.

Now Troop A's long line of flashing sabres advanced to salute. At this moment the church bells began their deepening wail. A short service was just concluding within the McKinley home. Dr. Manchester had said a brief prayer while Mrs. McKinley, prostrated by grief and her long ordeal, listened from an adjoining room. She was not to attend the church services. Although she had wished to accompany her dearly loved husband's body to its final resting place, she had at last yielded to the urging of her relatives and Dr. Rixey. This was the time of the final parting. A double file of pallbearers raised the casket and carried it to the hearse.

Amidst a tolling of bells the mile-long procession started for the Methodist Church, moving under giant black arches and between solid banks of townspeople and visitors who packed the sidewalks and spilled over onto front lawns and porches.

The line swept on, past sobbing men and praying women, past maudlin signs that bore the inscriptions, "We Love Him" and "He Loves Us," past the courthouse, halting at last before the small granite church where the McKinleys had worshipped. Under lifted sabres the coffin was borne past President Roosevelt and cabinet members up the church steps, through the tunnel-like vestibule, under the draped nave, and, as the music of Beethoven's Grand Funeral March pulsated from the organ, placed upon a catafalque smothered in flowers.

In filed the mourners: the President, Senators, Congressmen, admirals, generals, diplomats, townspeople, and remnants of McKinley's regiment bearing aloft their torn battle flags. Only the McKinley pew, the fourth from the front of the church, remained vacant.

At 2:00 the Rev. O. B. Milligan, pastor of Canton's First Presbyterian Church, where the McKinleys had been married, rose and prayed. From the pulpit, Bible in hand, the Rev. Dr. John A. Hall, in a full, strong voice read the 19th Psalm, after which the Rev. E. P. Herburck read verses 41-58 of the 25th Chapter of First Corinthians.

Dr. C. E. Manchester, the President's Civil War companion in arms, delivered the funeral sermon. "Our President is dead," he began, then after a pause, "the silver cord is loosed, the gold bowl is broken, the pitcher is broken at the fountain, the wheel broken at the cistern, the mourners go about the streets.

"One voice is heard—the wail of sorrow from all the land; for the beauty of Israel is slain upon the high places. How are the mighty fallen."

For 24 minutes Dr. Manchester eulogized his old friend and "the people's friend."

After a prayer and the benediction the mourners moved on to Willow Lawn Cemetery, marching to the cadence of Chopin's Funeral March.

At 3:30 as cannons boomed and taps were sounded, the President's body was borne into the gigantic receiving vault in the family plot, situated at the crest of a gentle knoll overlooking the city he loved.

September 19, by President Roosevelt's proclamation, was designated a day of mourning throughout the country. During the hour of the funeral millions bowed reverently in the hushed silence of churches or places of business. Everywhere the Stars and Stripes hung at half-mast; buildings, private homes, and churches were draped with sable streamers. From thousands of pulpits preachers in the loftiest cathedrals and in the humblest chapels raised their voices in memorial services as choirs intoned President McKinley's favorite hymns.

A unique feature was the silencing of all telephones throughout the country for five minutes as the President's body was lowered to its last resting place.

Again the world joined in demonstrations of sorrow and respect. In Berlin, in St. Petersburg, in London, memorial services were held. Banks and the stock exchange in distant Bombay closed. The British embassy in Constantinople conducted a service of its own, and the guns of Gibraltar boomed forth a farewell salute.

21

"You Are Charged With the Crime
of Murder"

McKINLEY'S BATTLE FOR LIFE was over. Now society eagerly awaited the retribution that the state would certainly exact. There could be no doubt as to the end result, but the decorum and form upon which the law prides itself had first to be satisfied. The state made its initial move in this direction on September 16 with the convening of the Grand Jury.

Up to this time, Czolgosz had been held without counsel and without charge. This legal anomaly was explained, but only partially by District Attorney Penney on September 10, when a *Buffalo Express* reporter raised the question of the prisoner's arraignment.

"Has Czolgosz been arraigned?"

"He has not," answered Penney.

"Can you say approximately when he will be arraigned?"

The District Attorney's course of action was revealed in his reply: "We do not intend to arraign him until the results of the President's injuries are more fully determined."

The interview ended with a discussion of the possibility of the President's taking the stand against Czolgosz. The prosecutor explained that McKinley would not necessarily have to do so, adding, "Had the injuries to the President resulted fatally, we should have had to prove the facts without his testimony."

Penney did not explain why the prisoner had not been charged with felonious assault or possession of a dangerous weapon, either of which charge might have been placed and later superseded by a murder charge.

Since on September 10 McKinley appeared to be recovering

189

and the press and doctors were trumpeting the fact, the press began to stir up lively conjecture on the penalties that Czolgosz and any possible accomplices might face. "One of the best known lawyers in this part of the country," yet unidentified, when consulted by *The Express* answered in a prepared statement that the prisoner might draw a sentence of up to ten years, but this relatively light sentence could be augmented by assault charges laid by the Buffalo detectives with whom Czolgosz, armed with his revolver, had scuffled on the Temple floor.

As for Czolgosz's accomplices, the lawyer explained that their punishment would be the same as that prescribed for Czolgosz— death if the President were to die, and imprisonment not exceeding ten years if the President recovered.

The most notable case on record, he explained, where individuals not present but actually participating in the commission of a crime were convicted as principals was that of Spies and others (the Haymarket rioters) against the people, reported in Vol. 12, N.E. Rep. 865, known as the Anarchists' case. "The Illinois statutes under which the Anarchists' case arose are substantially the same as the New York Penal Code," he stated.

Actually on the night of September 13, when the President was known to be dying and police were successfully aborting all attempts of mob violence, Czolgosz was no longer at Police Headquarters, the focus of the mob's fury. Though it was not revealed until several days later, the prisoner had been secretly removed from his cell at Headquarters and was then in the Erie County Penitentiary on Trenton Avenue about a mile distant on the west side of the city.

Shortly before noon of that day (Friday, September 13) Chief Bull had telephoned C. W. Miller's livery stable on Huron Street and ordered a carriage to be sent around to the Headquarters entrance.

Czolgosz was brought up a rear stairway from his "dungeon" cell to the chief's office. As he entered, the prisoner managed a slight bow to Chief Bull and Assistant Chief Cusack, who alone was to be his escort during the transfer. He looked more presentable at this time than he had at any time since the shooting, for he wore a clean shirt, bought for him in the meantime.

Cusack put no handcuffs upon his charge, but showed him a

revolver, which he explained he would not hesitate to use if necessary. At Cusack's direction Czolgosz turned and started down the stairway with his sole guard about a foot behind him, a revolver in his pocket.

Out of the front entrance and onto the street the two moved inconspicuously. Passersby were unaware that the world's number one criminal was being so casually released from his close imprisonment of the past few days.

Two knots of men, in reality plain clothesmen, were chatting within twenty feet to the north and to the south of the waiting vehicle.

Cusack spoke to the driver after Czolgosz had preceded him into the carriage. "The man in there is Czolgosz who shot the President. You are to drive us to the Penitentiary. Do you want a revolver?"

"No, sir," the driver answered and hopped quickly on to the box.

Inside, Cusack threatened his charge, "You move and I'll kill you," as he held the revolver about three inches from Czolgosz's head. "You understand?"

Czolgosz continued his granite-like imperviousness. There was no response.

The horses trotted but were not driven with undue haste to the penitentiary.

Here the two emerged from the carriage and in the same manner in which they had departed from Superintendent Bull's office they entered that of Sheriff Caldwell, whose responsibility the prisoner had now become and would remain until the day of his indictment.

Since the proceedings of the Grand Jury were conducted without observers, voracious newspapermen covering the case had to content themselves by waiting outside the Grand Jury room, recording the names of witnesses called from among those subpoenaed, checking the time each spent in being queried, and speculating on the evidence that each was presenting.

The whole procedure was accomplished with the utmost expedition, for in four hours and 43 minutes, 28 witnesses had appeared, the revolver which had fired the fatal shot and the clothing worn by the President at the time of the shooting had been examined, and the statements to police made by the culprit at the time of his arrest had been presented.

Assisting District Attorney Penney were the members of his staff—Attorneys Sickman, Haller, Ticknor, and Hinkley.

During the morning session, which opened at 10:15 on Monday, September 16, the first witnesses to disappear into the jury room were Doctors Mynter, Gaylord, Matzinger, and Mann. As these were the medical men who had performed the operation and those who had performed the autopsy, presumably during the hour their testimony consumed (fifteen minutes each) the cause of death was well established.

There followed a series of actual witnesses to the crime. Why Secret Service man Albert Gallaher was selected rather than George Foster as the next witness is not entirely understandable, but he also was held for fifteen minutes.

The star witness of the morning was James L. Quackenbush, committee member, attorney and witness to the crime, whose cool presence of mind had prompted him within minutes after the shooting to order the Temple doors to be closed and to scan the crowd pressing toward the President for a possible accomplice. Quackenbush's evidence must have proved rewarding, for he was detained from 11:30 to 12:15, three times as long as each of the medical men, as well as Louis L. Babcock, who followed him.

Next was Major Alexander R. Robertson, assistant commandant of Exposition police in charge of the detail of Exposition policemen inside and outside the Temple on the afternoon of the fatal reception. From the inside detail of patrolmen, all of whom had been subpoenaed, only James and Westenfelder, as well as Captain Damer, would be called later in the day, although McCauley, Sullivan, Merkle, Warner, Dougherty, Smith, Mahoney, and Taylor were also in readiness to give their versions of the crime.

Major Robertson's evidence lasted only seven minutes and brought to a close the morning session of the Grand Jury, which recessed for dinner at 12:38.

The afternoon session reconvened at 2:00. However, for twenty minutes no witnesses were called.

Then in jig time twenty witnesses were ticked off within two

hours, no one person being detained for more than ten minutes.
First, H. F. Henshaw made a five minute appearance. The length
of time consumed by each of the five members of the 73rd Coast
Artillery who had been present at the Temple and witnesses of
the crime ranged from Fenenbaugh, one minute, to O'Brien, ten
minutes.

Of the scores of visitors possible to be chosen from those in the
Temple one E. C. Knapp, a medium-sized, middle-aged man,
described by the *Express* reporter as having a "thin sallow face,
black hair and mustache and wearing black clothes" was closeted
in the jury room for seven minutes.

Mrs. Van Dozen Davis, a Negress in charge of the toilet room
at the Temple, and James Branch, a Negro porter in the Temple
who had stood within twenty feet of the President, were the next
witnesses. A notable omission, however, was James Parker, whose
act of prowess on the Temple floor had been at first featured by
the press but was now coming under question.

The next three to make brief appearances were not witnesses
to the act itself but were obviously connected with the prisoner
immediately after he had been seized: Chief of Exposition detectives James Valelly, who made a three-minute appearance; Chief
Bull, a seven-minute one; and Assistant Chief Cusack, who was
on the stand for three minutes.

A string of eyewitnesses again was called, headed by Fred H.
Leiter, a timekeeper for the Exposition company. He was followed
by the Superintendent of the Temple, Charles J. Close. Then
came the Exposition policemen Westenfelder and James, and
police detectives Geary and Solomon. Geary had stood just to
the left and a little behind the President and had caught him as
he was about to fall. However, his partner, Solomon, gave the
longer testimony of the two—ten minutes.

A small, dark young man with a dark mustache and wearing
gold-rimmed spectacles awaited his turn to be called quite ap-
prehensively and refused to reveal his identity to newsmen. Police
officers respected his wishes and likewise refused to divulge his
name, although they said he was not an important witness.

"I have very good reasons for not wishing to be known in this
matter," he told an *Express* reporter. "I am a Buffalo man. I did
not see the shooting and my testimony is really unimportant—at

least I believe so and hope so. I don't expect to be called for the trial and so do not wish to have my name dragged into the case."

When this mystery witness had finished his seven-minute testimony, it was 4:10 and the prosecution had also concluded its presentation of the case to the Grand Jury. Penney, Haller, and Hinkley left the jury room and crossed the hall to the District Attorney's office. Chief Bull, who had remained in there after having given his testimony in the jury room, now appeared at the door of the office and beckoned to Detectives Geary and Solomon. They immediately left the building. Their mission was obvious.

Meanwhile Penney went on into the county court room on the same floor, where Judge Emery was waiting, having dismissed his trial witness in order to keep his court clear for the Czolgosz case.

In five minutes' time the Grand Jurors filed out of their room and into the County Court room. The clerk called the roll of the 21 jurors. Then Judge Emery asked, "Have you any report to make?"

Foreman Theodore Krehbiel arose and answered, "Yes, Your Honor, we have a partial report." He handed a three-page typewritten document to the judge.

Glancing at it briefly, Judge Emery nodded to the jury and said, "Gentlemen, you may be excused."

However, the jurors remained seated as Judge Emery passed the report to his clerk, who made a record of it. It was the indictment prepared by Penney. In order to cover the situation properly Penney had reverted to an antiquated form of indictment with more circumlocution and repetition than in the current form. Nevertheless, the first paragraph was relatively straightforward and simple: "The grand jury of the county of Erie by this indictment accuse Leon F. Czolgosz, alias Fred Nieman, of the crime of murder in the first degree. . . ."

Meanwhile, preparations were being made for Czolgosz's immediate arraignment. The police, in line with their previous policy of keeping Czolgosz hidden from public view as much as possible, had already removed him from the county penitentiary and had driven him to the jail, across the street from the City Hall. To avoid attention, Czolgosz was led through the "Tunnel of Sobs," a narrow subterranean passageway leading from the jail and under Delaware Avenue to the City Hall. The 300-foot tunnel, which *Leslie's Weekly* described as a "dank, reeking passage," was about six feet wide, nine feet high. It had been built in 1878 when the jail was constructed.

The police took no chances on Czolgosz's escape, or a possible lynching. Burly Captain Regan, commanding a squad of policemen, joined the prisoner's escort in the passage through the tunnel.

At 5:35, Czolgosz reached the City Hall basement. Spectators noted that he was wedged between Detectives Geary and Solomon and handcuffed to the latter with Cusack forming a rear guard.

As Czolgosz reached the first floor, he was confronted by a huge pillar swathed in black and white crepe. Those around him were amazed when he passed the signs of mourning with no display of emotion. His head was bent and his eyes fixed on the floor. The escort led him eastward to the foot of the north staircase leading to the second floor, passing enroute a few feet from the place where less than twelve hours before his victim's body had lain in state.

A reporter noted: "The detectives spurned the elevators for they wanted to get the prisoner to the court as obscurely as possible." A spectator described the prisoner as "hatless, mussy-haired and somewhat slovenly in his gait." As the prisoner was about to enter the court, Regan and his detail formed a barricade to prevent others from entering the courtroom. The prisoner was hustled along and taken inside the railing before Judge Emery. At this point, Penney chided an attorney who was attempting to photograph Czolgosz.

The prisoner stood sullenly before the bench, oblivious to his surroundings and the fact that Detective Solomon was having difficulty in removing his handcuffs. His face looked thinner than newspaper photographs had shown. Since his own clothes had been torn to shreds, he was wearing a borrowed coat of bluish striped material and trousers of the same color but of different pattern. He wore a laydown linen collar but no tie. Geary stood nearby, holding Czolgosz's light brown felt hat, which had fallen off during the passage through the tunnel. The prisoner's trousers were not fully buttoned and his shoes unlaced. He looked like a man who had dressed hastily.

When the handcuffs had been removed after a five-minute

struggle, Penney addressed the prisoner, asking, "Czolgosz, have you got a lawyer?"

The prisoner stared at the prosecutor and shook his head almost imperceptibly. His lips were parted as if to speak, but he said nothing.

The district attorney repeated his question more sharply, but the prisoner did not blink an eye.

"Czolgosz, you have been indicted for murder in the first degree. Do you want counsel to defend you?"

Chief Cusack shook the prisoner, urging him to speak up.

"Do the officers know whether or not this defendant has any counsel?" demanded the court.

"No, sir," said Chief Cusack, and Detectives Geary and Solomon shook their heads.

Judge Emery, addressing himself to Czolgosz, then said: "Czolgosz, you have appeared for arraignment in the court without counsel. The law makes it the duty of the court to assign counsel for you. The Bar Association of our county has considered the matter and has suggested the names of certain men of high character for such assignment. The court has seriously considered the question and after such consideration has concluded to follow the suggestions made by the association. The court, therefore, assigns the Hon. Loran L. Lewis and the Hon. Robert C. Titus as your counsel."

The prisoner showed no emotion, only an icy calm. His eyes were glued to the floor. He remained silent.

The judge addressed himself to the officers. "The officers," he said, "will notify Judge Lewis and Judge Titus of their assignment."

"I'll do that, Your Honor, or have done it," answered Penney.

The district attorney at this point signaled the officers, who handcuffed the prisoner and hurried him out of the courtroom. Captain Regan's squad moved into action, screening the defendant from onrushing spectators.

The prisoner had been in court slightly more than ten minutes. Now he was led back through the "Tunnel of Sobs" and incarcerated in a third floor cell of the jail, described as "well fortified." Patrolman James Mahoney of the First Precinct and two deputy sheriffs were assigned to guard detail.

There were various reactions to Czolgosz's strange actions while in court. Chief of Detectives Cusack felt that the prisoner was feigning insanity, recalling that before he had entered the "Tunnel of Sobs," he had been chatting freely with his escort, but as soon as he reached the City Hall he became "a clam."

"No," said Cusack," he is not insane. He is shrewder than some persons give him credit for."

Penney dismissed the idea that Czolgosz had been "doped" in order to obtain further information from him. "It seems to be purely a case of stubbornness. He has had several stubborn fits before during his confinement while under examination."

Assistant District Attorney Haller thought that Czolgosz's behavior was typically that of an Anarchist, taught to "preserve a stolid silence until it becomes apparent that there is no hope of avoiding the death penalty, then to get up in court . . . and say 'Long Live Anarchy!' and rant about the principles of that doctrine."

Emery had named Titus and Lewis at the suggestion of the Erie County Bar Association.

"We deem it of the utmost importance," Adelbert Moot, president of the association, had written, "that the counsel assigned shall be of such experience and of such a high sense of their professional obligations that the highest traditions of the profession shall be upheld and that the trial shall be dignified, just and impartial, . . . we respectfully suggest, that the Hon. Loran L. Lewis and the Hon. Robert C. Titus, former justices of the Supreme Court of the State of New York be assigned as counsel, and be requested to act."

Moot added that neither attorney had yet been consulted.

While the two attorneys were to be given a "choice," in reality they had practically no alternative but to accept or place themselves in a position of being fined by the court, though such a course was unlikely.

The pair chosen to defend Czolgosz were both beyond the prime of life. While both had served as Supreme Court justices, it had been years since either had appeared as a trial lawyer. Titus first learned of his assignment while attending a Masonic convention in Milwaukee and made no effort to conceal his repugnance at the idea.

"I can't understand why I have been selected for this unpleasant duty," he remarked. "I am very much depressed by the announcement. He should be defended by one of his own kind—an anarchist," then added hopefully that his reported assignment might be a mistake.

Lewis was no more enthusiastic, but he consented to appear for the prisoner's arraignment before Judge Emery on the following day.

Czolgosz was led through the tunnel to the jail, as he had been on the previous day. When he neared the basement of City Hall and noted spectators who formed a gauntlet through which he and his escort had to move, he reacted much as he had on the first occasion—he bent his head and lowered his eyes. Quite evidently he realized the potential force of the crowd, for he cringed at sight of it.

On Czolgosz's arrival at the courtroom Judge Emery was in the midst of a jury trial, in which Patrick J. McMahon was bringing an action for more salary from a grain shovelers' union. Judge Emery immediately suspended the action and turned his attention to Czolgosz. Meanwhile, Penney, Judge Lewis, his son, Loran L., Jr., Quackenbush, and other Buffalo lawyers, as well as Sheriff Caldwell, had gathered inside the railing.

Penney, holding in his hand the indictment, addressed the prisoner, "Leon Czolgosz, you have been indicted by the grand jury of this county for the crime of murder in the first degree." The prosecutor then droned through the lengthy indictment, and as he ended, asked, "How do you plead?"

The defendant was silent.

"Do you understand what I have read to you?"

Since few would have been able to comprehend the labyrinth of words through which the prosecutor had just waded, it is not surprising that Czolgosz gave no indication that he understood it.

The exasperated prosecutor asked sharply, "Czolgosz, do you hear me? Do you understand that you are charged with the crime of murder in the first degree?"

The prisoner stuck out his tongue to moisten his dry lips but made no reply.

"You can say 'yes' or 'no'," said Penney.

The defendant took neither choice.

At this point Judge Lewis arose and addressed the court: "Your honor has designated Justice Titus and myself to defend this defendant. I have called upon the prisoner and have not been able to ascertain any wish upon his part as to the employment of counsel. Justice Titus is out of town. A dispatch has been sent to him and I appear here informally to enter the plea of not guilty for the defendant, the law requiring that such a plea should be entered under these circumstances. I reserve the right, however, after consultation with Justice Titus, if after such consultation we conclude not to make an application for the designation of other counsel, to withdraw the plea of not guilty and interpose, if it is thought advisable, another plea in the case, in the way of a demurrer to the indictment or whatever it may be.

"I learned only this morning of my designation and regret my name has been named to attend upon this trial, for, as Your Honor well knows, I have been out of practice for some considerable time. Reserving this right to change the plea, if it is thought advisable, I enter the plea of not guilty."

The district attorney then advised the court that he intended to move the transmission of the indictment to the Supreme Court and intended to serve notice for trial on the ensuing Monday.

Lewis acquiesced, then said, "There is one other remark that perhaps I ought to make. I am informed by the district attorney that some eminent physicians, alienists, have had interviews with the defendant, and who will perhaps be called as witnesses. After consulting with my associate, if we continue in the case, it might be deemed advisable to consult other alienists, and if so, I would like an order of the court permitting such consultation."

"I have already told Mr. Lewis I would grant him every favor that he deemed advisable in that direction," said Penney.

"The trial court will undoubtedly grant any order you desire in that regard," said Judge Emery.

"Take the prisoner away," ordered the district attorney.

Detectives Geary and Solomon obeyed his instructions.

When Lewis spoke of the alienists called by the district attorney, he was referring to Drs. Floyd S. Crego, professor of Insanity and Brain Diseases at the University of Buffalo, James W. Putnam, professor of Nervous Diseases at the same university, and

Joseph Fowler, police surgeon. These local experts had already made several examinations of the prisoner, their first being within a few hours of the shooting.

Like others who had heard his confession at that time, the doctors found Czolgosz communicative and ready to discuss his motive for the crime. On this occasion Dr. Crego had taken measurements of his head and eyes and made a general physical examination.

The next day, September 8, Czolgosz had repeated substantially what he had said the day before. He appeared fastidious about his clothing, expressing indignation at not having been able to change it since his arrival, and refused to reenact his crime with his own soiled handkerchief. Given a clean one, however, he was perfectly willing to demonstrate for them his method of concealing his weapon.

There had been a change on their third consecutive day's examination, for now he refused to admit he had shot the President until the end of the interview when he capitulated, saying, "I am glad I did it." Subsequently, he refused to discuss the crime with the alienists, although he was voluble enough on other subjects.

Meanwhile, the subject of Czolgosz's sanity was being definitively settled by the Buffalo press from certain innuendoes and out-and-out statements by law enforcement officers and lawyers, if not by the alienists themselves.

An item in the *Buffalo News* on September 10 was headlined "Czolgosz Sane Beyond Doubt," and purported to give the verdict of Drs. Crego, Fowler, and Putnam.

Two days later the *Buffalo Commercial,* more conservative in its reporting of Dr. Fowler's examination of that day, as well as his and Dr. Crego's several examinations of Czolgosz, stated, ". . . the opinion is gaining ground that they [the doctors] are not thoroughly satisfied yet as to his insanity." Nevertheless, Superintendent Bull was quoted in the same article as stating without reservation that Czologsz was sane.

The permission granted to the defense by the court to call alienists resulted in the arrival in the city of Dr. Carlos F. Mac-Donald, professor of Mental Diseases and Medical Jurisprudence in the University-Bellevue Medical College. He was extolled in a

Buffalo Express article of September 22 as standing "at the head of his profession in that specialty and . . . universally regarded to be the leading alienist in the United States."

Actually, Dr. MacDonald had come at the behest of Adelbert Moot, acting for the Erie County Bar Association.

On the Saturday afternoon previous to his trial Czolgosz underwent an examination by the New York alienist, held, rather significantly, in the office of the district attorney. Afterward, Dr. MacDonald, prodded by newsmen about whether he would appear at the trial, was properly uncommunicative. However, Titus gave out a newsworthy gem in answer to the same question: "We are not calling adverse witnesses."

22

"If There Should Be Reasonable Doubt..."

IT IS AXIOMATIC that police exert more vigilance after than before a crime. Law enforcement officers thought that they were showing great vigilance before the President was murdered; after his assassination their circumspection knew no bounds.

Their increased watchfulness was especially evident on the mild, pleasant morning of September 23 when 80 policemen, selected for their size and brawn, were assigned to guard City Hall and the courtroom where the President's assassin was to stand trial on a charge of first degree murder. Bull's placement of men was strategic. His five huskiest bluecoats were stationed at the main entrance, among them Patrolman Daniels, tallest man on the force.

The bandage ruse had been used once with spectacular success and catastrophic results. Bull was determined that no such subterfuge would be used again. The police, therefore, were instructed to check anyone who looked even vaguely suspicious.

A big crowd was expected, but, oddly enough, it did not materialize. At 8:00 A.M. the streets around City Hall contained no more people than usual.

The Supreme Court of New York State was on the second floor, almost directly over the spot where the President's body had lain in state. The courtroom was at the south end of the building, and although light was admitted by four large windows facing Church Street and two each on the Delaware Avenue and Franklin Street sides, the room appeared dingy that morning. A thick wooden rail separated the actors in the forthcoming courtroom drama from the spectators who would view it.

Justice Truman C. White would be the presiding judge.

Expecting new and dramatic developments, 53 newsmen had crammed their way into the open space before the bench. A table directly before the witness box had been assigned to Attorneys Titus and Lewis. Attorney Carlton E. Ladd, Titus's law partner was also to act as counsel. A chair to the rear of Lewis had been assigned to the defendant. At the district attorney's table places had been assigned to Cusack, Haller, Drs. Mynter and Mann, and the alienists—Dr. Arthur W. Hurd, Dr. Allan McLane Hamilton, and Drs. MacDonald, Crego, Fowler and Putnam—who might or might not testify to Czolgosz's mental condition. About 200 had been fortunate enough to obtain cards enabling them to gain entrance to the spectators' section.

All sorts of lively conjecture was bandied about by the spectators as they awaited the defendant's arrival: Would he possibly implicate Emma Goldman? What were the alienists prepared to say? It had been widely assumed that the defendant was sane, but would defense counsel come up with ingenious arguments to prove he was not? Would the defendant make one of those ranting speeches defending Anarchism? Would the trial be characterized by those wild outbursts that had punctuated the trial of Garfield's assassin, Charles J. Guiteau?

At 10:13 cries of "here he comes" were heard along the corridors. Seconds later, shackled to Solomon and Geary, Czolgosz was hustled into the courtroom amidst hisses and boos. Once the defendant was seated, Penney arose and read the charge—murder in the first degree. The crime had been committed on the sixth day of September, 1901 . . . the prisoner had killed one William McKinley . . .

After the charge had been read, Penney, turning to the prisoner, asked: "How do you plead, guilty or not guilty?"

Judge Lewis arose.

"I believe the defendant was about to speak," said Justice White, whereupon Lewis sat down.

"Do you understand what the district attorney has read to you, Czolgosz?" asked Justice White.

The prisoner shook his head. Penney again stated the charge and again asked him how he pleaded.

"Guilty," blurted the prisoner, though only those close to the bench heard him. The *Commercial* reporter, seated along with 52 other newsmen within the rail, reported that the plea, when whispered to the spectators, "created a decided sensation."

"That plea can not be accepted," said Justice White and instructed the clerk to enter a not guilty plea, explaining that a guilty plea to murder was contrary to New York State law.

Once this technicality had been smoothed out, Penney explained that the prisoner had already been arraigned in the County Court, where counsel had been appointed. The court then formally ratified the appointment of Titus and Lewis.

At this point, Titus addressed the court, "not in the way of apology, but as a reason" for his and his associate's appearance. "At the time of our assignment," he explained, "I was out of the city and neither of my associates was consulted about the assignment. I, at first, declined to take part in the defense of this case, but subsequently it was revealed that it was my duty to the public, the profession and the court, to accept the assignment, unpleasant as the task is.

"We, therefore, appear here to see that the conviction, if he is proven guilty, occurs only by due process prescribed by the law of the land; that no evidence be admitted unless such as would be introduced and accepted in the trial of a lesser criminal."

Justice White responded: "Those views accord with the views of this court, and it is proper that gentlemen such as you should guard the rights of the fundamental laws of the land.

"The public will understand that the defense will be such as the law demands.

"The plea of guilty entered by the prisoner indicates that he anticipates no escape from the penalty that the law provides. That plea can not be accepted. The trial must be conducted as though the prisoner had pleaded 'not guilty.'

"The question has been raised in the public press as to the jurisdiction of the county court. I believe there is no doubt as to the legality of all proceedings there, so that, if necessary, I will confirm or even appoint the same counsel. Anything further, Mr. District Attorney?"

"I move the trial of Leon F. Czolgosz," said Penney.

Thus the law started to deal with Leon F. Czolgosz.

The selection of jurors now began. The first juror called, Frederick V. Lauer, a 60-year-old plumber, 1048 Michigan Avenue, Buffalo, under questioning by Penney revealed that he felt himself capable of being fair and impartial in his decision about the defendant's guilt.

During cross examination Lewis brought up the question of insanity. "If a reasonable doubt is raised in your mind as to the sanity of this defendant would you be willing to convict this defendant?" he asked.

"If a reasonable doubt is raised I might not," replied Lauer.

"But if the testimony indicates that this man is insane, would you convict him?"

"No, sir."

"I am satisfied," said Lewis.

As the district attorney was also satisfied, Lauer was sworn in and took his place in the jury box as Juror No. 1.

The *Buffalo Commercial* reporter commented that Lewis was "not inclined to be captious concerning the qualifications of the jurors," but he did question Richard J. Garwood, a 45-year-old street railway foreman, also from Buffalo, rather extensively:

"Have you formed an opinion in this case?" asked the defense attorney.

"Yes, sir, I have," was the answer.

"Have you expressed your opinion?"

"Yes, I think I have."

"Is that opinion so strong that evidence could not change it?"

"I think not."

"Notwithstanding that opinion could you carefully weigh the evidence and render an impartial verdict?"

"I could."

"We accept."

So Garwood became Juror Number 2.

However, a farmer from North Collins, Joshua Winner, who had read all about the case and already formed a strong opinion was not satisfactory to Lewis.

Henry W. Wendt, a Buffalo manufacturer, became Juror Number 3. He confessed to an opinion about the case, but supposed evidence might remove that opinion in the face of "reasonable doubt."

A farmer from Elma, Horatio M. Winspear, expressed some doubt about capital punishment and was excused by Penney.

Justice White excused the next prospect who had too strong an opinion, and Penney did the same for a farmer from Grand Island who at first denied that he would vote for conviction if it meant the death penalty.

Silas Carmer, of Clarence, another farmer, 65, had formed a "pretty strong" opinion, but would vote for acquittal of the defendant if the evidence in his favor likewise was "pretty strong." Carmer was sworn in as Juror Number 4 at 11:00.

Although both of the next two examined believed in the United States government and felt that they could render fair and impartial judgments, both were excused, the first by the court and the second by the district attorney. Herman Tauber's opinion of the guilt of the defendant was firmly fixed while Dennis T. O'Reilly had formed only a kind of opinion but he simply did not "want to sit on this case."

From a record of his responses to Lewis, Frederick Langbein, a farmer from Hamburg, would appear to be the ideal juror. He had formed no opinion, limited his newspaper reading to once a week, had discussed the case with his neighbors but had himself refrained from any expression of opinion to them.

"Are you a married man?"

"Yes, sir."

"Have you not expressed your opinion to your wife?"

"No, sir."

"Nor to your children?"

"No, sir, not to them."

"No objection," said Lewis.

But evidently Penney felt otherwise. "We will excuse him, sir," said the district attorney.

On the other hand, Assemblyman George Ruehl's occupation of barber appeared to present doubt to Lewis.

"You are a barber?"

"Yes, sir."

"Heard people talk about it in your shop and have talked with them, have you not?"

"More people have talked to me than I have talked to," retorted the barber.

"You must be one of those barbers who do not talk," said Lewis, then added, "We will excuse Mr. Ruehl."

Wallace Butler, a farmer from Sardinia, would require pretty strong evidence to conform to the requirements of the law, was challenged by Lewis and so excused by the court.

A plumber from Normal Avenue, James S. Stygall, Jr., 45,

went through the "opinion" and "benefit of a reasonable doubt" grilling so satisfactorily that he was seated as Juror Number 5.

At about 11:30 John G. Milburn strode into the courtroom, walked up to the court clerk's desk and then sat down in a press seat. In order to get a better view of the defendant he put on his glasses. His long, slow appraisal was described by *The Commercial* reporter as "an odd mixture of sorrow, contempt and pity."

Lewis was not satisfied with the self-contradictory statements of Frank Lutz and the next possibility was excused by the district attorney.

When queried about his belief in capital punishment, William Loton, an Eden farmer, 65, answered "I do" with a snap of his teeth. He had formed an opinion but proved satisfactory to both sides and was seated at 11:45 as Juror Number 6.

After two more rejections based upon technicalities, William E. Everett, a 39-year-old blacksmith from 176 15th Street in Buffalo, was accepted as Juror Number 7.

Ben C. Ralph, 40, an assistant cashier from 310 Woodward Avenue, in Buffalo, was about to be examined as potential juryman Number 8 when Lewis interrupted the business at hand to address the court on the subject of the hours for the court sessions: "Now about the hours we are to sit here. Neither Judge Titus or myself is a young man, especially myself, and neither of us is in perfect health. We have had very little opportunity to consult with each other since we concluded to abide by our designation as counsel for the defendant. Now, we believe, that the trial will not be injured by having short hours. We need some time for consulting, and after conversations with the district attorney, we have concluded to ask your honor during this trial to sit from 10 to 12 o'clock in the morning and from 2 to 4 o'clock in the afternoon. I mention 4 o'clock in the afternoon because my home, my summer home, is in Lewiston, and my train leaves at 4:40, and I am not inclined, unless absolutely compelled to do so, to find an abiding place here in the city while my family is in Lewiston.

"That is our request, that those be the hours fixed, and we believe that the trial can be as expeditiously concluded as if we were compelled to work here longer than our health would permit."

Justice White acquiesced to this request, stating that the court was "inclined to grant any reasonable request" counsel might make, owing to the "onerous and unpleasant task" that they had assumed. The hours were accordingly fixed as requested.

Since only a few minutes intervened before noon, Ralph speedily satisfied the district attorney with his qualifications. Again the defense, this time represented by Titus, brought up the question of insanity: "If there should be a reasonable doubt as to the sanity of the defendant, would you give him the benefit of the doubt?"

"I would," said Ralph, and was forthwith sworn in as the eighth juryman.

Justice White advised the jurors not to talk with each other about the trial or to allow anyone to speak of the trial in their presence, then recessed the court until 2:00.

Czolgosz was returned to the courtroom slightly earlier than he had been expected so that his entry would be as inconspicuous as possible. It was a duplicate of his morning appearance. He was preceded by Cusack and shackled to Solomon and Geary. When Solomon removed the handcuffs from his wrist, the prisoner was heard to murmur, "Thank you," in a low, soft voice.

Most of the distinguished guests of the morning had returned for the afternoon session, Senators Timothy L. Ellsworth, and George A. Davis, Judge Hammond of the Supreme Court, and Judge Sherman of the Superior Court of Massachusetts. Attorney Ansley Wilcox was now added to their number.

At 2:03 the noisy courtroom quieted down as Justice White made his appearance. The examination of jurors resumed with Titus continuing to cross examine for the defense.

A Lancaster farmer, John Bergtold, was excused by Penney after he had responded to Titus that he had "partly formed" an opinion.

Samuel P. Waldow, 59, of Alden, another farmer, said that he had definitely formed an opinion that would need evidence to alter. Nevertheless, he felt that he could sit upon the jury and pass the evidence. He was accepted as the ninth juror.

The case of juror Number 10 was similar to that of Farmer Waldow. Andrew J. Smith, 60, of 140 Leroy Avenue, a dealer in butter and eggs, had read about the case and had an opinion that would require evidence to change.

After a short consultation with his colleague, Titus accepted him.

"We are satisfied," said the district attorney, and Smith was sworn in.

When the clerk called the name of Truman D. Keyes several times there was no answer.

"Enter an order imposing a fine of $25 upon the juror for failing to appear," said Justice White, sternly.

The district attorney had evidently done some sleuthing in regard to the qualifications of Peter Feidt. "I have a paper here showing that he made certain statements which I would not care to have published. They disqualify him," said Penney, who then challenged him peremptorily.

Penney excused the next prospect and Titus the following two.

Joachim H. Mertens, 42, a boot and shoe dealer, of 945 Exchange Street in Buffalo, stated that he had formed an opinion but said that he could set it aside in the interest of a fair trial; he was accepted as Juror Number 11.

A contractor of 200 Purdy Street, Robert J. Adams, had a partial opinion that would yield only to considerable evidence, yet he considered himself competent to be a jury member. Evidently his inquisitors agreed, for he was sworn in at 2:43 as Juror Number 12.

Crier Hess then announced, "Jury all ready, your honor."

The thorny process of picking a jury to sit upon a murder case, usually slow and laborious, had been accomplished with considerable dispatch, having occupied only two hours and 29 minutes. Yet the element of time still seemed a consideration of importance to the presiding justice. As a stir of excitement and expectation filled the courtroom, the presiding justice asked the district attorney, "How much time will you require in presenting your case?"

"If we adjourn at four o'clock I think we will be able to finish our case by noon tomorrow," answered Penney.

Turning to the defense attorneys, Justice White inquired, "And how much time will the gentlemen for the defense require?"

"That will depend very largely on the turn the case takes," said Titus. "We can not tell now how long we will require."

Justice White then turned to Penney and said, "Mr. District Attorney, the case is with you."

Assistant District Attorney Frederick Haller opened for the prosecution with a brief preview of the case against Leon F. Czolgosz, who had committed assault upon "one William McKinley, with a certain weapon or firearms, causing a wound from which the said William McKinley, languishing, did die." The evidence presented would show "beyond the shadow of a doubt" that the crime had been premeditated. There was, however, a minimum of legal clichés in Haller's short prologue which ended: "We will show you, gentlemen, pictures of the scene of the shooting and explain every detail of the crime and when we have finished we are confident that you will agree with us that this man is guilty."

District Attorney Penney called his first witness, the chief engineer of the Pan American Exposition and former city engineer, Samuel J. Fields. Court officials had already tacked up an outsized floor plan of the interior of the Temple of Music. Fields, who had been called to the Temple between 5:00 and 6:00 on the day of the shooting, pointed out the placement of furniture, drapery, and flags and gave measurements, which he had taken at the time.

During the cross examination Titus pointed to the map and asked, "Did you mark that spot?"

"Yes, sir."

"What for?"

"There was a spot of blood on the floor there."

The second witness was a personable, clean shaven, dark young man, Harry A. Bliss, the photographer who at 9:00 A.M. on the day after the shooting had taken pictures of the interior of the Temple of Music. He identified five of his photographs. These were passed to defense counsel, then to the jurymen and were subsequently admitted as Exhibits A, B, C, D, and E.

Having established the setting of the crime, the prosecution now turned to the results of the shooting. Dr. Harvey B. Gaylord, who had performed the autopsy upon the body of McKinley, was the first of the group of medical men to be called. A tall, smooth-shaven young surgeon, already well-known in the field of cancer research, Gaylord answered promptly in a full, clear voice.

Obviously in rebuttal to allegations by some of the yellow journals, the line of questioning pursued sought to show that the medical treatment of the President had been of the best and had caused no complications.

Lewis's cross examination of Dr. Gaylord was long and penetrating, even demanding an explanation of the first bullet wound:

Q: Now, this wound that you first described, did that enter the body?

A: No, sir. That perforated the skin and had destroyed or caused the destruction of a small amount of fat beneath it, but did not reach down to the muscles.

Q: That wound you dismissed as one of no great importance?

A: We described it and passed over it.

At the time of the post-mortem examination, the second wound it was established from the standpoint of the operation was in good condition, the edges properly united and in the process of healing. Parts near the wound were in a "condition of necrosis," however.

Q: Is that what is properly known as gangrene?

A: That is, sir.

Q: Doctor, in your testimony will you be kind enough to use as plain language as you can, leaving out the scientific language?

The condition of the kidney and pancreas was explored. Finally, Lewis asked, "What organ was injured by the bullet coming in contact with it that caused the death of the President?"

A: I don't think that I could state specifically that the death of the President was due to injury in any organ made directly by the bullet. That is, I could not make that statement. The changes caused by the bullet, which resulted from the passage of the bullet through that space back of the stomach was what caused his death, and that was largely because of the fact that the pancreas was involved. It was caused by the absorption or breaking up of the material back of the peritoneal cavity.

The man of law and the man of medicine very nearly reached a verbal impasse on the subject of the use of antiseptics, Lewis demanding a yes or no and Gaylord hesitating to commit himself to either of these absolutes.

Lewis finally took up the subject of the President's general condition of health, then veered in a direction apparently unexpected by the doctor:

Q: Did I understand you to say that you found cancerous germs?

A: That I found what, sir?

Q: Cancerous germs?

A: No, sir.

This concluded Lewis's cross examination of Gaylord, but before the doctor left the stand Penney evidently wished to pinpoint conclusively the cause of the President's death:

Q: What is your conclusion as to the cause of death?

A: He died as a result of absorption of this breaking-down material in this area of the stomach.

Q: What was the cause of the breaking down of the material-

A: The cause of the breaking down of the material was, in the first place, injury to the tissues and was probably facilitated by the escape of the secretion of the pancreas into this cavity.

Q: What was the cause of the injury to the tissues?

A: That I should attribute to the bullet.

Q: Well, getting back to primal causes, then, the result or cause of death rather, was the bullet wound?

A. Was the bullet wound.

During cross examination Dr. Gaylord had already set Lewis right upon the proper location of the pancreas; now as a final nugget of physiological information Penney demanded, "Doctor, one thing more. Tell us the office of the pancreas?"

A: The office of the pancreas is in digestion, intestinal digestion. It secretes certain ferments which act upon the fluid which passes out of the stomach into the intestinal tract.

"That is all, doctor," said Penney.

"That is all," echoed Lewis.

Dr. Gaylord had been on the stand for 21 minutes when he stepped down at 3:28.

The black-mustached, sturdily built Dr. Herman Mynter was the next witness and proved to be the most interesting of the day. He was decisive and dramatic, using gestures to mark out on his own person the areas of the President's body he was describing.

Without too much prompting by the district attorney the entire narrative from Dr. Mynter's viewpoint flowed forth—his arrival at the hospital, his part in the operation, his participation in the subsequent council of doctors, his version of the autopsy down to the question of the moment: What was the cause of death?

A: Cause of death was what we call toxemia, kind of blood poisoning from absorption of poisonous products from the gangrene, produced by the bullet wound.

Q: Well, in simple language it was the gunshot wound?

A: It was the gunshot wound primarily.

Q: The cause of death of President McKinley was the gunshot wound that occurred on the sixth day of September of this year?

A: Yes, sir.

The cross-examination by Titus resulted in some exciting but friendly verbal parrying, during which the 12 men in the jury box leaned forward attentively.

Asked about the advisability of locating the second bullet at the time of the operation, Dr. Mynter explained bluntly that to have done so would have proved fatal to the President. "We couldn't have done that without taking all the intestines out," said the doctor. "The President would have died on the table if we had gone further. We would have had to make a large incision, ten inches long, take all his intestines out. He was already under the influence of shock at that time. He would have died on the table if we had gone further."

Q: What was the object or what would have been the object in locating the bullet and removing it?

A: To get rid of it that it might not raise any disturbance afterward.

The use of X-rays would not have helped the situation for "even if we had known where the bullet was," said Dr. Mynter, "not one of us would have thought at the time of trying to remove it."

Titus hit upon the drainage question:

Q: If there had been an open drain and the passage of the bullet had been clearly diagnosed and determined, would there have been so much liability of his death as when the wound was closed and no access to it?

A: I do not suppose it would have made the slightest difference either one way or another. The gangrene of the stomach would have occurred anyway.

As to what had brought about the gangrenous condition, unusual and unexpected in such a case, Dr. Mynter presented three possible causes: "I attribute it, perhaps, to what Dr. Gaylord said, to leakage of the pancreatic fluid, although, to my idea, the pancreas was not wounded by the bullet, but it might have got into a state of injury by simply the wave of the bullet striking it—*contre coup,* as we call it—and in that way injury to the pancreas occurred. That is one idea. Another idea is that the bullet—or that the injury—was followed with bacterial growth. That we can not say yet, because the bacteriological examination is not finished. Another thing is that the proximity of the large solar plexus, the large ganglia near the heart, near the stomach wound, might have certain deleterious influence upon the nervous system, which already was weakened and in that way favored gangrenous processes."

The defense counsel referred to the reopening of the wound on September 10.

Q: You opened the wound, after a number of days, did you?

A: We only opened the outer wound.

Q: You opened it sufficiently to look into the first wound?

A: No; Oh, my no.

Q: To the stomach?

A: Oh, my, no. Only sufficient to open the incision in the skin, in the subcutaneous tissue, down to the muscles of the abdominal wall.

Titus returned to the subject of the location of the bullet, now asking why the bullet had not been located during the autopsy.

A: Well, they tried their level best for four hours and could not find it, and at last they were told to desist. The family of the President would not have allowed that we go on any longer and would not permit them to injure the corpse any longer; therefore, they desisted.

When Dr. Mynter concluded his testimony at 3:49, he had been on the stand for 21 minutes.

During the physician's testimony, perhaps the most attentive person in the courtroom was the prisoner himself. Since he had probably not known of the President's death until the day of the indictment, and had not been permitted to read any of the deluge of news stories being poured out hourly about his victim's condition after the shooting, this was all fresh information to him. Others were glad to learn the true version of the President's treatment, given under oath by the surgeons most intimately associated with the entire case.

The next witness, Dr. Matthew D. Mann, whose small, steady hand had wielded the knife during the President's operation, was the object of a special interest to all in the room. A quiet, gray-bearded, self-possessed little man, he answered the lawyers' questions without hesitation. His account varied in no detail from Dr. Mynter's.

When first naming the President's consulting physicians, he omitted Dr. Park's name until prompted by the district attorney.

Q: Dr. Park was in the consultation?

A: Oh, Dr. Park; yes, Dr. Park was in the consultation from the first.

Then Penney tried to establish the idea of a joint consultation for the President.

Q: All you gentlemen consulted together and treated the President as the result of your whole consultation?

A: We did so. We made a point that two of us should stay each night with the President and the rest of us met three times a day.

Just as Dr. Mann was concluding his description of the autopsy, Justice White interrupted, "We will suspend here." Apparently it was 4:00.

Penney requested one more question as the doctor was at the point of giving the cause of the President's death.

"The cause of death," said Mann, "was the bullet wound in the stomach and in the parts behind it."

Q: The cause of death of the late President was this bullet wound that you operated for at the Pan-American grounds?

A: Without any doubt.

Again Justice White interrupted, "We will suspend here."

It would be necessary for Dr. Mann to return at 10 the next morning to complete his testimony.

The *Buffalo Commercial* in its reporting of the first day of the trial rightly surmised that insanity would not be used by the defense in order to try to save the life of the "dastard." Drs. Mac-

Donald and Crego would be the medical men called by the district attorney if the defense did pursue that tack. Since Dr. MacDonald had originally been called by the defense but was now "retained by the people," it was now "perfectly clear that in the judgment of this great alienist Czolgosz is not insane." Dr. Hamilton would not be called, the newspaper said without reservation.

After the noon adjournment the alienists had met in Penney's office. When they emerged half an hour later Dr. MacDonald was asked if it had been decided to call the doctors to the witness stand.

"We may all be asked to testify," he said, "The matter rests with the counsel for the defense and the district attorney. Of course, we can not announce any decision as to the mental condition of Czolgosz. It would be unprofessional and disrespectful to those two noble men who have undertaken to uphold the dignity of the law by defending the assassin. But there are very few people who have not formed the proper opinion as to what our verdict will be."

ii

On the second day of the trial, September 24, the defendant was led into the crowded courtroom at 9:37. He appeared to be drowsy, sulky and less placid than on the preceding day.

Ten minutes later the jury filed in, led by Frederick V. Lauer, Juror Number 1. "The first night we lodged on Delaware Street," he remarked jocosely as he looked across at the jail, where the jury had slept the night before.

After the defense lawyers had entered, accompanied by several of the medical men, Lewis attempted to speak to Czolgosz, who only shut his eyes and turned away his head.

Two minutes before the thumps of the tipstaff announced the approach of Justice White, Penney and Haller took their places within the rail. There followed the usual court ritual—the announcement by the court crier, the archaic "hear ye" as the presiding judge was seated, the calling of the roll of the jury by the clerk, the naming of the prisoner, who, in this case, sat silent and unflinching.

Since Penney had managed to conclude the direct questioning of Dr. Mann on the afternoon previous, the first business of the court was the cross examination of the surgeon by defense attorney Lewis.

In agreement with Dr. Mynter, Dr. Mann characterized the gangrenous condition of the President's wound as unusual and unexpected, but shied away from a specific cause. Further investigation would be necessary to explain it, he said. In any case it was the duty of the pathologists who had made the autopsy, not himself, who had been only a spectator.

The defense attorney veered slightly in his questioning to probe into the reason for the sanguine reports carried in the newspapers during the days following the President's operation.

Q: I conclude, therefore, that the optimistic bulletins that were issued from time to time by the physicians, were without any knowledge or any sufficient knowledge of those symptoms that were finally discovered?

A: The bulletins which were issued were not optimistic, in that they gave no ideas of what was to come, they expressed no opinion, they merely stated facts, but the opinions that were held by the staff seemed to be fully warranted by the condition of the President. We had no reason to suspect the existence of any such state of affairs, within the abdomen.

Q: Whether they appeared in the bulletins or not, they certainly appeared in the press extensively, that the physicians were quite confident, in fact, almost certain that the President would recover?

A: Yes, that was so, in the press, but a good deal was attributed to the physicians by the press which was not always quite correct.

Then Lewis returned to press Mann for his opinion of the causes of the gangrene. Mann named three: "invasion of the parts by germs . . . a very low state of vitality . . . the action of the pancreatic juice."

In breaking down each of these causes under Lewis's questioning, he further elucidated on the germs: "There are remedies which will kill germs, but it is very difficult to apply them deep down in the tissues of the body and impossible, once they get a lodgment in the tissues, to dislodge them and kill them."

As to the President's state of health, which the physician considered undoubtedly to have been a contributory factor, he answered: "The President probably was not in a very good physical condition; he was somewhat weakened by hard work, want of exercise and conditions of that kind."

Lewis pushed on to the third cause, injury to the pancreas. "You agree with the other physicians," he queried, "that that organ was not actually mutilated or struck by the ball?"

A: As well as could be determined, the ball did not enter it. It is impossible to say positively, but it was injured in some way.

Q: By concussion?

A: Very possibly by concussion. Once the organ is injured, then the pancreatic juice, the secretion of the gland, will pass through the gland and can enter other parts. One portion of it being healthy, another part diseased, the healthy part would secrete while the diseased portion will allow the secretion to pass through it and attack other parts. Food cannot be digested, if it does not secrete.

In redirect examination Penney was able to extort the note of finality everyone wished to believe.

Q: Every known method of the latest surgical and medical science was applied in the treatment of the President?

A: I think that is true.

Q: From your knowledge of the autopsy and the history of the case, was there anything that would have saved the life of the President known to medical or surgical science?

A: There was not.

And with this statement Dr. Mann concluded his testimony.

Louis L. Babcock and Edward R. Rice both related the story of the crime from their own points of view and each was asked to identify the defendant. For the most part they were not interrupted by Penney or cross examined to any extent by the defense. In fact, Babcock was not cross examined at all.

Babcock described his own action: "Just as soon as the prisoner was down on the ground I ran towards the east and motioned to the guards and cried: 'Everybody out!' And the guards immediately cleared the Temple of Music toward the east."

Upon his return he found the defendant on his feet, surrounded by artillerymen, Secret Service men, Exposition guards and (he thought) by some Buffalo city detectives. A controversy ensued as to who should assume custody of the prisoner, but this "was soon settled and then the prisoner was taken by three or four of the officers in plain clothes . . . toward Mr. Henshaw's office . . . which is right where I indicate on this diagram."

At the moment of the shooting Rice was in the act of exchanging signals with Cortelyou to indicate that the reception should end. "I took my watch out of my hand," testified Rice, "indicating to Secretary Cortelyou that the time we had agreed upon was about up, and as I remember he took his watch from his hand, indicating that he understood." Immediately the two revolver shots sounded so close together that he "could hardly distinguish one from the other." He saw an object that looked to him "black and white" and the people around it all dropped to the floor in a mass. His first thought was that the revolver had been concealed in a newspaper.

Rice also ran toward the east door where people were entering and shouted, "Close the door and clear the aisle." Then he turned toward the south entrance and asked whether an ambulance had been summoned. It had, so he returned to find that the President had been removed to a chair in the aisle leading toward the stage, the second chair from the end.

The star witness of the day was James L. Quackenbush, Exposition committee member and attorney, who had not only been present at the time of the crime but had subsequently heard Czolgosz's confession at Police Headquarters.

He gave a precise account of the positions of all those near the President at the time of the tragedy, identifying each and describing vividly their actions. He himself had been standing to Rice's right and directly opposite McKinley, south of the line of chairs forming the aisle, and resting his left foot on one of those chairs.

After the President had been removed to the hospital and Czolgosz to Police Headquarters, he had stayed on at the Temple with the district attorney, taking measurements and hearing statements from witnesses. He and Penney had arrived at Headquarters between 10 and 11 that night where they found Czolgosz seated at a table in Bull's inner office.

The greater part of Quackenbush's testimony was based upon the confession the prisoner had made that night. "He described in detail," said Quackenbush, "in a conversation of about two hours, his movements during the day of the shooting and for some time previous. He himself, with a handkerchief, which he had, showed how he concealed his revolver and how he fired the shot. He stated that he had gone to Niagara Falls on the morning of the day of the shooting, with the intention of shooting the President at the Falls, but that he was unable to carry out his purpose there, not being able to get near enough to the President. That he took a street car from Niagara Falls to Buffalo, transferred to a car going to the exposition grounds and went to the Temple of Music for the purpose of shooting the President. He said he waited outside in the line, that he had placed his revolver in his right hand, covered it with his handkerchief, placed his hand covered with the handkerchief and holding the revolver in his right-hand pocket and stood that way while in the crowd outside of the entrance to the Temple, and as he entered the Temple, but that when he got to the point where the people were singled out in a single file, he took his right hand from his pocket and held the hand covered with the handkerchief cross his stomach until he reached the President, when he fired."

Quackenbush recounted biographical details of Czolgosz's life, his theories of government, marriage, and the church. These did not differ from those already publicized. The witness did not recall the names of the papers Czolgosz had read except *Free Society*.

Here Penney prompted the witness, "He mentioned some places he had been to where he had heard those subjects discussed, didn't he?"

A: Yes, places in Cleveland, Ohio. He stated before he came to Buffalo he had been in Chicago. He said he had been influenced by the teachings of Emma Goldman and another woman living near Cleveland, whose name I do not recall at this moment.

Titus began to cross examine at this point. Had the prisoner volunteered information, he wished to know, or had it been extracted from him in response to questions put by the district attorney.

The witness made a rather surprising comparison: ". . . he talked just as I talk now."

Q: You mean at first.

A: Yes, sir; when he did answer he answered not in monosyllables but gave direct, positive answers.

In answer to further questions by the defense about the prisoner at the time of his confession Quackenbush described him as not appearing to be disturbed mentally, but evidently suffering from some physical pain from the blows struck him at the Temple of Music. He was constantly applying his handkerchief to the side of his face and complained that his eyes hurt him. During the two-hour grilling he did not become "excited" or "stirred up."

Q: Was he upbraided or condemned by anybody there in your presence?

A: Not by anybody.

Quackenbush recalled the circumstances of the prisoner's statement which by now had become well-known. "I asked him to make a statement for publication. I told him that we couldn't hold the newspapers all night to wait for his statement. He thought, evidently, that I was a newspaper-man. And he then dictated a statement.

Q: Without interrogatories?

A: Yes, sir. I would prefer to refresh my recollection about that, if I could be permitted.

He was permitted, whereupon Penney handed him a paper which he examined.

Q: You recollect that that is the statement independent of what you see there, I suppose?

A: By looking at this statement it refreshes my recollection so that I am able to state what it was.

Q: Go on.

A: "I killed President McKinley because I done my duty. I didn't believe one man should have so much service and another man should have none." This statement he signed.

In further cross examination Titus asked about the prisoner's statement with regard to Anarchy.

Q: I want to ask you one other question. You said that he made the statement that he was an anarchist. Was that it?

A: I don't think I made quite that statement.

Q: Well, he believed in anarchy?

A. I don't——

Q. Well, won't you repeat what you did say.

A: What he did say was that he didn't believe in any government, that he didn't believe in rulers; he thought that all rulers were tyrants and should be removed and that he had done his duty in removing the President.

Q: Then he said nothing about anarchy—you have used the expression in your evidence?

A: Yes, well, the district attorney on several occasions used the word "anarchy" and talked with him about anarchists of note, mentioning them by name to him; asking him if he knew them. Whether he himself used that precise term or not I would not state positively.

Q: Did he say anything upon the subject as to whether it was his duty, belonging or owing allegiance or believing in that society, to slay the heads of governments; did he say anything upon that subject?

A: He did not put it on any ground of allegiance. He put it on the ground of belief, and he claimed it was a result of his own individual theorizing and reflection on the subject; not that he used those terms, but that is the substance of it.

Penney concluded the evidence of Quackenbush by establishing the source of the prisoner's theorizing.

Q: In connection with that he did speak of the lectures and speakers he had heard?

A: Yes, sir.

Q: The things that he had heard in these places, that he was meditating upon?

A: Yes.

Quackenbush had been on the stand 40 minutes, the center of rapt attention by everyone in the room—even on several occasions by the prisoner himself.

Next Secret Service men Gallaher and Foster appeared on the witness stand to tell of their swift action in helping to bring the assassin under control. Although someone had grabbed the revolver from his grasp, Gallaher had managed to keep a hold on the handkerchief. This he produced and passed to Penney, who had it introduced as evidence, and then handed it to the jurymen. It was not a woman's handkerchief, as some rumors had stated, but an ordinary man's white handkerchief, now blackened and burned in two spots by the revolver fire.

Foster's contribution was the first bullet, which the President had located himself in the ambulance and which had later fallen out in the hospital when the President was being undressed.

Titus cross examined Foster about the suspicious-looking black-mustached man who had engaged the Secret Service men's attention just previous to the shooting.

Q: Was he near this man here?

A: No, sir, I don't think he was. I think he was ten feet in front of him. In fact, I put my hand on his shoulder and passed him past the President?

Q: Why did you do that?

A: I didn't like his general appearance. And I motioned to Gallaher to take care of him after I left him.

Titus then asked about Parker.

A: I noticed a colored man in the line, but it seems to me he was in front of this man.

Q: Instead of behind him?

A: Instead of behind him. I never saw a colored man in the whole fracas.

Q: Then you were the man instead of those artillerymen that crushed this defendant to the floor?

A: No, sir. When we settled down, I noticed a man by the name of O'Brien—Sergt. O'Brien of the artillery—was lying along side of me.

Q: On the floor?

A: On the floor. That was the only artilleryman that was seen though.

The three artillerymen—O'Brien, Neff, and Bertschey—were then called. The only artilleryman whom Foster had seen in the fracas, Private (not sergeant) Francis P. O'Brien, a smooth shaven Irishman from Massachusetts, identified the revolver produced by Penney as the one he had seized when he and the defendant went down on the floor together.

A red-mustached German, Private Louis Neff, had been keeping the women in line and the people passing and so had not noticed Czolgosz before the shots were fired, but he too had lunged for the revolver.

Corporal Louis Bertschey bore out the evidence of O'Brien and Neff. He himself had grabbed the defendant by the shoulder and pulled him backward.

Superintendent of Music at the Exposition Harry F. Henshaw had actually seen the whole assassination. Several other witnesses appeared to be looking in some other direction at the precise moment when they heard the shots. Henshaw had jumped over the rail, but the artillerymen had already knocked Czolgosz to the floor. Others were crowding around, so when he reached the "bunch," he could not even see the defendant.

The Negro janitor, John Branch, who had appeared before the grand jury, added a touch of humor to the morning session when under Titus's cross examination he told what he had heard the President say about his assailant.

Q: What did you hear the President say?

A: He didn't say anything only just "Be easy with him, boys." That is all I heard him say.

Q: What is that?

A: "Be easy with him, boys."

Q: "Be easy with him, boys?"

A: Yes, sir. "Be easy with him, boys." That is all I heard him say.

The same truly Christian sentiment had been attributed to the President by the press and commented on by the pulpit; usually it was couched in stiff, formal phrasing like "Let no one hurt him." It was good to hear this homely colloquial expression, which might have been expected from a long-time politician and man among men.

This ended the morning session.

During the afternoon session the courtroom was packed. Many notables of the area bench and bar mingled with outstanding Buffalo citizens. Several women also were in the audience, among them the wife of Justice White. Although all was in readiness to continue the business of the court, there was an eight-minute wait while prosecution and defense conferred about the advisability of calling alienists to the stand.

It was evidently agreed that this would be unnecessary, for none was called.

At 2:12 Captain James F. Vallely of the Exposition detective bureau was sworn in. He added little in the way of new evidence about Czolgosz's statements in Bull's office on the night of September 6.

Superintendent Bull himself became the last witness of the prosecution and, as it developed, the last witness of the trial.

Bull's evidence consisted mostly of a repetition of the prisoner's statements made during their talks since his arrest. Penney drew Bull out particularly on Czolgosz's anarchistic beliefs and their supposed sources. After cross examination by Titus, Bull told of the visit to Headquarters of Albert Nowak, of Cleveland, of Nowak's reproach of Czolgosz, and of Czolgosz's reaction to Nowak.

Had the defendant said anything about wishing to see a lawyer, friends, or his parents, Bull was asked.

"He said," Bull replied, "he didn't wish to see a lawyer, didn't need a lawyer, that he had no friends, and did not care to see his father or mother."

"The people rest," said the district attorney quietly at 2:37 P.M.

Judge Lewis then turned to the defendant, asking whether he wished to take the stand. For answer, Czolgosz only closed his eyes and turned away his head.

"If Your Honor please," said Lewis, "the defendant has no witnesses that he will call, so that the testimony is closed at the close of the testimony of the people."

Lewis admitted that his colleague and he were "somewhat embarrassed, disappointed in the people's testimony closing at this point." They had not had much opportunity to consult, so he asked that each be allowed to make some brief remarks by way of summing up the case.

Reputed to have once been a trial lawyer of note, Judge Lewis, however, had not addressed a jury in this capacity in many years. Now he stood, a strikingly dignified figure with his white hair, white beard, black garb, as he spoke deliberately, impressively. Although he had promised to be brief his "remarks" trailed on for 27 minutes.

After a short apology for his lack of practice in addressing a jury in such a capacity, he presented the decision they would have to make about the defendant in an exceedingly unusual manner, especially since no evidence had been admitted on the subject of the prisoner's mental state. "A great calamity has befallen our nation. The President of the country has been stricken down and died in our city. It is shown beyond any peradventure of doubt that it was at the defendant's hand that he was stricken down, and the only question that can be discussed or considered in this case is the question whether that act was that of a sane person. If it was, then the defendant is guilty of the murder and must suffer the penalty. If it was the act of an insane man, then he is not guilty of murder, but should be acquitted of that charge and would then be confined in a lunatic asylum."

Much comment had been raised about the propriety of any defense at all for such a culprit. Lewis then reviewed the circumstances under which Titus and he had entered the case.

"A defendant," he explained, "no matter how enormous the crime that he may have committed is, under our laws entitled to the benefit of a trial. In a case of murder in the first degree he must have a trial. You sat here and listened to the defendant's plea of guilty when he was arraigned by the learned District Attorney, but the law of our state will not permit a man to plead guilty of such a crime as this."

Lewis then launched into a condemnation of "lynch law," which did not exist in their community, but unfortunately did in other parts of "this free and independent country."

He admitted that Anarchy was dangerous but not so dangerous as the rule of the mob without recourse to law and the courts of justice.

Some people have an erroneous idea of the purpose of the lawyer in defense of the criminal. They think he is in court to impede the administration of law and raise technicalities, "but no man who understands and knows the better class of the members of the bar entertains any such notion." He and his associates were there in the same capacity as the district attorney (and he might have added in this case as his helpers) to see that the trial progressed in a legal, orderly and proper manner.

Here the jurist launched into a lengthy anecdote about William H. Seward, a one-time contender for the Presidency and later Secretary of State under Lincoln. Lewis had been a young law student in the city of Auburn when Seward was one of its residents. News came that a Negro named Freeman had killed nearly an entire family upon the shore of Owasco Lake and was to be brought into the city to be jailed. Crowds gathered upon the streets and might have lynched Freeman, had not Seward appeared among them and "counselled moderation." Not only had Seward saved the Negro from the mob, but he later appeared as Freeman's counsel in a trial which lasted at least two months.

Judge Lewis recalled that the selection of a jury alone had consumed three weeks. The young Lewis had "sat by during almost the entire length of the trial and listened to the defense that Mr. Seward interposed."

The relevance of the anecdote was obvious. Seward cared nothing for the defendant personally, "but he wanted to teach the people of the country the sacredness of the law; he wanted to impress upon them the importance of maintaining the law and putting down mob violence."

A short paean of praise followed to the President for his considerateness in coming to the city to assist in promoting the Exposition. "He submitted to being met by the people who desired to see him, in order to help on this great enterprise in which we have been interested, and he was stricken down and died from the effects of the wounds. It has touched every heart in this community and in the world, and yet we sit here today . . . quietly considering . . . whether this man is responsible for the act which he committed, and that question, gentlemen, is one that you are called upon to decide."

The defense attorneys had not been able to present any evidence, since the defendant had stolidly refused even to talk to his counsel. All he could say to aid the jury in its decision was "that every human being . . . has a strong desire to live. Death is a spectre that we all dislike to meet, and here this defendant, without having any animosity against our President, without any . . . personal motive, we find him going into this building, in the presence of these hundreds of people. and committing an act which, if he was sane, must cause his death."

Upon what, other than their own intuition, the jury's finding the defendant insane could be based, the attorney did not say, but he suggested that such a decision would "aid in uplifting a great cloud off from the hearts . . . of the people of this country and of the world." If the President had met with some accident, everyone would have deeply grieved, but not so deeply as they were now grieving. However, could they "find that he had met his fate at the hand of an insane man, it would amount to the same as though he met it accidentally, by some accident, and passed away under such circumstances."

Lewis then concluded with yet another panegyric on the dead President, whose career he had watched for twenty years or more. "One of the noblest men that God ever made," "a man of irreproachable character," "a loving husband," "a grand man in every aspect that you could conceive of" were appellations used by the jurist, who finally ended "and his death has been the saddest blow to me that has occurred in many years."

The eloquent voice wavered, then broke as the venerable counsel sat down with his handkerchief to his eyes.

The courtroom was silent.

Then Judge Titus arose and added his summation, which was, in fact, brief: "If the court pleases, the remarks of my distinguished associate have so fully and completely covered the ground and so largely anticipated what I intended to present to the jury myself, that it seems entirely unnecessary for me to reiterate what has already been said upon this subject and we, therefore, rest with the remarks made by Judge Lewis."

As soon as Titus was seated, the district attorney arose, bowed to Justice White and faced the jury and began his 17-minute summation:

"If the court please, gentlemen of the jury: It is hardly possible for any man to stand before his fellow men and talk without the deepest emotion concerning the awful tragedy that has come upon the entire world. A remarkable exhibition of feeling has just been made to you by the distinguished jurist who was forced by his duty as a citizen, as a lawyer and a judge to carry out the absolute mandates of our law. . . . He says to you that there is no question, no question that it has been proved beyond any peradventure that this man was the instrument that caused the death of our beloved President and he simply leaves you with the statement that if this man was mentally responsible, then he is fully and absolutely guilty of the crime of murder in the first degree."

Penney then reviewed the evidence presented by the prosecution, all pointing to such a verdict and all set forth with just the proper balance of expeditiousness and thoroughness. Just exactly what the district attorney meant by the term "diseased heart" is not clear when in reciting the details of the prisoner's background he said, "We have shown you that he had gone to these anarchistic or socialistic meetings and that there had been embedded in his diseased heart the seeds of this awful crime. . . ."

Certainly it was not synonymous with "diseased brain," for he immediately followed with an answer to the insanity implication in Lewis's summation, ". . . and the counsel says to you, gentlemen, that if—IF—the man was sane then, he is responsible. He says to you that this man must be presumed to be innocent, that that is a presumption of our law. But it is also a presumption of our law that every man is sane until proved insane."

The question then appeared "simple" to the district attorney. "What evidence is there in this case that the man is not sane?" he asked. "Under the presumption of the law that he is sane . . . how brief ought to be your meditation, how brief ought to be your consultation about the responsibility and criminality of this individual?"

Penney did not feel this was the place for oratorical flights or vivid imagination. All sensationalism, he said, had been eliminated by both sides. He reiterated the defense counsel's excoriation of lynch law, as well as his praise of the orderliness of the people of Buffalo. But the time had now come for the vindication of the law, to make a certain class of people "feel the strong arm of justice, the strong arm of the law," before something terrible would happen to "our beloved country."

There followed a brief resumé of that grand man who had stood but a few days before in the Temple of Music, with praise for his "strength and courage" in rising unaided from the lowly walks of life to become a lawyer, a judge, a Congressman, a Governor, and the President, "more than all else" praise for him as a loving husband and praise for the noble character demonstrated upon his deathbed by his words of resignation to God's will, and the great praise for one so great that could forgive his own assassin. He then pronounced the President, in his estimation the "noblest man that God ever created on the soil of the United States."

At this point, evidently, the district attorney was so over-wrought that he forgot his earlier statement that this was not the place for oratorical flights or vivid imagination and indulged in both. He concluded a 205-word sentence as follows: ". . . and I am convinced, if I never was before, that there is such a thing as a national heart and that great national heart has been weeping as it never wept before, the great heart is broken and it will take God's own time and God's own way to heal it, such a great calamity has been brought about."

Czolgosz's situation, the district attorney pointed out, was an ironical one, for here was a man who had repudiated the very institutions that were attempting to protect him. He had been represented by two "of the ablest and most respected jurists in our city with all the legal formalities just the same as if he were the most respected and highly thought of man heretofore."

Now that the duty of both defense and prosecution had been performed, it only remained for the jurymen to perform their duty and he expressed confidence in their decision.

The time for Justice White's charge to the jury had now arrived. As the jurist rose the jury also stood up and faced him. His voice was calm and restrained. Czolgosz, sweating, seemed to slump deeper into his chair and show signs of increased nervousness.

The justice spoke for 21 minutes.

Like Lewis and Penney before him, he recalled the prisoner's legally unacceptable self-condemnation at the time of his arraignment, smugly reminding the jurymen not to take it into consideration in their decision. Neither should the high position of the victim sway them from their duty.

He explained the term "reasonable doubt," which would be grounds for acquittal: ". . . it means so far as the application of the principle here is concerned, that you are bound to sift, compare and examine all of the evidence and all of the circumstances which have been developed upon this trial; and if, when you have done that, there exists in your mind a doubt as to the criminal responsibility of this man, you are bound to acquit him."

The justice broke into his explanation of the questions to be pondered by the jury to praise the decorum and respect for the law which up to that time had marked the "progress of this lamentable affair." No higher tribute might be paid to the dead President than "to observe that exalted opinion and reverence for the law which he would ask if he were here."

At this point the speaker's voice quavered and tears filled his eyes. For a moment he was forced to pause. But he went on to condemn mob rule as Anarchy in embryo. "The man who is ready to go out on the street today and commit a crime because some other man has committed a crime is as guilty in his heart as the man who already has committed the act."

Now came the definition and elucidation of the three possible verdicts pertinent to the case, each couched in approximately the same repetitive legal phraseology, yet each unique in designating a special gradation of guilt.

"So let me say in closing," said the jurist, "that if on the sixth day of September, 1901, the defendant did wrongfully, without justifiable cause or excuse assault, shoot and wound William McKinley at the place, in the manner and by the means alleged in the indictment upon which he is being tried, and such assault, shooting and wounding were committed from a deliberate and premeditated design to effect the death of the said William McKinley or of another, and if the said William McKinley thereafter died from the effects of such assault, shooting and wounding, and such assault, shooting and wounding were the sole and proximate cause of his death, and if at the time of such assault, shooting and wounding the defendant was not laboring under such a defect of reason as not to know the nature and quality of the act he was doing or that it was wrong, he is guilty of murder in the first degree."

The second proposition was worded in a manner almost identical to the first; so, for the benefit of any juryman who might have become entangled in the verbal thicket, Justice White elucidated: "The second proposition, as I read it to you, eliminates premeditation and deliberation," and defined "murder in the second degree."

If, however, there was "reasonable doubt" in the minds of the jurymen about either of these propositions, a third choice, "manslaughter in the first degree" was open to them. This, formally stated, was practically indistinguishable from the second except the phrase "with design to kill" became "without design to kill."

The justice called to the attention of the jury that each proposition was subject to the "test of responsibility."

"In other words, if he was laboring under such a defect of reason as not to know the nature and quality of the act he was doing or that it was wrong, it is your duty, gentlemen of the jury, to acquit him in this case."

Finally, he commended the jurymen's patience and attentiveness and closed with a plea for the continuance of the same seemly behavior that had characterized the proceedings to that point.

The jury sat down at 3:46.

The subject of the defendant's sanity now caused legal quibbling. Penney asked the court to charge the jury "that the law presumes every individual sane."

The court complied. "The law in this case presumes that the defendant was sane," said Justice White.

"I ask, Your Honor to charge the jury that the burden of overthrowing the presumption of sanity and of showing insanity is upon the person who alleges it," the district attorney further pressed.

"The burden of showing insanity is upon the person who alleges it. Is that all?"

Titus here interposed to ask, "You do not want that charged in that way?"

"I concede that that last part be stricken out," said the district attorney. "The counsel objects to it."

The Court said, "The burden in the first place, gentlemen of the jury, upon that proposition is with the defendant to give some evidence tending to show insanity on his part, or irresponsibility; but in that connection, when evidence of that kind is given, if it is given at all, it is incumbent upon the people to rebut or meet it with other evidence and remove all doubt in your minds—all reasonable doubt in your minds upon the subject."

Titus now requested, "I did not intend to ask Your Honor to charge anything before the counsel got up to request Your Honor to charge, but I now ask Your Honor to charge that if the jury are satisfied from all the evidence in the case that at the time of the committing of this assault he was laboring under such a defect of reason as not to know the quality of the act he was doing or not to know the act was wrong, that then he is not responsible and they must acquit him."

"I so charge," said Justice White. "I intended to make it very plain to the jury in the first place. Is that all, Judge Titus?"

"That is all, sir."

Justice White, turning to the jury, said. "You gentlemen may now retire with the officers."

Preceded and followed by court officers, the jurors filed out and were led to the second-floor jury room. The door was shut on them at 3:50.

Lauer, Carmer, and Waldow, as well as others, favored instant action in a verdict of guilty of murder in the first degree and return immediately to the courtroom.

Wendt, Everett, and others favored action only after a deliberated discussion. Wendt, without opposition, was chosen foreman after which the discussion began not as to the guilt of the prisoner but over the form or manner of finding him guilty.

The jurors who favored slower, more deliberate action wanted the matter of the defendant's sanity settled—but there was a cleavage on this point. Part of the jury thought this already had been settled and there was nothing further to discuss. Lauer urged finding the defendant guilty and others agreed.

Finally the slow-action jurors suggested a ballot on the sanity question. In all, four ballots were taken. On the first the jurors voted that Czolgosz was sane and they were unanimous in agreeing he was guilty. The third ballot was on whether the defendant's crime was murder in the second degree; all voted it was not. On the fourth ballot the jury voted Czolgosz was guilty of murder in the first degree.

The Buffalo Courier observed that during the taking of the ballots, a number of jurors indignantly insisted that the balloting was a waste of time and that they should simply find him guilty as charged and return immediately with their verdict.

"They overcame," *The Courier* reported, "the opinion of the two or three who thought it wise to wait an hour before bringing in the verdict. The few who favored delay had no doubt of the assassin's guilt. They desired to avoid any appearance of unseemly haste or lack of proper deliberation and consultation. So deep was the disgust of some of the jurors that they were loth to linger even in discussion of the wretch's case."

In the eyes of the same observer the prisoner seemed "to become of secondary moment. The law was first. Its working had been perfect. Its machinery had proved flawless."

Meanwhile, the crowd in the courtroom had increased and many made no secret of the fact that they were surprised that, after 15 minutes, the jury had not yet brought in its verdict. Finally, at 4:17, two thumps of the tipstaff sounded. Three minutes later, Justice White, who had taken a brief respite from his judicial labors, returned to the bench. At 4:24, the jury filed in, led by Juror Lauer. A moment later, Clerk Fisher called the names of the jurors, then asked, "Gentlemen of the jury, have you reached a verdict?"

"We have," responded Foreman Wendt.

"How do you find?"

At this critical moment a fly lit on Czolgosz's right cheek. He brushed it aside with a hand that shook visibly, but otherwise he showed no emotion as Wendt, holding up a piece of paper containing the verdict, read, "Guilty of murder in the first degree as charged in the indictment."

A murmur, subdued, then hushed, fell over the room, indicating to The Express reporter, "a thrill of exultation over the vindication of the supremacy and majesty of the law."

Then Clerk Fisher spoke up, "Gentlemen, listen to your verdict as the court has recorded it. You say you find the defendant guilty of murder in the first degree as charged in the indictment. So say you all?"

"We do," chorused the jurors.

Then Justice White told the jury "That ends your services, gentlemen," and a moment later the jurist left the room after scheduling the assassin's sentence for 2:00 P.M. Thursday.

The jury's deliberation had been brief—but too long to please Juror Lauer, who, upon leaving the courtroom, was heard to say, "If we had done it my way, we would have declared the ballot right here without leaving our seats." Several other jurors murmured assent.

"It was only a few minutes either way," remarked one. "He'll be dead a long time."

As defense attorney Lewis was making his "dignified, impressive speech, worthy of study and preservation," the defendant's father, his brother Waldeck, and his sister Victoria, accompanied by Constable Jacob Mintz of Cleveland, were arriving at the New York Central station. Constable Mintz had volunteered to be their escort, to help protect them from possible violence. The three members of Leon's family had not been subpoenaed, but, according to reporters, were principally interested in clearing themselves of any implication in or sympathy for Leon's unaccountable act. Victoria, a personable, intelligent young woman of 17, was deeply apprehensive of their being spotted and perhaps molested by the crowds at the station. However, her fears were unfounded. Neither there nor at the small nearby restaurant, where they were taken for a lunch after their arrival, did anyone recognize them, even though they were being escorted by Buffalo detectives and two or three newspapermen. Waldeck became separated from the others after murmuring something about wanting a drink. The elder Czolgosz and Victoria were taken to the district attorney's office.

When Bull learned of Waldeck's disappearance, he sent Detective Geary to find him and bring him to Headquarters. Eventually, all were reunited there. Meanwhile, the verdict against Leon had been brought in, and they were informed of it.

They had intended to remain in Buffalo but a few hours and return to Cleveland on an evening train, but Assistant District Attorney Haller informed them, "You certainly can't see Leon tonight and I make no promise as to tomorrow."

After they had submitted to some interrogation at Headquarters, the head janitress, Mrs. Reilly, prepared a supper for them. Since they hadn't brought enough money for overnight lodgings, Cusack offered them accommodations at Headquarters.

During the grilling by newsmen and authorities, the older Czolgosz, who could speak no English, spoke through an interpreter, either Sergeant Fredericks of the Eighth Precinct, or his daughter Victoria. The police and Haller thought Waldeck much brighter than his father but not so bright as Leon. To 62-year-old, Irish-born Patrick Cusack, Victoria made a special appeal. "The little Czolgosz girl is far above the general run of her class in intelligence," he commented.

Paul Czolgosz steadfastly denied he was an Anarchist, as had been reported. Waldeck emphasized the same thing about his father, who, he said, had no understanding of Anarchist principles. He himself had Socialist leanings but had no time to indulge in the realm of ideas. Both he and his father had voted the Democratic ticket, never the Socialist.

As far as supplying biographical details about Leon, the father thought he had been born in May 1872, but he did not know the day of the month. Waldeck told of his brother's education—two years of school in Alpena and night school in Cleveland during the winter of 1896-1897. Their own mother had died 17 years before. Waldeck was glad she had not been present to witness the tragedy. She had been a good mother and taught them right from wrong. She had been "awful good" to Leon and had, in fact, liked him best of all.

Leon had talked little about Emma Goldman, although after reading a report of her Cleveland appearance, he had told Waldeck he thought that kind of speech "pretty fair." Waldeck did not know whether his brother had heard the speech, but admitted he might have.

Waldeck told about the farm money, also of a $10 money order which he had sent to Leon in West Seneca the previous August. That his brother had requested him to address it to "Frank Snyder" did not strike Waldeck as unusual since Leon probably was unknown in West Seneca and was using the name of his landlord.

That night—the night after the verdict was returned—Czolgosz did not sleep so well as he had, but rolled about and awoke several times.

At 11:00 the next morning Jailer Mitchell appeared before Leon's cell on the third floor of the jail to tell him his relatives had come to visit him. A smile of pleasure flitted across his face.

Victoria was the first to greet him. "Leon," she said, accenting the second syllable, "Leon, what have you done?"

She kissed him and, sobbing, buried her head on his shoulder. He shoved her gently aside, but his lip quivered as he said, "There is father. I must speak to him."

Paul took his son's hand but said nothing. Leon spoke to him in Polish. Paul still made no answer. It was one of the many ironies of Leon's case that the same kind of taciturnity that he had been displaying toward the authorities was now directed toward him by his father.

Waldeck spoke up, "I am sorry you have come to this, Leon."

Leon made no answer. However, observers noted that his lip was again quivering. Then he asked about the members of the family at home.

Waldeck's belief that he might be able to extract from Leon what no one had yet been able to do—the names of possible accomplices—was shattered. Leon answered his questions simply, "I was alone in this." But he hung his head and twisted the button on his coat as Waldeck called his act deplorable.

To Victoria, who was sobbing so uncontrollably that even the two guards were moved by her emotion, he turned and asked her to stop for his sake.

When it was time to part, Leon grasped the hands of both his brother and father. Victoria broke out crying afresh as she kissed him goodbye.

In an interview with a *Buffalo Courier* reporter, Waldeck, who had spent the night in the witness room at Police Headquarters, expressed his sorrow at his brother's crime. "Leon was my chum in the old days," he said, "and I liked him."

It was not true, Waldeck answered to a query on the subject, that Cleveland grocers refused to deliver groceries to his family. They would continue to deliver, he said, as long as they had the money to pay for their purchases.

At 2:00 P.M. on Wednesday, September 25, Detective Solomon escorted the trio to the New York Central Exchange Street station, where they boarded a Lake Shore Railroad train for their return to Cleveland.

With the jury box filled with well-known lawyers and the courtroom jammed to standing room only, at 2:00 P.M. Thursday, September 26, Justice White was about to sentence Czolgosz.

Leaning forward the jurist spoke to Penney, "Mr. Penney, the court is at your service."

"I move sentence in the case of the people against Leon F. Czolgosz," promptly responded the district attorney. Then turning to the assassin, he said, "Stand up, Czolgosz, please."

Once the assassin had complied, he was ordered to place his

hand on the Bible, but he did not respond to the court oath. Penney then began what appeared to be a belated probe of the defendant's background.

The assassin answered slowly, haltingly, giving data that was already known to millions—his age, place of birth, last address, and occupation.

Q: What schools have you attended?

A: Small, common school.

Q: Been to the church school, too?

A: Yes.

Q: Catholic Church?

A: Yes.

Q: What church were you educated in? Did you used to go to the Catholic Church?

A: I did.

After answering, in response to further questions, that his father was living and his mother dead, he was asked, "Do you drink much? Drink intoxicating liquors much?"

"No, sir, don't drink too much."

Penney tenaciously pursued—rather inexplicably—the matter of drinking. "You never get drunk. Have you been in the habit of getting drunk? You are not, are you?"

Czolgosz, probably puzzled by this line of anticlimatic quizzing (which would have been more apropos to the preliminary questioning of a vagrant upon precinct booking) closed his eyes and remained mute.

Justice White, relieving what appeared to be an impasse, now ordered Penney to pass to something else.

"Have you been convicted of any crime before this?" asked Penney.

"No, sir."

Here Clerk Fisher took up the questioning, but the throng in the courtroom became so noisy that his voice was inaudible. After the spectators had been rebuked by the court, Fisher repeated his question. Then the prisoner made a surprising retort, "I would rather have this gentleman speak," he muttered with a nod toward District Attorney Penney.

"The clerk asks you if you have any legal cause to show why sentence should not be pronounced against you?"

"No, sir."

It was obvious now that the prisoner wished to make some sort of statement, so Penney encouraged him. "Make your statement then," said Penney.

The judge then explained the legal grounds he might claim for exemption from judgment at that time—first, insanity; ". . . the next is that you have good cause to offer either in arrest of the judgment about to be pronounced against you, or for a new trial. . . . you have the right to speak at this time, and you are at perfect liberty to do so freely."

Though he appeared not to be listening, Czolgosz answered, "I have nothing to say about that."

Since he seemed to wish to speak further, both the justice and the prosecutor urged him to do so. Finally, Titus, who was appearing alone on this day as his counsel, arose and standing next to him asked him what he wished to say.

"My family," said Czolgosz in a barely audible whisper, "they had nothing to do with it. I was alone. I want to say I was alone and had no one else, no one else but me."

As Czolgosz spoke in a low whisper, his counsel had to relay his words to the court. Finally, however, the prisoner falteringly with prompting by his counsel exculpated not only his family but anyone else from complicity in the crime.

He concluded, "I never told anything to nobody; I never told anything of that kind. I never thought of that until a couple of days before I committed the crime."

This, too, was repeated by Titus, then there was complete silence in the courtroom. The prisoner clutched the back of a chair.

"Anything further, Czolgosz?" asked Justice White.

"No, sir," murmured the prisoner.

Now the justice pronounced the sentence that all had been waiting to hear, as *The Express* described it, "without waver, without emotion, without expression either of pity or disgust, the voice of the law, the voice of justice, the voice of fate."

"Czolgosz, in taking the life of our beloved President, you committed a crime which shocked and outraged the moral sense of the civilized world. You have confessed your guilt, and, after learning all that can at this time be learned of the facts and circumstances of the case, twelve good men have pronounced your confession true and have found you guilty of murder in the first degree. You declare, according to the testimony of credible witnesses, that no other person aided or abetted you in the commission of this terrible act. God grant it may be so. The penalty of the crime of which you stand convicted is fixed by statute, and it now becomes my duty to pronounce its judgment against you. The sentence of the court is that in the week beginning on October 28, 1901, at the place, in the manner, and by the means prescribed by law you suffer the punishment of death. Remove the prisoner."

Justice White had omitted the usual commiserative evocation, "May God have mercy on your soul!"

Detective Geary eased the drooping body of the prisoner into his chair, then slipped the handcuffs over his wrists.

"Czolgosz, goodbye," said Titus.

The prisoner answered huskily, "Goodbye," then shook Titus's outstretched hand listlessly.

Back at his jail cell door, he bade goodbye to the two detectives, Solomon and Geary, then stepped into his cell, removed his coat, and sat down, his head buried in his hands.

23

A Model of Justice

THE DEFENDANT had hardly left the courtroom before the trial evoked a chorus of praise.

Even though Lewis had delivered a maudlin apology for his appearance as defense counsel, and both he and Titus had appeared to find it impossible not to help the prosecution, praise was lavished on them for their altruistic efforts.

From the sidelines, where he eagerly awaited the trial's outcome, Elihu Root was so pleased that he hastened to express his praise in a letter to Governor Odell, asking him to convey to the state and county officers charged with the administration of justice "an expression of satisfaction and approval." Root was convinced that the "law had been vindicated and the ends of justice attained."

"The court, the prosecuting attorney, the officers who had the prisoner in charge—all appear to have performed their duties with effectiveness and decorum and particular credit seems due to the distinguished gentlemen, who, upon the request of the bar of Erie County, undertook the disagreeable task of protecting the legal rights of the wretched culprit under the assignment of the court."

The Nation, in its leader of October 31, observed, "The people wanted only justice . . . but they wanted it speedily and surely. They got it."

"The time was wonderfully short for our system of punishing criminals," *The New York Times* commented, hailing the trial as a model of justice carried out in a "dignified way."

Dr. MacDonald praised and criticized the conduct of the trial. The alienist thought that the preparation and trial of the case by District Attorney Penney and his assistant, Haller, was "well neigh

241

faultless." MacDonald pointed out that shortly after Czolgosz's arrest Penney procured a statement from the prisoner of several pages in length. "This statement gave in detail facts concerning his premeditations and preparations for the crime, also his movements for some time prior, and up to the time of the shooting. The District Attorney also, within a few hours after the crime . . . proceeded to put the prisoner under the observation of local experts in mental disease."

These physicians, MacDonald observed, over a period of three weeks had free access to Czolgosz, and made a careful study of his case, and he added that Penney allowed experts on either side to confer together freely and the defense to have free access to all facts, a proceeding equivalent to the appointment of a commission of five experts.

"This course on the part of the District Attorney, marks a new departure in the methods of getting expert evidence in criminal trials where the question of mental responsibility is involved, which is to be highly commended as a practical measure tending to eliminate much superfluous testimony and at the same time to minimize the danger of contradictory expert opinions."

But MacDonald felt it was regrettable that no experts were called to testify to the prisoner's mental condition so it might appear on the record that Czolgosz's mental condition had been inquired into by competent authority.

Turning to the defense, MacDonald felt that substantially no preparation was made "beyond a fruitless effort of counsel to confer with the prisoner and the examination made of him at their request by Dr. Hurd and the writer with reference to his mental condition. . . . It also appears that no plea was entered by the attorneys for the defense, but Czolgosz speaking for the first time in court, entered a plea of guilty to the indictment which plea the court promptly rejected and directed that one of not guilty be entered. . . .

"Each juror on qualifying said, in answer to the usual question, that he had formed an opinion as to the guilt of the prisoner, but that this opinion could be removed by reasonable evidence tending to show that the defendant was innocent. And yet, to one accustomed to being in court . . . it was difficult to avoid the impression that each of the jurors in the case held a mental reservation to convict the prisoner."

MacDonald's reaction was that if Czolgosz had been on trial for the murder of an ordinary citizen, not one of the jury would have been accepted by the defense. In such a case, he felt, the selection of the jury would have consumed several days instead of approximately one hour and a half.

MacDonald, a veteran observer of murder trials, felt he had never witnessed such an anomalous defense. "Having in view the nature and importance of the case, the fact that no testimony was offered on the defendant's behalf and that practically no defense was made, beyond a perfunctory examination of jurors and a mild cross-examination of some of the people's witnesses, which was limited to efforts to elicit information respecting the President's condition during his illness and of his body after death, and a summing up by one of the counsel—Judge Lewis—which consisted mainly of an apology for appearing as counsel for the defendant and a touching eulogy of his distinguished victim, renders the case, in this respect, a unique one in the annals of criminal jurisprudence."

Dr. Allan McLane Hamilton in his autobiography, *Recollections of an Alienist,* published 17 years after he had viewed the trial, bitterly denounced it. "I really do not think in all my experience that I have ever seen such a travesty of justice," he wrote. The defense attorneys were particularly the objects of his condemnation: "The two superannuated and apparently self-satisfied ex-judges assigned for the defence apologised freely and humbly for *their appearance in behalf of this wretched man,* referred to 'the dastardly murder of our martyred President,' and really made nothing more than a formal perfunctory effort, if it could be called such. Long and fulsome perorations were indulged in by these remiss members of a great and dignified profession, and others who praised the dead President, and flattered each other, the District Attorney, the Presiding Judge, the Medical Faculty of Buffalo, and every one they could think of."

On the other hand, Louis L. Babcock, himself a witness for the State, discredits Hamilton as just "a disappointed job seeker" who had come to Buffalo to proffer his services to examine Czolgosz, but whose offer, Babcock insists, was rejected. Many thought that Hamilton (who was, incidentally, the grandson of both Alexander Hamilton and Louis McLane) was probably "seeking notoriety."

24

"Are You Sorry?"

ON SEPTEMBER 26, 1901, at 10:06 P.M. Sheriff Caldwell, Jailer Mitchell, and several guards hustled Leon Czolgosz aboard an Auburn-bound train. The "journey to the tombs," as it was called by one of the newspapermen who accompanied the party, had started. Except for the sullen silence of the prisoner the spirit in general was one of an outing. Car 1509 was amply stocked with sandwiches, pickles, and cheese—and a good supply of cigars. As the train rolled on through the night, the sheriff and his deputies settled back, lit cigars, and either ate or joshed with each other. The prisoner, handcuffed to Jailer Mitchell, sat between the law enforcement officer and Louis Seibold, correspondent of *The New York World*.

Czolgosz drew on a cigar, glaring at a reporter who asked if he had any message for the public.

"Was it a mistake?" asked the newsman.

"Yes."

"Are you sorry?" Jailer Mitchell prodded the prisoner, "Go ahead, Leon, speak up."

"Yes, I am," replied the prisoner. Then he lapsed into silence, his eyes fixed upon the fields, farmhouses and woods all bathed in eerie moonlight.

Until the party reached Rochester the trip was uneventful enough. At that city, a railroad brakeman, porter, and conductor gained entrance to the car and stood staring at the prisoner.

At Victor, eight blood-red lanterns had been hung outside the station. But until the train reached Canandaigua only a few spectators were abroad. As the train slipped into Canandaigua depot at 1:21, shouts and jeers arose.

A deputy sheriff poked his head out of the car window.

"What's this all about?" he demanded.

"Czolgosz," roared the crowd.

"Czolgosz," exclaimed the sheriff. "Why, he won't leave Buffalo until Saturday."

Across from the train lay a graveyard, bathed in soft moonlight. The black limbs of the trees surrounding it looked "like crepe" to one observer and caused the prisoner to shudder at the mournful scene.

At 2:10 the train passed Geneva. Fifty-five minutes later it chugged into Auburn, where an ugly crowd of 1500 waited, determined if possible to seize Czolgosz before he reached the prison. Four guards had been dispatched by Police Chief McMaster of Auburn to offset any such eventuality. The guards had slipped aboard the train as it reached the city's outskirts.

Cries of "kill him" rent the air as the train ground to a stop. The rear door of Car 1509 was flung open, and Czolgosz, surrounded by guards, emerged. The mob rushed forward. In the gloom broken only by the prison gate lights, Jailer Mitchell and the prisoner, protected by a phalanx of guards, moved forward step by step amidst a surge of angry cries. Punches were thrown and one struck Mitchell.

"Don't shoot," cried Sheriff Caldwell, to the guards. "Use your clubs."

"Keep close to me," Mitchell yelled to his prisoner above the uproar.

As he heard the cries and screaming threats and saw the mob clawing frantically to reach him, the prisoner wavered, then stumbled to his knees. "Oh, Oh," he moaned.

A few feet ahead, a big guard waited at the gate, ready to swing back the barrier when Czolgosz reached it. It was a race against death.

Now Mitchell and the guard were dragging the prisoner forward, foot by foot, "like a bag of salt." As they neared the gate, Prison Guard John Martin reached out and grabbed the prisoner and "with a mighty heave tossed him through the gate with Mitchell beside him."

The prisoner, still inert, half-conscious and moaning with terror, was dragged up the stairs to the prisoners' entrance, where a fresh shock awaited him. There, overhead at the main entrance, hung a large outsized picture of the man he had murdered. The assassin shuddered. The portrait was framed in black crepe and draped with American flags. Beside it hung a picture of the assassinated Garfield.

A minute later the prisoner began to shriek, then broke into hysteria. The guards summoned the prison physician, Dr. John Gerin. The doctor found Czolgosz writhing on the floor, crying and kicking his legs and waving his arms.

"Save me, save me," he was crying, each plea culminating in a shriek.

The prisoner's face was ashen. Sweat dropped from it like water. Spittle drooled from his chin. To a reporter who viewed the scene Czolgosz looked like a mad dog.

Warden J. Warren Mead had intended to read the death warrant upon the prisoner's arrival, but that plan was shelved and the prisoner was led toward Deputy Warden Allan J. Tupper's office. The door on the left of the vestibule swung back. Guard Morton stopped and picked up Czolgosz as if he were "a kitten" and carried him through the door.

Still screaming, the prisoner was clamped into a chair. His clothes were peeled off and he was jammed into a prison suit. At 3:26 Dr. Gerin, dressed in a blue and red military cloak, entered the room, eyed the prisoner for a minute, smiled, then injected a hypodermic. Within seconds the prisoner slumped to the floor, his head and lips twitching convulsively.

"Well, what is it?" someone in the room asked the doctor.

"Half fright—half fake," the doctor replied.

Guards now stepped forward, picked up the inert body and removed it to the chamber of the condemned, which consisted of five cells—each eight feet square and facing the west side of the building.

Czolgosz was placed in a vacant cell between two murderers, Clarence Egner, who had killed Keeper Benedict, and Fred Krist of Waverly, New York, the slayer of Kittie Tobin of the same village.

At 3:50 A.M. Dr. Gerin found the prisoner sound asleep. At 8:00 A.M. he was awakened, served breakfast, then measured for the Bertillion records. Hardly reassuring was the news that Cornell University already had asked for his skull and that Syracuse University would be interested in securing his body.

25

Czolgosz Executed

DURING THE AFTERNOON HOURS of October 28, the killer allowed Fathers Hickey and Pudzinski to visit his cell. He remained adamant, however, when the clerics pleaded with him to ask divine forgiveness. Despite the prisoner's surliness, the clerygmen offered to answer his call at any hour, should he repent. His brother Waldeck visited him a few hours before the execution. "Tell us, Leon, who got you into this scrape?" Waldeck asked.

"No one," came the sullen answer.

"Do you want to see the priest again?" asked Waldeck. Czolgosz began to pace his small cell. "No, damn them. I don't want them and don't have them praying over me when I'm dead. I don't want any of their damned religion."

His jailors reported the assassin slept soundly on the eve of his execution. He was still slumbering in the small gray hours of October 29 when the jailors unlocked his cell door. He sat up, rubbing and blinking his cold blue eyes, listening as the warden read the death warrant.

Czolgosz's request to see Waldeck again was denied. As last-minute preparations proceeded he told Superintendent Collins, "I want to make a statement."

"Well," demanded Collins, "what do you want to say?"

Czolgosz replied that he wanted to make his statement when there were "a lot of people around."

Collins was not impressed; he shook his head.

"Well, then," said Czolgosz, "I won't talk at all."

The prison guards now were summoned. Grasping the prisoner firmly by the arms, they led him to the electric chair. When he stumbled twice, the guards carried him forward to the rubber-covered platform upon which rested the chair.

247

248 THE MAN WHO SHOT MC KINLEY

As the straps and electrodes were adjusted Czolgosz cried out, "I am not sorry. I did this for the working people. My only regret is that I haven't been able to see my father."

Some witnesses claim that Czolgosz went to his death screaming curses and foaming like a maniac; others say he preserved his outward composure until Warden Mead gave the signal to switch on the 1700 volts of electricity. An observer who stood next to the chair recalled that the assassin in his last moment on earth ground his teeth as he muttered a curse.

The man who shot President McKinley died at 7:12 A.M. A surge of electric power hurled his body against the electric chair straps so violently that they cracked. Czolgosz's hands clenched; his body stiffened. The full current was maintained for 45 seconds, then slowly reduced. Upon the lessening of the current the body collapsed. Dr. MacDonald stepped forward and felt the assassin's heart. He could detect no pulsation, but he suggested that the current be restored for a few seconds. Czolgosz's body grew rigid. Two minutes later the warden pronounced him dead.

Dr. Edward A. Spitzka of New York City, conducted the three-hour examination of the assassin's brain and body organs, which revealed a healthy state of all the organs, including the brain. All of the physicians who attended the execution were present at the autopsy and all concurred in the findings of the examiners.

Czolgosz was buried in the prison cemetery in accordance with the following agreement with Waldeck Czolgosz.

"Auburn, New York, October 28—J. Warren Mead, agent and warden of Auburn Prison—I hereby authorize you as warden of Auburn Prison to dispose of the body of my brother, Leon F. Czolgosz, by burying it in the cemetery attached to the prison as provided for by the law of the State of New York.

"This request is made upon the express understanding that no part of the remains will be given to any person or society, but that the entire body will be buried in accordance with the law in the cemetery attached to the prison." Waldeck Czolgosz. Witnesses, John A. Sleicher, George E. Graham.

The assassin's clothing and his meagre belongings were burned: a carboy of sulfuric acid was dropped into the casket after it had been lowered into the grave. The assassin's corpse, doctors said, would disintegrate in about twelve hours.

Although removed by many miles at the time of Czolgosz's execution, Emma Goldman wrote in her autobiography (published thirty years later) a dramatic account of the event:

It was early dawn, October 29, 1901. The condemned man sat strapped to the electric chair. The executioner stood with his hand on the switch, awaiting the signal. A warden, impelled by Christian mercy, makes a last effort to save the sinner's soul, to induce him to confess. Tenderly he says: "Leon, my boy, why do you shield that bad woman, Emma Goldman? She is not your friend. She has denounced you as a loafer, too lazy to work. She said you had always begged money from her. Emma Goldman has betrayed you, Leon. Why should you shield her?"

Breathless silence, seconds of endless time. It fills the death chamber, creeps into the hearts of the spectators. At last a muffled sound and an almost inaudible voice from under the black mask.

"It doesn't matter what Emma Goldman has said about me. She had nothing to do with my act. I did it alone. I did it for the American people."

A silence more terrible than the first. A sizzling sound—the smell of burnt flesh—a final agonized twitch of life.

26

"I Didn't Want McKinley Killed"

AFTER FIFTEEN DAYS of incarceration, a relatively brief period for her, the High Priestess of Anarchism walked out of jail minus a tooth, which an overzealous Chicago policeman had knocked out.

On the fifth day after her arrest she found an unexpected champion in Chief O'Neill, who after listening to a detailed account of her activities from May 5 up to her arrest professed to believe in her innocence. "Unless you're a very clever actress, you are certainly innocent," Chief O'Neill told her. "I think you are innocent, and I am going to do my part to help you out."

To his offer, Emma replied, "It would indeed be a strange experience to have help from a chief of police."

Emma's treatment after this interview was in direct contrast to what she had received before. Attentions were lavished upon her.

"The officer on night duty now appeared with his arms full of parcels, containing fruit, candy, and drink stronger than grape-juice. 'From a friend who keeps a saloon around the corner,' he would say, 'an admirer of yours.' The matron presented me with flowers from the same unknown. One day she brought me the message that he was going to send a grand supper for the coming Sunday. 'Who is the man and why should he admire me?' I inquired. 'Well, we're all Democrats, and McKinley was a Republican,' she replied. 'You don't mean you are glad McKinley was shot?' I exclaimed. 'Not glad exactly, but not sorry, neither,' she said; 'We have to pretend, you know, but we're none of us excited about it.' 'I didn't want McKinley killed,' I told her. 'We know that,' she smiled, 'but you're standing up for the boy.' I wondered how many more people in America were pretending the same kind of sympathy with the stricken President as my guardians in the station-house."

Meanwhile Emma had refused two offers. The first came from Hearst, who was willing to give her $20,000 if she would go to New York for an exclusive interview. Her friend Max Baginski explained that Hearst was anxious to whitewash himself of the charge of having incited the assassin. The second was an offer of advice from Clarence Darrow delivered by a representative from his office—a warning to cease defending Czolgosz. ". . . the man was crazy and I should admit it. 'No prominent attorney will accept your defense if you ally yourself with the assassin of the President,' he assured me; 'in fact, you stand in imminent danger of being held as an accessory to the crime.'"

Emma describes her reaction to the Darrow emissary: "His talk was repugnant to me. I informed him that I was not willing to swear away the reason, character, or life of a defenseless human being and that I wanted no assistance from his chief."

She records further, "The country was in a panic. Judging by the press, I was sure that the people of the United States and not Czolgosz had gone mad."

"It was a repetition of the dark Chicago days. Fourteen years, years of painful growth, yet fascinating and fruitful years. And now the end! The end? I was only thirty-two and there was yet so much, so very much undone. And the boy in Buffalo—his life had scarce begun. What was his life, I wondered; what the forces that drove him to this doom 'I did it for the working people,' he was reported to have said. The people! Sasha [Berkman] also had done something for the people; and our brave Chicago martyrs, and the others in every land and time. But the people are asleep; they remain indifferent. They forge their own chains and do the bidding of their masters to crucify their Christ."

An interviewer was amazed by Emma's ambivalent attitude toward Czolgosz and McKinley. Next day his story appeared under the headline, "Emma Goldman Wants To Nurse President; Sympathies Are With Slayer." Emma's explanation was entirely reasonable, at least to herself. Czolgosz had acted unselfishly, idealistically. On the other hand, "William McKinley, suffering and probably near death, is merely a human being to me now. That is why I would nurse him."[1]

Meanwhile, District Attorney Thomas Penney persisted in trying to extradite Emma to Buffalo to be tried for conspiracy. The Chicago authorities steadfastly refused to comply. Nevertheless, she was placed under $20,000 bail. Added to the $15,000 for the Isaak group it made too large a sum for their friends to raise, so she was transferred to the Cook County Jail.

The night before her transfer, Emma's saloon-keeper admirer (who was also a ward heeler and a rabid Democrat) sent her a turkey dinner, including wine and flowers—also an offer of $5000 toward her bail. Emma shared the dinner with a number of her keepers. Other compensations she discovered were that she was being held in the same place as the Haymarket martyrs (even with one of the same guards) and that next day she would be in the same jail in which four of them had been hanged.

Although her removal from the Harrison Street station was not attended by the riots predicted by the press, Emma did engage in an altercation with a guard. Protesting the rough treatment he was giving another prisoner, she was knocked to the floor of the patrol wagon. "He had landed his fist on my jaw, knocking out a tooth and covering my face with blood. Then he pulled me up, shoved me into the seat, and yelled: 'Another word from you, you damned Anarchist, and I'll break every bone in your body!' " she later recounted.

Emma's reaction to the news of McKinley's death was characteristic: "Is it possible . . . that in the entire United States only the President passed away on this day? Surely many others have died at the same time, perhaps in poverty and destitution, leaving helpless dependents behind. Why do you expect me to feel more regret over the death of McKinley than of the rest?"

She was in despair at the thought of Czolgosz's certain doom now and even more at the torture of body and spirit he would endure before the end came. A sudden realization of Czolgosz's possible motive brought her further anguish. Perhaps, she reasoned, the warning against him printed in *Free Society* had

---

1. Emma had studied both midwifery and nursing in Vienna in 1895–1896.

prompted him to prove himself a true Anarchist to those who had suspected him of being a spy.

"But why," she wondered, "had he chosen the President rather than some more direct representative of the system of economic oppression and misery? Was it because he saw in McKinley the willing tool of Wall Street and of the new American imperialism that flowered under his administration? One of its first steps had been the annexation of the Philippines, an act of treachery to the people whom America had pledged to set free during the Spanish War. McKinley also typified a hostile and reactionary attitude to labour; he had repeatedly sided with the masters by sending troops to strike regions. All these circumstances, I felt must have exerted a decisive influence upon the impressionable Leon, finally crystallizing in his act of violence."

The next morning she was still pacing her cell, "Leon's beautiful face, pale and haunted, before me."

After the President's death another demand for extradition by Buffalo authorities met with no success; this time as a result Emma was set free.

Emma grumbled at the scanty treatment given by the press to her release—scanty at least in comparison with the flaming headlines that had accompanied her arrest and followed her imprisonment.

The Isaak group having also been dismissed, all the comrades enjoyed a reunion at the Isaak home.

However, she was soon disillusioned by Chief O'Neill's motives when a journalist friend informed her that O'Neill had been anxious to have several of his captains brought to justice for perjury and bribery. Rather than allow them to use the Anarchists' arrests to their own advantage he backed Emma's cause.

Their next consideration must be what they could do for Czolgosz. Thwarted by the circumstances surrounding the prisoner in Buffalo, as well as a plan to hold a public meeting in Brand's Hall, Emma wrote an article, "The Tragedy of Buffalo," which she turned over to Isaak for publication in *Free Society*.

"Leon Czolgosz and other men of his type . . . far from being depraved creatures of low instincts are in reality supersensitive beings unable to bear up under too great social stress. They are driven to some violent expression, even at the sacrifice of their own lives, because they cannot supinely witness the misery and suffering of their fellows. The blame for such acts must be laid at the door of those who are responsible for the injustice and inhumanity which dominate the world. . . . As I write, my thoughts wander to the young man with the girlish face about to be put to death, pacing his cell, followed by cruel eyes:

> Who watch him when he tries to weep
> And when he tries to pray,
> Who watch him lest himself should rob
> The prison of its prey.

My heart goes out to him in deep sympathy, as it goes out to all the victims of oppression and misery, to the martyrs past and future that die, the forerunners of a better and nobler life."

On checking the proof for the article, Emma discovered that it had been toned down to such an extent that it had lost its impact. She suspected Isaak, who readily admitted to having edited it in order to save *Free Society*. "And incidentally your skin!" snapped Emma. It took some persuasion to have "The Tragedy of Buffalo" appear in its original form, but eventually Emma won out.

On her way back to New York she stopped in Rochester for a month with her family, who had endured much embarrassment and even persecution on her account. Her father's furniture business had suffered, and he had been excommunicated from his synagogue.

In New York Emma discovered that no one would rent a room to so notorious an Anarchist. Finally, she approached a young prostitute she had once nursed, who, Emma records, was "tickled to death" to let Emma have her flat.

But Emma's quest for help on Czolgosz's behalf was to no avail. American and Jewish Anarchists were not interested—in fact, they felt that Czolgosz had done the Anarchist cause much harm. The only groups who felt sympathetic were the Italian, Spanish, and French Anarchists; but they had no way of influencing the general American public.

27

Was Czolgosz Insane?

AFTER THE TRIAL Dr. Crego summarized concisely the work and decisions of the six alienists involved in the case in a statement to a *Buffalo Express* reporter: "The three doctors called in by the District Attorney, Drs. Fowler, Putnam and myself, examined Czolgosz four times. Each time we had him under observation for two hours. We applied all the known tests. Our first examination led us to believe he was sane. Each of our subsequent inquisitions confirmed that conviction.

"The two experts called by the Bar Association and the defendant's attorneys, Drs. MacDonald and Hurd, examined Czolgosz three times, two hours at a time. Their conclusion was the same as ours. In fact, there was but one conclusion reached by all six doctors—that Leon Czolgosz was sane."

Had Dr. Hamilton examined him, the reporter queried.

"No, he did not," Dr. Crego answered, and went on to explain Dr. Hamilton's position. "He was called here by the prosecution. Had Drs. MacDonald and Hurd reached the conclusion that the prisoner was insane, Dr. Hamilton would have been called upon to examine the defendant and if his conclusion confirmed that of the alienists for the prosecution, his testimony would have been sought to strengthen our position."

On November 2, the official report of the Buffalo alienists was filed in the office of the District Attorney and its salient points made known to the public. It simply detailed what had been well established (at least outside of the courtroom) during the trial—that Czolgosz was sane.

The doctors felt that their early opportunity to interview the prisoner—within a few hours of the crime—had been an advantage,

255

for then he had been willing to talk freely about his seemingly unmotivated act.

The next day he repeated what he had said during their previous examination, thereby showing that his memory was "perfect." His fastidiousness about his dress and person was cited as not characteristic of insane persons.

Although after September 8 he refused to discuss the crime with them, from their two examinations and reports filed with them by observers of him during his incarceration, they concluded that he was sane before the crime, at the time he committed the crime, and during his trial. His actions were consistent with his belief in Anarchy. Anarchist leaders and propagandists had found in Czolgosz "a willing and intelligent tool; one who had the courage of his convictions, regardless of personal consequences."

He was not a victim of paranoia "because he has not systematized delusions reverting to self, and because he is in exceptionally good condition, and has an unbroken record of good health. His capacity for labor has always been good, and equal to that of his fellows."

Neither was he to be classed as a degenerate, because their examinations revealed none of the stigmata of degeneration; "his skull is symmetrical; his ears do not protrude, nor are they of abnormal size, and his palate not highly arched."

"He is the product of anarchy; sane and responsible" was their conclusion.

Dr. MacDonald's association with the case and his conclusions regarding it were the subject of an article appearing in *The Philadelphia Medical Journal* for January 4 of the next year, and published jointly with the report of the post-mortem examination by Edward Anthony Spitzka. His essential conclusion recorded here "unqualifiedly," that "Leon F. Czolgosz . . . was in all respects a sane man—both legally and medically—and fully responsible for his act," was, of course, already known. His reasons for this opinion and the means by which he had arrived at it furnish interesting reading for the reader of today and must at the time have seemed to present the final word of authority on the subject of Czolgosz's mental state.

What Czolgosz said as he was about to die, that the President had been "an enemy of the good and working people," was, Dr.

MacDonald admits, the expression of a delusion; but it was not an "insane delusion or false belief due to disease of the brain. On the contrary, it was a political delusion . . . founded on ignorance, faulty education and warped—not diseased—reason and judgment —the false belief which dominates the politico-social sect to which he belonged and of which he was a zealot. . . . The course and conduct of Czolgosz from the beginning down to his death are entirely in keeping with this [the Anarchists'] creed."

Dr. MacDonald made his last examination of the assassin together with Dr. John Gerin, the Auburn prison physician, on the night before the execution. At that time he found nothing to change his opinion from that expressed at Buffalo. Dr. Gerin, who had observed Czolgosz carefully during the four weeks of his imprisonment, concurred with Dr. MacDonald in judging the prisoner to be sane.

Under the direction of Drs. MacDonald and Gerin and in the presence of five other doctors, Edward A. Spitzka, an eminent alienist associated with the College of Physicians and Surgeons in New York City, conducted a four and a half hour post-mortem examination. In compliance with the Czolgosz family's wishes and for "reasons of a sentimental nature on the part of State authorities," Warden Mead refused to allow any portion of the body to be removed for further microscopic examination and study. While Dr. MacDonald considered this regrettable, he felt the State had been fortunate "to secure the services of so able a brain anatomist and skilled operator and draughtsman as Mr. Spitzka to make the post-mortem examination."

Spitzka's report, with plates of drawings and photographs to illustrate it, gave a fully detailed description of the dissection and complete physical structure of the body with special attention to the brain of the assassin. Other than scars probably indicating a form of venereal disease (although Czolgosz had admitted only to gonorrhea in his examinations by Dr. MacDonald), his body was normal; and nothing about the structure of the brain indicated abnormality. In his conclusion Spitzka was somewhat cautious. "Of course," he wrote, "it is far more difficult . . . to establish sanity upon the results of an examination of the brain, than it is to prove insanity. It is well-known that some forms of psychoses have absolutely no ascertainable anatomical basis; and the assumption has been made that these psychoses depend rather upon circulatory and chemical disturbances. So far as this question touches upon the body and the brain of Czolgosz, there have been found absolutely none of those conditions of any of the viscera that could have been at the bottom of any mental derangement. Taking all in all, the verdict must be, 'socially diseased and perverted, and not mentally diseased.' "

The painstaking research of Drs. Walter Channing and L. Vernon Briggs has already been cited. Their conclusions controverted those previously established on two pivotal points; namely, that Czolgosz was an Anarchist and that he was sane.

The essence of Dr. Channing's article about their study, published in the October 1902, issue of the *American Journal of Insanity* is expressed in ten conclusions with which he closes. These are in substance:

1. The opinion of the experts who examined Czolgosz cannot be accepted as final.

2. The shortness of time forbade an investigation of Czolgosz's early life which would have revealed that some of his own statements about it were inaccurate.

3. He was not a true Anarchist. Anarchy was not the true cause of his act or an adequate explanation.

4. For several years he had been in ill health, which changed him from an industrious and fairly normal young man into a sickly abnormal one.

5. In this sickliness and abnormality it is probable that he conceived the idea of performing a great act for the common working people.

6. This resulted in the true delusion that it was his duty to kill the President because he was the enemy of the people.

7. His conduct after the crime was not inconsistent with insanity.

8. His history furnishes a good illustration of the typical regicide or magnicide as described by Régis.

9. The post-mortem examination threw no light on his mental condition and would not invalidate the opinion that the existing delusion was the result of disturbed brain action.

10. From all the facts that had come to his [Dr. Channing's] attention insanity appeared the most reasonable and logical explanation of the crime.

Dr. Allan McLane Hamilton, who had been one of the battery of alienists summoned in the Guiteau case, was also (he claims) called to Buffalo to examine Czolgosz. However, he had not been allowed to see the McKinley assassin. He was permitted to sit in on the trial, and did so.

In his autobiography published in 1916 he expresses agreement with the Channing opinion, stating, "Had I been allowed, and had the trial not been hurried on with such indecent haste, I would have made the same examination subsequently undertaken by Dr. Walter Channing, the learned psychiatrist of Brookline, Mass., who after the execution established without doubt the family's degeneracy and the prisoner's mental disease, but the newspapers were impatient and something had to be done and at once to appease the vengeful and restless public."

28

Aftermath

THE EXPOSITION, which had swung back its gates with rosy prospects on a snowy May 1, closed them under a pall of gloom six months later. A brief ceremony at midnight on November 2, 1901, brought to an end the giant fair; and although over eight million people had passed through its turnstiles, it was a failure—at least from a financial standpoint—haunted, as it were, by the tragedy that had at once blighted its gaiety and its hopes.

The sadness caused by the death of the President extended across the nation, but was particularly evident in the capital. The oldest citizens of Washington could not remember when that city had been plunged into a depression more profound. The excitement that had gripped the city after Lincoln's murder was more intense but even the Great Emancipator's death had not so depressed the people. President Garfield had been widely admired, but his death was not mourned as was McKinley's.

Capital hostesses looked forward with misgivings to a bleak winter and a social season bereft of its usual vivacity. The new President, following the precedent set by President Chester Arthur two decades before, it was thought, would extend the official mourning until March 14, 1902.

It was inevitable that the world-wide publicity accompanying so exalted a patient as the President of the United States should cause his case to become the subject of endless wrangling, both in and out of medical circles.

The Buffalo doctors who attended McKinley, following a meeting at the home of Ansley Wilcox on September 17, 1901, issued a statement denying dissension among themselves: "The undersigned, surgeons and physicians who were in attendance on the late President McKinley, have had their attention called to the

260

certain sensational statements published in the daily papers and particularly in one New York paper, indicating dissension and mutual recrimination among them.

"We desire to say to the press and the public, once and for all, that every such publication and all alleged interviews with any of us containing criticism of one another or of any of our associates, are false and are nothing but scandal mongering.

"We say again that there was never disagreement among the professional attendants as to any of the symptoms or as to treatment of the case, or as to the bulletins which were issued. A very unusual harmony of opinion and of action prevailed all through the case.

"The unfortunate result could not have been foreseen before the unfavorable symptoms declared themselves late on the sixth day and could not have been prevented by any human agency.

"Pending the completion and publication of the official reports of the post-mortem examiners and of the attending staff we shall refuse to make any further statements for publication, and alleged interviews with any of us may be known to be fictitious."

The statement was signed by Drs. Mann, Mynter, Park, Wasdin and Stockton.

An article in the *Journal of the American Medical Association*, which examined the case and compared it to the Garfield case, commended Dr. Mann's method of enlarging the original wound, irrigating the cavity, and his use of interrupted sutures. Full confidence was expressed in the judgment of the attending surgeons' decision not to provide for further drainage of the wound. The length of the operation (an hour and a half) suggested that each step had been considered judiciously. The cutting off of further search for the bullet was thought praiseworthy. Failure to use the X-ray machine to locate the exact position of the ball was understandable in the light of the practice of "the greatest of military surgeons" of the day. A second operation to extract the bullet from the muscles of the back would under the circumstances have been "censurable," for an encysted bullet that was doing no harm at the time of its removal.

The article stated: "The public was fairly and candidly treated from beginning to end. The unexpected happened."

The "courageous action of Dr. Mann and his associates in performing an immediate laparotomy" was termed "more to be commended now than it would have been three years ago." Although Emil Theodore Kocher of Berne had first operated successfully for a pistol shot wound of the stomach in 1884, the general treatment of such wounds by military surgeons during the Spanish-American and Boer Wars did not usually involve surgery. The fortunate outcome of such a case depended upon the bullet becoming encysted. However, the article continues: "A rule which is applicable and proper in military surgery cannot always be accepted in civil practice. The wounds are different; the facilities and environments are different. The modern rifle ball is small, conical . . . of great velocity, and cuts like a knife. Such a wound occurring in soldiers with comparatively empty gastro-intestinal tracts—brought about by starvation and diarrhea, common conditions in soldiers—might be recovered from; whereas, a pistol ball, which is usually larger, rounder, and of less velocity, makes a greater and more ragged opening, through which extravasation from any of the hollow viscera injured would almost surely take place. It is also far more likely to carry in clothing and other foreign material which would have a tendency to cause irritation and even sepsis."

American Medicine, a medical journal of Philadelphia, recalled that statistics of gunshot wounds of the abdomen had not been encouraging. "For a long time the results were so unfavorable, whether cases were treated by exploratory laparotomy or by the 'do nothing' system, that surgeons were divided as to the proper plan of procedure; but present increased knowledge and experience have brought better results, and all are now agreed that early and rapid operation with arrest of hemorrhage, toilet of peritoneum, removal of irritant and septic material and careful closure of any and all openings in the viscera, offer the best hope of saving life. All observations show that the chances of recovery rapidly diminish in proportion to the lapse of time before operation, the patient rarely surviving a section done a half day or more subsequent to the injury."

The *Medical Record,* published in New York City, although terming the suturing of the stomach wounds as "brilliant," criticized the failure of diagnosis. The AMA *Journal* responded to the *Record* article by calling the criticism "premature," since it had been published before the final autopsy reports had been made known.

In the proceedings of the staff meetings of the Mayo Clinic January 12, 1944, Dr. S. B. Harper reexamined the cases of Presidents Lincoln, Garfield, and McKinley in the light of modern medical and surgical knowledge. He praised Dr. Mann's decision to operate at once, stating it would "be considered entirely correct today while under the circumstances of the times his decision was remarkable." As to the possibility of saving McKinley's life in 1944, Harper believed that though the surgery might be the same, improved X-ray, sulfa drugs and penicillin, plasma or whole blood, anticoagulant drugs, and intravenous use of adequate amounts of fluids would undoubtedly have played an important part in the treatment of the patient. On the drainage question Dr. Harper agreed with Dr. Mann, who at the time of McKinley's death had justified his decision not to drain the wound by stating that there was nothing to drain—no bleeding or oozing—also that drainage could do harm as well as good.

Dr. Park's reminiscences, written in 1911 but not published in their entirety until 1945, revealed some of the differences of opinion among the attending physicians.

Dr. Park's position in not pushing drainage was understandable since he had witnessed only the conclusion of the operation. However, he termed the decision not to drain one "which subsequent events proved to be probably unfortunate." No one present, he said, had practiced posterior or through and through drainage though he conceded this might have been difficult because "the patient's body was so stout."

"While therefore," he stated, "probably no one would, at that time, have drained posteriorly it certainly would have been wiser had an anterior drain been made. Whether this would have saved the patient or not I cannot say, but I have always regretted that it was not put into practice."

Several weeks after McKinley died, Dr. Park recalled that he had treated a gunshot case similar "in every respect as nearly as could be made out, of a woman who attempted suicide by firing a bullet into the upper abdomen. I found perforation of the stomach and injury to the pancreas; at all events I closed the stomach perforation and made posterior as well as anterior drainage; this case recovered without an untoward symptom."

For Dr. Edgar Wallace Lee's aggressiveness Dr. Park expressed disdain although Dr. Lee's action and attitude before Dr. Park's arrival must have been recounted to him by others:

"Regarding this Dr. Lee, he happened to be on the grounds as a visitor; he had been medical director of one of the western expositions, and was on his way to New York where he proposed to, and did locate. He manifested a tremendous amount of nerve in almost forcing his way into the operating room, talking with the president, and virtually offering to do the operation himself, it even appearing as though he tried to bring this about. He left for New York the same evening, and, in spite of our injunction to reticence and secrecy, he did a lot of talking the following day in New York. In reality he was more hindrance than help although it was a somewhat difficult matter to eliminate him."

As to Dr. Mann's and Dr. Mynter's general competence to perform this operation, Dr. Park's reminiscences suggest his own reservations: "I do not believe that Dr. Mann had ever done a gunshot case before. Dr. Mynter had, however, of course, seen them and handled them, but neither of them insisted upon a clean excision of the bullet track and tissues immediately surrounding it through the whole thickness of the abdominal covering, i.e., some three inches and this contused and minutely ragged tubular wound was closed with the rest of the incision which all seemed to me unfortunate."

Relying upon reports from Drs. Parmenter and Wilson Dr. Park commented, too, upon their allegation that perspiration from Dr. Mynter's forehead had dropped into the open wound. "Mynter by the way always perspired freely when doing any of this work in a warm room. I do not recall caps or gauze were worn by anyone in the room. I mention this fact about the drops of perspiration because they might be supposed to have produced septic infection but nothing of the kind was shown at the autopsy, nor by the bacteriological examinations made by Dr. Matzinger."

Of the inadequate facilities for so difficult an operation, Dr. Park observed: ". . . and while the operating room was practically sufficient for all ordinary purposes it must be acknowledged that both light and equipment were not all that could have been desired.

"Had I been present at the time the president arrived at the hospital all this would have been changed or else I should have insisted upon his being taken to the General Hospital where the admirable facilities would have permitted easier work."

A few, wrote Park, "have not hesitated to express their unreserved opinions to the effect that it was simply a matter of jealousy rather than of urgent haste because of the president's symptoms" that caused the surgeons to plunge into the operation before Park's arrival. The President was in fact gaining in strength and his pulse steadily improving, "and there was no reason to fear immediate collapse nor to suspect serious internal hemorrhage. It was known that I was hurrying to the scene as rapidly as possible and would soon be there, but perhaps with these few words enough has been said on this score."

In response to Dr. Park's published reminiscences, which seemed to cast aspersions upon her father's work, Mrs. Agnes Mynter Robertson wrote some of her own recollections and comments:

First, she recalled that Dr. Park was not present during most of the operation. "This disposes of his statements that Dr. Mann and my father did sloppy, peevish work, that other doctors were urging him to take the operation away from them, and that he urged the wound be left open and drainage tubes put in."

As to the operation having been done with unnecessary haste, she said simply, "this is not true. The president would have died within half an hour except for the speedy operation. Dr. Simpson confirms this. When my father arrived the two young internes were frantic, realizing that the president was at the point of death."

Her father had wanted drainage tubes himself, but the other doctors outvoted him.

As to the sweat that dropped from her father's forehead into the wound during the operation she admitted that her father did perspire during the operation. "Therefore he invariably wore a towel about his head, and kept a nurse wiping off his brow."

She was quite certain that her father had had "plenty of experience" with gunshot wounds but admits that in this case she could not speak with authority.

That the wound had not been cleaned properly, Mrs. Robertson branded "an absurdity." This was proved by the fact that the wound had healed perfectly, "though inside, where it was impossible to trace it without cutting too far, the path of the bullet was gangrened."

Mrs. Robertson's seventh point refers to her father's magnanimity in consigning the operation to Dr. Mann. "My father, who was first to arrive, was all ready for an emergency operation when Dr. Mann came. He did the biggest thing of his life when he said, 'Dr. Mann, you are the older man. Will you perform the operation?' The minutes of the Medical Society, which I have, give him full credit for this in a speech by Dr. Hopkins."

This concession on Dr. Mynter's part, though possibly performed, could not have been rightly based upon age, for Dr. Mann was less than two months older than Dr. Mynter. Dr. Mynter's practice in Buffalo was actually of longer duration than Dr. Mann's.

As recently as March 1963, Dr. Selig Adler[1] reexamined the McKinley case in an article published in *The Scientific American.* After reviewing the chief cause of death as discovered by the autopsy—injury to the pancreas with complications—in the light of Dr. Mann's unsatisfactory explanation that the President's vitality had been weakened by years of sedentary life "to the point where nature failed to provide a normal healing process," Dr. Mynter's bluff expression of mystification of what had gone wrong, Dr. Wasdin's firm opinion that the bullet had been poisoned, Dr. Park's conviction that "toxic products escaping from the pancreas had resulted in terminal toxemia," Dr. Adler adds:

"In the light of our present knowledge, according to a leading Buffalo pathologist, fluid and electrolyte imbalance must also be taken into account in explaining the unexpected fatal outcome.

"In passing judgment on McKinley's physicians, one must always recall the limitations under which they worked. Laboratory determination for measuring changes in body chemistry, intravenous feedings, blood transfusions, antibiotics, effective postoperative technics, and medical therapy for acute damage to the pancreas all had to wait for the future."

Dr. George E. Moore, then director of Roswell Park Institute

---

1. Dr. Adler is the Samuel P. Capen Professor of American History in the State University of Buffalo.

in Buffalo, answered the question of whether McKinley's life could have been saved today by referring to the use of "modern antibiotic drugs and improved surgical techniques" which might have produced a more fortunate result. He believes that a bullet through the pancreas would not necessarily be fatal, though he concedes there are opposing schools of thought on this. However, he expressed doubt as to whether any surgeon could have saved the President's life in 1901.

The payment of McKinley's doctors by Congressional appropriation was not entirely without distasteful publicity, though unmarked by the acrimony and lack of professionalism that had characterized the Garfield case. In the case of the 1881 assassination exorbitant demands by the medical men met a severe bluepenciling by a Board of Audit. Dr. D. W. Bliss of Washington was pared down from $25,000 to $6500; Dr. D. Hayes Agnew of Philadelphia from $14,700 to $5000; Dr. Frank Hamilton from $25,000 to $5000; Dr. Robert Reyburn of Washington from $10,800 to $4000; and Dr. Susan G. Edson, who acted as nurse, from $10,000 to $3000. Dr. Silas Boynton's more modest demand of $4500 was reduced by only $500; while the $1000 claim of D. S. Lamb, surgeon of the U.S. Army, for the post-mortem examination was disallowed.

Milburn, to quash the rumor that he and Hanna were to act as bluepencilling agents, issued a statement on February 28, 1902, denying that this was the case. After conferring with doctors he said that certain figures had been made which were agreed upon all around.

"There is no basis whatsoever," he stated, "that the bills for services of doctors who attended the late President were referred to Senator Hanna and myself; that any bills rendered had been revised or cut down; or that I have anything to do with the preparation of any bill to be submitted to Congress. Some time ago I was requested to confer with the doctors about their compensation. No bills have been rendered by them. We met and talked the matter over. . . . As the result of our talks certain figures were made which were agreed upon all around, and those figures I sent to Washington, which is the last I have heard of the matter."

An article on May 4, 1902, in *The Buffalo Courier* presumed to take up the cause of Dr. Mynter, who, information from Washington revealed, would receive $6000 from a Congressional appropriation of $31,000, as contrasted to Dr. Mann, who would receive $10,000. Dr. Mynter, the article pointed out, had been present 25 minutes before Dr. Mann's arrival and had already secured the President's permission to operate. The article quoted from Dr. Mann's own statement in *American Medicine* (October 1901) acknowledged Dr. Mynter's assistance: ". . . not only was he an assistant, but he was much more and helped me greatly as a consultant with his good judgment and extensive knowledge of abdominal work. Although called first, he waived his claim and generously placed the case in my hands, willingly assuming his share of the responsibility."

Although mention was made of articles which charged that Dr. Mynter had been "buncoed out of the operation through the machinations of a clique," no statements were available from any of the principals involved. "None presumed what they or anyone else will get."

In the same article, *The Courier* listed amounts to be given the doctors—purportedly based upon information from Washington:

Dr. Mann	$10,000
Dr. Mynter	$ 6,000
Dr. Park	$ 2,500
Dr. Parmenter	$ 2,500
Dr. Janeway	$ 2,500
Dr. McBurney	$ 2,500
Dr. Johnson	$ 2,000
Dr. Stockton	$ 2,000
Dr. Gaylord	$ 1,000
Total	$31,000

Finally, an appropriation of $45,000 to cover the unpaid McKinley expenses was passed by Congress. Of this $10,000 would go to Dr. Mann with the other medical men to be paid "proportionately," *The Buffalo Express* reported on July 20, 1902. Exact amounts were kept secret, however.

Dr. Rixey's and Dr. Wasdin's services did not figure in the bill, since both were in the service of the United States.

Within 36 years three Presidents—Lincoln, Garfield, and Mc-
Kinley—had died by assassin's hands. In the past, assassinations
had been associated in the American mind with the autocratic
rulers of foreign countries; but no record could approach this.
The public was aghast. It had learned a bitter lesson—one which
by the time of Theodore Roosevelt's accession to office was to result in formal protection by the Secret Service. Roosevelt, with
characteristic fearlessness, reluctantly consented to protection
until the expiration of his term in 1909.

In 1912, seeking a third term as the Progressive Bull Moose
candidate, the hero of San Juan Hill, who had braved the dangers
of war and African big game hunting, felt scant need for protection as he set out on a cross-country campaign tour. He might
have felt different had he known of the murderous design lurking
in the mind of a mild-mannered, part-time New York City bartender who considered a third term iniquitous and who further
considered Roosevelt as McKinley's murderer.

John Nepomuk Schrank, then 36, later described by a sanity
commission as "self confident, profoundly self-satisfied, courteous
and kindly" had first shown signs of his aberration when he experienced a weird dream 24 hours after McKinley's death. In his
dream Schrank saw McKinley rise from his coffin, point an ac-
cusatory finger at Roosevelt and name his Vice President as his
murderer.

The dream made a profound impression on Schrank. He
brooded over it for years. On the morning of September 14, 1912,
the eleventh anniversary of McKinley's death, the part-time bartender was penning a poem when he experienced another strange
visitation, which he interpreted as a command to kill Roosevelt.
The ghost of the martyred McKinley seemed to flit before his eyes,
admonishing him that the murderer should not again become
President.

The next day Schrank wrote a note which he addressed "To
The People of the United States." It read:

Sept. 15, 1901—1:30 AM in a dream I saw president McKinley
sit up in his coffin pointing at a man in a monk's attire, in
whom I recognized Theo. Roosevelt.
    The dead president said This is my murderer, avenge my
death.

Sept. 14, 1912, 1:30 AM: While writing a poem someone tapped me on the shoulder and said Let not a murderer take the presidential chair, avenge my death. I could clearly see Mr. McKinley's features.

Before the Allmighty god I swear that the above written is nothing but the truth.

So long as Japan could rise to be one of the greatest powers of the world despite her serving a tradition more than 2,000 years old, as General Nogi so nobly demonstrated It is the duty of the U.S.A. to uphold the third term tradition. Let every third termer be regarded as a traitor to the American cause Let it be the right and duty of every citizen to forcibly remove a third termer. To prevent is better than to defend. Never let a third term party emblem appear on an official ballot.

I am willing to die for my country. God has called me to be his instrument, so help me God.

Eine Feste Berg ist unser Gott. (A Mighty Fortress Is Our God.)

Schrank's strange missive, which was found on his person 29 days later when he was arrested was signed "Innocent Guilty."

After the second manifestation Schrank was convinced that he was the one designated to kill Roosevelt. At first, he considered shooting the Bull Moose candidate in New York City, but abandoned this plan because he feared that it might be thought he was an assassin hired by Wall Street interests.

Roosevelt was scheduled to appear in New Orleans on September 27, during a speaking tour through some of the Southern states. Originally, Schrank decided upon shooting the former President in New Orleans. After scribbling a note which read in part: "We want no King. We want no murderer," he bought a 38-caliber revolver in a Broadway gunshop. Attired in an ill fitting gray tweed suit and a fedora hat, he boarded the ship *Comanche*. Disembarking at Charleston he abandoned his plan to go to New Orleans. Instead he remained in Charleston two days, then moved on to Augusta and finally, Chattanooga, Tennessee, where for the first time he sighted his quarry. He stood within a few feet of his intended victim, but, as he later confessed, he lacked the nerve to fire.

On October 13, Schrank again caught up with his prospective victim, this time in Milwaukee. He arrived in the Wisconsin city on Sunday and idled away the evening in a small tavern, tipping a band of musicians to play a medley of his favorite airs, among them "The Stars and Stripes Forever," and "Die Wacht am Rhein." He even joined in and sang when the band played one of his special favorites, "Where the River Shannon Flows."

At 5:00 P.M. the next afternoon Roosevelt arrived in his private railroad car, *Mayflower*. He set out at once by automobile for the Hotel Gilpatrick to attend a dinner in his honor. Moving about in the milling crowd in front of the hotel marquee, Schrank waited until Roosevelt was leaving the hotel about 8:00, then stepped forward and squeezed the trigger of his revolver.

Fired at a distance of only six feet, the bullet struck the former President in the right breast to the right of the nipple, fracturing his fourth rib. The crowd surged forward and pounced upon the would-be assassin, who might have been lynched on the spot but for Roosevelt's intercession. "Don't hurt him," cried the Presidential candidate as Schrank was hurried away.

Roosevelt waved aside any suggestions that he go to a hospital; instead he drove off to a Bull Moose rally, where with his shirt stained with blood he blasted the tobacco, sugar, and oil trusts. His life had been saved by a folded 50-page manuscript and the spectacle case in his vest pocket.

Schrank, a Sanity Commission later agreed, was "suffering from insane delusions, grandiose in character."

The mild-mannered barkeep later was committed to the Central Hospital in Waupun, Wisconsin, where, except for a temporary upset in 1940 when Franklin D. Roosevelt sought his third term, he whiled away his later years reading about politics. During his 31 years at Central Hospital, Uncle John, as Schrank was called, proved an exemplary patient.

Ida McKinley, shattered by the harrowing week at Buffalo, passed the remaining years of her life at the McKinley North Market Street home, dreaming of the past and ready for death when it came on May 26, 1907, a few days before her sixtieth birthday.

The assassination had fallen heavily upon John Hay. Life had opened brilliant prospects for this able man but it had also unfolded tragedies almost too crushing to bear. Hay had served under three martyred Chief Executives; and his son, Adelbert,

had died under tragic circumstances. As he looked back he wondered if his life—even such a brilliant life as his—had been worth
living. In a moment of dark despair he told a friend, "Do you
know that if a horoscope had foretold to me thirty years ago
the future of my life I gladly would have given it all up to have
escaped it all."

Hanna survived his political protege by only a few years. During the early days of Roosevelt's administration the new President
frequently sought Hanna's counsel and aid. To all appearances
the two were reconciled. Gradually, however, the new President
assumed the real rather than the titular leadership of the party.

Roosevelt may have sensed in Hanna a rival for the Presidency
and although the Republican boss regularly denied any such
aspirations, the Lords of Wall Street quietly but firmly went about
advancing his candidacy. After a secret conclave in the Waldorf-
Astoria Hotel, ten railroad presidents offered their purses and
their influence to support Hanna if he would consent to become
a candidate. "Stop making Presidents and become one yourself,"
the magnates told Hanna.

In November 1903, Hanna, mellowed somewhat by the passing
years and now tolerated by the press, was returned to his Senate
seat after a fierce campaign, but soon after, in January 1904, after
returning to the capital, he succumbed to a serious illness.

As the obdurate old political chieftain lay dying, his power
crumbling, his misty eyes upon the past, he was touched when
the young President, "a medium of the strange new times" called
at his home and left his card. The great Republican "Receiver-
General" replied with a a few words hastily scribbled in his own
hand. On February 15, 1904, the great man died. Now, with Platt
sidelined and Matthew Quay dead, Roosevelt reached out to take
the helm of the mighty political machine that Hanna had forged.

Cortelyou, who had served McKinley so faithfully, went on to
act as President Roosevelt's private secretary until February 1903,
when he was moved up the political ladder to the cabinet as Secretary of the newly formed Department of Commerce and Labor.
He served too as Roosevelt's liaison agent with the Overlords of
Wall Street, whom the new President alternately kicked and
courted.

For some time after Czolgosz's execution Emma Goldman's personal fortunes fared little better than her agitation on his behalf. In order to secure permanent lodgings and continue her work of nursing, she became Miss E. G. Smith. Even then many doctors refused to recognize her. However, the most shattering blow was a letter from Berkman, still in the Western Penitentiary in Pittsburgh for the shooting of Frick.

Berkman expressed admiration of Emma's offer to nurse the wounded President, adding that this sentiment showed a change in her thinking with which he was in accord. "How impossible such a thought would have been to us in the days of a decade ago! We should have considered it treason to the spirit of revolution; it would have outraged all our traditions even to admit the humanity of an official representative of capitalism."

This admission of change Emma looked upon as "big and brave," but his stand on Czolgosz was crushing: "I have read of the beautiful personality of the youth, of his inability to adapt himself to brutal conditions, and of the rebellion of his soul. It throws a significant light upon the causes of the Attentat. Indeed, it is at once the greatest tragedy of martyrdom and the most terrible indictment of society that it forces the noblest men and women to shed human blood, though their souls shrink from it. The more imperative it is that drastic methods of this character be resorted to only as a last extremity. To prove of value they must be motivated by social rather than individual necessity and be aimed against a direct and immediate enemy of the people. The significance of such a deed is understood by the popular mind, and in that alone lies the propagandistic, educational import of an Attentat, except if it is exclusively an act of terrorism."

Could he mean that McKinley was not an enemy of the people? She read on: "The scheme of political subjection is subtle in America. Though McKinley was the chief representative of our modern slavery, he could not be considered in the light of a direct and immediate enemy of the people. In an absolutism the autocrat is visible and tangible. The real despotism of republican institutions is far deeper, more insidious, because it rests on the popular delusion of self-government and independence. That is the source of democratic tyranny, and as such it cannot be reached with a bullet. In modern capitalism economic exploitation rather than political oppression is the real enemy of the people. Politics is but its handmaid. Hence the battle is to be waged in the economic rather than the political field. It is therefore that I regard my own act as far more significant and educational than Leon's. It was directed against a tangible, real oppressor, visualized as such by the people."

What an irony had placed in Berkman's words the same sentiments which Most had used nine years before about the Frick affair!

Emma found a further irony in the attitude of Theodore Roosevelt. Anarchistic motives had placed him on the "Presidential throne," yet how had he reacted? "In gratitude for that involuntary service Roosevelt turned savage. His message to Congress, intended largely to strike at Anarchism, was in reality a death-blow to social and political freedom in the United States," she declared.

As hysterically wrought citizens demanded the exportation of Anarchists to remote Pacific islands, and as Senator Joseph R. Hawley offered $1000 for a shot at an Anarchist, Congress, spurred by Roosevelt, went on to enact legislation against the radicals. The Federal Anti-Anarchist law passed by Congress on March 3, 1903, provides: "No person who disbelieves in or who is opposed to all organized government, or who is a member of or affiliated with any organization entertaining or teaching such disbelief in or opposition to all governments . . . shall be permitted to enter the United States."

McKinley, the supple agent of big business, was dead. Czolgosz had "done his duty" and even though he never could have suspected it, the two shots he fired on a sunny September afternoon in 1901 produced results more far reaching than many wars.

As the Lords of Finance, like J. P. Morgan, shuddered and swore mighty oaths, the former cow puncher moved into the White House, where, with "the breathless drama of a Western movie," he proceeded to smash the Northern Securities Co., distinguish between good and bad trusts, halt railroad mergers, enact the Meat Inspection and Pure Food Laws, establish the Department of Commerce and Labor, conserve the nation's dwindling forest and water supply, and, as Clinton Rossiter observes, "put the Presidency on the front page of every newspaper in America."

He was delighted, the new Chief Executive said, to show any courtesies to Pierpont Morgan, Andrew Carnegie, or James J. Hill—but he would never regard them with the affection he reserved for Professor Bury, Admiral Peary, or the historian, Rhodes.

In the days ahead, as Roosevelt protested to his friend, British historian George Trevelyan, he did not usurp power, he extended it. "I think the President should be a very strong man who uses without hesitation every power that the position yields," he said.

In the future even the atmosphere of the capital was to change in a political revival which brought bright young men swarming to the new President's reform banner. Speaking softly, the youthful Chief Executive kept the big stick in reserve as he brought to the country a new, dynamic concept of government.

Bibliography

Books about McKinley

1. Campaign and Memorial Biographies

Halstead, Murat. *The Illustrious Life of William McKinley.* N.P. 1901.
——— *Life and Distinguished Service of William McKinley.* H. L. Barber, 1901.
McClure, Alexander K., and Morris, Charles. *The Authentic Life of William McKinley.* W. E. Scull, 1901.
Pell, Edward Leigh; Buel, James W.; and Boyd, James P. *McKinley and Men of our Times.* Historical Society of America, 1901.
Russell, Henry B. *The Lives of William McKinley and Garret A. Hobart.* (A campaign biography). Hartford, Conn.: Worthington & Co., 1896.
Townsend, G. W., *Memorial Life of William McKinley,* D. Z. Howell, 1901.

2. Later Books about McKinley

Dawes, Charles G., *A Journal of the McKinley Years.* Chicago: Lakeside Press, R. R. Donnelly & Sons, 1950.
Glad, Paul W. *McKinley, Bryan and the People.* Philadelphia: J. B. Lippincott, 1964.
Leech, Margaret. *In the Days of McKinley.* New York: Harper and Brothers, 1959.
Morgan, H. Wayne. *William McKinley and His America.* Syracuse, N.Y.: Syracuse University Press, 1963.
Olcott, Charles S. *Life of William McKinley.* 2 vols. Boston and New York: Houghton, Mifflin Company, 1916.
Spielman, William Carl. *William McKinley, Stalwart Republican.* New York: Exposition Press, 1963.

Further Biographical Material

Beer, Thomas. *Marcus Alonzo Hanna.* New York: Alfred A. Knopf, 1929.
Coblenz, Edmond D., ed. *William Randolph Hearst, a Portrait in His Own Words.* New York: Simon and Schuster, 1952.

277

Croly, Herbert. *Marcus Alonzo Hanna.* New York: Macmillan and Co., 1912.

Depew, Chauncey M. *My Memoirs of 80 Years.* New York: Charles Scribner's Sons, 1924.

Drinnon, Richard. *Rebel in Paradise, A Biography of Emma Goldman.* Chicago: University of Chicago Press, 1961.

Goldman, Emma. *Living My Life.* New York: Alfred A. Knopf, 1931.

Hagedorn, Herman. *The Roosevelt Family of Sagamore Hill.* New York: The Macmillan Company, 1954.

Hamilton, Allan McLane. *Recollections of an Alienist.* New York: George H. Doran, 1916.

Jessup, Philip C. *Elihu Root.* New York: Dodd, Mead & Co., 1938.

Kane, Joseph Nathan. *Facts About the Presidents.* New York: H. W. Wilson & Co., 1959.

Satterlee, Herbert Lee. *J. Pierpont Morgan.* New York: The Macmillan Company, 1939.

Stoddard, Henry L. *As I Knew Them; Presidents and Politics from Grant to Coolidge.* New York: Harper and Brothers, 1927.

Swanberg, W. A. *Citizen Hearst.* New York: Charles Scribner's Sons, 1961.

Tebbel, John. *The Life and Good Times of William Randolph Hearst.* New York: E. P. Dutton and Co., 1952.

Thayer, William Roscoe. *The Life and Letters of John Hay.* 2 vols. Boston: Houghton Mifflin Company, 1915.

Thompson, Charles. *Presidents I've Known and Two New Presidents.* New York: Bobbs-Merrill, 1929.

Winkler, John K. *William Randolph Hearst, A New Appraisal.* New York: Hastings House, 1955.

Books Furnishing Background Material

Allen, Frederick Lewis. *The Lords of Creation.* New York: Harper and Brothers, 1935.

——— *The Big Change: America Transforms Itself 1900–1950.* New York, Harper and Brothers, 1952.

Carr, E. H. *Michael Bakunin.* New York: The Macmillan Company, 1937.

Donovan, Robert J. *The Assassins.* New York: Harper and Brothers, 1955. Popular Library Reprint, 1964.

Dumond, Dwight Lowell. *America in Our Time, 1896–1946.* New York: Henry Holt, 1947.

Faulkner, Harold Underwood. *The Quest for Social Justice (1898–1914).* In *A History of American Life,* vol. 11. New York: Macmillan and Company, 1931.

Hacker, Louis M., and Kendrick, Benjamin. *The United States Since 1865.* New York: Appleton-Century-Crofts, 1949.

Holbrook, Stewart H. *The Age of the Moguls.* Garden City: Doubleday, 1954.

Jensen, Amy LaFollette. *The White House and Its Thirty-two Families.* New York: McGraw Hill, 1958.

Josephson, Matthew. *The Politicos, 1865–1896.* New York: Harcourt, Brace, 1938.

—— *The President-Makers.* New York: Frederick Ungar, 1940.

—— *The Robber Barons.* New York: Harcourt, Brace, 1934.

Kohlsaat, H. H. *From McKinley to Harding.* New York: Charles Scribner's Sons, 1923.

Kropotkin, Peter. *Memories of a Revolutionist.* Garden City, N.Y.: Doubleday & Company, Anchor Books, 1962.

Lord, Walter. *The Good Years: From 1900 to the First World War.* New York: Harper and Row, 1960.

Mitchell, Edwin Valentine. *Encyclopedia of American Politics.* Garden City: Doubleday, 1946.

Moody, John. *The Masters of Capital.* New Haven: Yale University Press, 1919.

Moos, Malcolm. *The Republicans; A History of the Party.* New York: Random House, 1956.

Mowry, George E. *The Era of Theodore Roosevelt 1900–1912.* New York: Harper, 1958.

Peek, H. T. *Twenty Years of the Republic, 1885–1905.*

Plekhanov, George. *Anarchy and Socialism.* Chicago: Charles Kerr, 1908.

Rossiter, Clinton. *The Presidency.* Mentor Book Reprint. New York: Harcourt, Brace, 1956.

Siedel, Frank. *Out of the Midwest.* Cleveland: World Publishing Co., 1953.

Sparks, E. E. *National Development.* In American Nation Series, vol. 28.

Stern, Clarence A. *Resurgent Republicanism, the Handwork of Hanna.* Ann Arbor: Edwards Bros., 1963.

—— *Republican Heydey.* Ann Arbor: Edwards Bros., 1962.

Sullivan, Mark. *Our Times.* The United States 1900–1925, Vol. I. The Turn of the Century. New York: Charles Scribner's Sons, 1926.

Tuchman, Barbara W. *The Proud Tower.* New York: The Macmillan Company, 1966.

Vizatelli, Ernest Alfred. *The Anarchists.* London: John Lane, 1911.

White, William Allen. *The Autobiography of William Allen White.* New York: The Macmillan Company, 1946.

Magazine and Newspaper Articles

Adler, Selig. "Operation on President McKinley." *Scientific American* (March 1963), pp. 118–30.

Babcock, Louis L. "The Assassination of President William McKinley." *Niagara Frontier Miscellany* 34 (1947) :11–30.

Channing, Walter, M.D. "The Mental Status of Czolgosz, the Assassin of President McKinley." *American Journal of Insanity* 59 (October 1902) :233–78.

Goldberg, Arthur. "Perhaps McKinley's Life Could Be Saved Today." *Buffalo Evening News*, 30 June, 1945.

Morgan, H. Wayne. "The Civil War Diary of William McKinley." *The Ohio Historical Quarterly*, vol. 69, no. 3, July 1960.

Parmenter, John, M.D. "The Surgery in President McKinley's Case." *Buffalo Medical Journal* 41–57:205–6.

Potter, William Warren, M.D. "A Century of Medical History in the County of Erie 1800–1900" (Pan-American Exposition Hospital). *Buffalo Medical Journal* 41–57:507–8.

Reid, Babington. "A New Rear Admiral." *Munsey's* 27 (April 1902) : 75–76.

Roseberry, C. R. "TR's Famous Surrey Ride through the Adirondacks to Presidency." *Buffalo Evening News*, 14 June 1958.

VanPeyma, P. W., M.D. "Last Hours of McKinley." *The Daily Bazaar*, 28 November 1902, p. 5.

Wilcox, Ansley. "Theodore Roosevelt, President." *The Daily Bazaar*, Special Thanksgiving Supplement, November 1902, pp. 1–2.

Wilson, Nelson W., M.D. "Details of McKinley's Case." *Buffalo Medical Journal* 41–57:207–225.

Unsigned. "Dr. Mynter's Daughter Disputes Story of McKinley Operation." *Buffalo Evening News*, 14 November, 1945.

Unsigned. "The President's Case." *Red Cross Notes*, series 3, no. 9 (1901), pp. 191–96.

Unsigned. "The Official Report on the Case of President McKinley." *Buffalo Medical Journal* 41–57:271–93.

Unsigned. "What Wasn't Told about the McKinley Operation," (including reminiscences of Dr. Roswell Park). *Buffalo Evening News*, 15 September, 1945.

Pamphlets

James, Isabel Vaughn. *The Pan-American Exposition*. Buffalo and Erie Co. Historical Society Publications, Volume VI, 1961.

MacDonald, Carlos F., A.M.M.D. *The Trial, Execution, Autopsy and Mental Status of Leon F. Czolgosz, alias Fred Nieman, the Assassin of President McKinley*. Reprinted from *Philadelphia Medical Journal*, 4 January, 1902.

Nagle, Roy W. *The Pan-American Exposition*. n.p., n.d.

Unsigned. *Pan-American Exposition Book of 18 Special Privileges and Guidebook*. Endorsed by Pan-American Exposition Co., Buffalo, N.Y., The Visitors Information Company, 1901.

Newspaper Files
Buffalo Courier
The Buffalo Commercial
The Buffalo Enquirer
The Buffalo Evening Times
Buffalo Evening News
The Buffalo Express
Cleveland Plain Dealer
The New York Times
Police report of 1901 by Superintendent of Police William Bull.
Files of the District Attorney's Office, Erie County, New York State
Clipping files and scrapbooks were most helpful, especially those in the
    Private Collection of Roy W. Nagle, local historian
    The Buffalo and Erie County Public Library
    The Buffalo and Erie County Historical Association

Index

283